NOT ONLY GOLF

By the same author

MASTERS OF GOLF
THE LONG GREEN FAIRWAY
WORLD ATLAS OF GOLF (co-author)
ROYAL AND ANCIENT
SHELL GOLFERS ATLAS

NOT ONLY GOLF

an autobiography

Pat Ward-Thomas

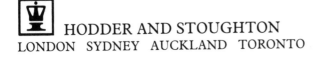
HODDER AND STOUGHTON
LONDON SYDNEY AUCKLAND TORONTO

British Library Cataloguing in Publication Data
Ward-Thomas, Pat
  Not Only Golf

1. Ward-Thomas, Pat
2. Golf – Biography
I. Title
070.4´49796352´0924   GV964.W/

ISBN 0 340 26756 9

Photosetting by Swiftpages Limited, Liverpool.
Printed in Great Britain for Hodder and Stoughton Limited, Mill Road, Dunton Green, Sevenoaks, Kent by The Thetford Press Limited.

Hodder and Stoughton Editorial Office: 47 Bedford Square, London WC1B 3DP.

For Jean, who else?

CONTENTS

ILLUSTRATIONS

Credits
 1   Taken by a German prison guard, Stalag Luft III
 2   Camera Press
 3   The *Guardian*
 4   The *Sunday Express*
 5   Portman Press Bureau
 6   D Ewart
 7   Barratt's Photo Press
 8   Links Country Park Hotel, Norfolk
 9   Julian P Graham
10   Kathryn Crosby
11   E D Lacey
12   Keystone Press
13   Author's collection
14   World Golf Hall of Fame, N Carolina.

INTRODUCTION
Alistair Cooke

Some lucky friends of old W-T know him as a fearless bridge player, stoical prisoner of war, bloodshot Tory, movie buff and a devil with the women. But the most characteristic memories of him, and of the hilarious split between his character and his prose, are the ones that have to do with his career as a golf writer. Without apology, therefore, I set down here my own most vivid memoir of him, written the weekend that he retired from the *Guardian*. The consolation for golfers who feel, correctly, that they have missed something must be that Ward-Thomas is temperamentally incapable of locking the desk, accepting the gold watch and retreating to the fireside slippers. So long as there is breath in his hacking bronchi, and ink in his typewriter ribbon, he will never surrender. Like Sarah Bernhardt, he will be back. Herewith, then, my premature obituary:

It is always hot inside an American telephone booth in summer, and the caller often pumps the split-hinged door like a concertina in the hope of wafting in gusts of bearable air.

That's what the man was doing. But it wasn't summer. It was spring in Georgia, which can be as intolerable as any Northern summer. And he wasn't making a social call, he was dictating copy to some cool girl at the Manchester end. He was pumping the door all right, but not just for relief. On the outside, close at hand, was a henchman or legman, clutching a bit of paper that bore hasty hieroglyphics, up-to-the-minute notes on what was going on outside.

What was going on outside was the annual Masters Tournament in Augusta, and the legman — name of Cooke — was trying to feed the latest birdies and bogeys, especially if they were being performed by an English golfer, to the desperate man inside the booth: a hawk-like figure with the exact profile of Goya's Duke of Wellington. This distinguished image was a little roughed up at the time, because the man's steel-grey hair had recently been subjected to a trim by a one-armed barber with blunt scissors, and from the poky strands of it rivulets of sweat were coursing through the clefts and canyons of a face that just then looked more like that of an impoverished Mexican farmer who was calling his landlord in a failing attempt to prolong the mortgage.

No wonder. It was 98 degrees outside, out along the rolling fairways and under the towering Georgia pines of the most beautiful inland course on earth. Inside the press building, it must have been a hundred and ten. And inside the man's booth, you could name any figure that might suggest a sauna on the blink or the inner rim of the crater of Vesuvius.

Imprisoned in this inferno the man was shouting, against the clatter of a hundred typewriters, the squawking amplification of the relayed television commentary, and the hullabaloo of other maniacs in other booths. He would shout out a phrase, glance at a paper, drop it, curse, bend over and crash his head, curse again, swing the door open and pant — 'Was Jacklin's birdie on the twelfth or — blast it! — the eleventh?' He'd get the legman's word, swing the door shut again, sweat some more and shout out the cadence of the sentence he was writhing through.

I say cadence deliberately, because even in the bowels of hell this is not a man to toss out unkempt sentences or sloppy subsidiary clauses. When the stuff was in print, you would always assume it had been written by some imperturbable oldster brought up on Hazlitt and Bernard Darwin: always the loving delineation of the landscape, the knowing adjective, the touch of Edwardian grace, and the meditative close.

He was coming to the close now. He was hunched against the door and I could see him mouthing the words with exaggerated articulation, like a goldfish waiting for the water to be renewed. I saw him chew on a word, wring his free hand, and glare at the mouthpiece with Max Wall's Bela Lugosi face. I opened the door to give him a breath. He was screaming: 'In the serenity of the Georgia twilight ... Ser-en-ity! SER-ENN-IT-TEE!!' He covered the mouthpiece and hissed at me: 'Bloody idiot! She can't get it.' Then back again and saying to the girl: 'That's it, yes, serenity, thnksvermuch. Goodbye.'

He emerges, the rivulets having now formed spreading lakes beneath his armpits. 'This goddam time-zone business!' he says. (For the further exasperation of the British correspondents, the Masters is always played during that brief interval between British and American (Eastern seaboard) summer time, so that the time difference is not the usual five but six hours. Since the climax of any day's play tends to happen around 6 pm, the impossible assignment is that of describing the finest hour to that cool girl transcribing it at Manchester's midnight.)

The reader may be puzzled to recognise in this raw slice of life the lineaments of his favourite golf writer. The alert *Guardian* subscriber might be expected to guess that there has to be some agile hole-hopping, some frantic checking of the leader board, behind the smooth account of a tournament and the planted hints of why it was inevitable that the victory should go to Watson's iron discipline or Nicklaus's competitive stamina. But the reader of Ward-Thomas's weekly musings in *Country Life* must believe that he is reading the oldest member, a gentle sifter of hot memories cooled by tolerance.

Well, the man in the booth is nobody but Pat Ward-Thomas on active service, from which he is now retiring, full of honour, fond memories and troops of friends. He is one and the same with the *Guardian's* austere reporter and *Country Life's* weaver of stately prose in the twilight. I must say that if there is a regret obtrudes about his talent, it must be that in print he always distilled his disgust at some idiotic rule, some passing vulgarity, into a mannerly sigh, leaving only those who know him well the relish of having seen the splendour of his original indignation.

That, in its raging pristine form, was reserved for nobody but himself. I see him now, the top of his spiky head rather, banging away in a bunker at Maidstone, with the sand flying and the seagulls wheeling away in dismay from the obscenities that were rocketing out at them. Any true account of a round of golf with him would require, before publication, more 'expletives deleted' than all the Nixon tapes.

The Masters at Augusta seemed more serene than usual because — the crack circulated — Pat was not there, for the first time in 14 years. Augusta was also considerably less fun than usual. In the press building, there were lots of the familiar cronies. But way down there, on the eighth row, there was an empty chair and a silent typewriter. No more the blacksmith's back bent over, the elbow leaning a millimetre away from a smouldering cigarette, the index finger poised for just the right verb. No more the smothered curses, but no more the quick smile, the bottle-blue eyes greeting chums and bores with equal good nature.

There were two things about his golf reports that set him apart from all the others. He tramped the courses, when most were settled in the press building scanning the big scoreboard and — on the basis of a figure change — tapping out 'he fired a birdie on the ninth.'

And he loved the landscape, all the landscapes of golf, from the ocean beauties of California's Pebble Beach to the Siberian wastes of Rye, from the pine and sand undulations of Swinley Forest to the yawning bunkers of Pine Valley and the cathedral aisles of Augusta. He knew the terrain, and made you know it, and how it shaped its peculiar form of golf, of every county of England and Scotland.

When others settled for 'this magnificent course,' he pictured the beeches and copses, distinguished an upland from a weald, weighed the comparative hazards of a cypress tree or a swale. Nobody has ever conveyed so easily the sense of being in Wiltshire or County Down or Fife or Arizona.

He will be greatly missed, but not by everybody. Only by those who care about the good earth and its cunning conversion into golf strategy, about the unsleeping conflict between character and talent, about the courtesies as well as the joys of the game, about many small favours, and about unfailing geniality to man, woman (especially) and beast.

AUTHOR'S NOTE

When my grandfather, William Thomas, went to the United States in 1867 I doubt that he was aware of Tom Morris's victory in the Open championship that summer. He would have been astounded at the seemingly frivolous sending of one of his numerous grandsons many times across the Atlantic in order to watch people hitting little balls in lavishly prepared parks. His business in Wolverhampton concerned malt and brewing. As a religious Welshman he was fascinated by the various denominations in America and usually went to two different churches every Sunday, but he was not without sporting instincts. After each addition to a large family he would reward his wife by taking her on walking holidays in Switzerland, presumably to ensure her fitness for their next creative act. She was a Stephenson from Northumberland. One of her brothers, who was several times mayor of Newcastle, was, I believe, the last person to be knighted by Queen Victoria.

My father inherited a love of high places and countryside. Having trained as an engineer, his first job was to introduce electric power to Keswick in the Lake District where he could indulge in fishing, cricket and exploring the mountains to his heart's content. Sadly he was never able to pursue a countryman's life to the full but, by an unusual chain of circumstances, his only son was more fortunate. It is with these and the pleasures, people, travel and the beauty of an outdoor life, rather than detail of the golf itself, that this book is mainly concerned. It raises no lids, exposes no scandals but is an account, broadly chronological in approach, of a rewarding period.

Before the Second War my life had followed a fairly common pattern — a happy home, devoted parents, school and readily forgettable jobs leavened by an ardent, if limited, pursuit of cricket and golf. Except for an occasional backward glance little of that time merits recall some forty years later, and so this story begins not with an account of childhood but on a November night in 1940 when a single German anti-aircraft shell changed the course of my life.

I am grateful to the editors of the *Guardian* and *Country Life* for allowing me to use material of mine which has appeared in their journals.

P. W-T

CHAPTER 1

SOMEBODY'S SITTING ON MY PARACHUTE

In common with many another in time of war I nursed the delusion that disaster was no part of my immediate future. Men might vanish, be killed or taken prisoner but I was immune. It cannot happen to me was the sustaining thought, but at dawn one high summer day in 1940 it certainly did so.

A bombing raid to the Ruhr had been uneventful and our Wellington was cruising peacefully back across the North Sea towards its base on Newmarket Heath when, for no apparent reason, an engine cut. At first there was no anxiety — a lightened aircraft with ample fuel could easily reach England on one engine — but when the second engine expired a few moments later our thinking was sharpened, to say the least.

Swift, hopeful calculation estimated, falsely as it proved, that we were only about ten miles from the English coast. Cloud cover was low over the sea, and as we broke it at a thousand feet six pairs of eyes searched anxiously for a sight of land. Greyness was all; there was no trace of a long dark welcoming line on the horizon, and no alternative but to ditch.

The captain was Percy Pickard, who later won great distinction as a pilot and became known as 'F for Freddie' after a film in which he took part. As we descended towards an unfriendly sea he told me to go back into the body of the aircraft and be ready to work the dinghy release, a cord that one pulled. I clutched it and with three other members of the crew waited for the gentle swish as the aircraft kissed the waves; but such innocence was rudely shattered by the crash as it struck.

Within seconds we were floundering up to our waists as water came rushing through the aircraft. It was no fault of Pickard's; the choppy sea had smashed the front turret. Fortunately the release worked and the dinghy popped out on to the water. As we clambered into it Pickard

15

laughed and said that there was nothing to worry about and that we would soon be found.

The wireless operator had sent out Mayday calls, bravely staying at his post until the last second, and was certain they had been received. The six of us settled in the dinghy and looked forward to the tale we would have to tell. Hours passed, aircraft passed and we saw ships on the horizon, but no one saw us. The auxiliary hand pump and distress flares had vanished at the ditching and water was seeping through a tiny hole in the floor of the dinghy. We took turns in baling out with shoes.

Without doubt we owed our lives to the navigator, who on leaving the aircraft had grabbed the Verey pistol and one cartridge, but this was soaked. Not until some cardboard had been stripped from it would it fit into the breach. And so we waited; someone sang softly but mostly we felt a deepening sense of resignation. We had no food or anything to drink but mercifully the June skies remained overcast or our plight would have been much worse.

Surely, if we were only ten miles out and the signals had been received, we should have been found. For the only time in my life I thought we were on our way, and later Pickard said that he felt the same. It was a strange experience. In common with most aircrew I had faced moments of danger, when life had been threatened, but mostly they were brief; whereas in the dinghy there was time to reflect on the irony of being young, in perfect health and totally helpless with nothing to do until fatigue became the final mercy. As it was we were dulled by lack of sleep, and memory tends to reject the unpleasant, but I clearly recall wondering whether there had been any purpose to life thus far. For it to end in such a fashion seemed so futile.

Suddenly, after some eight hours, a Wellington from our own squadron appeared. It was flying low and obviously looking for us. By the grace of God the Verey pistol fired its vital message, the Wellington swung towards us, skimming low over the waves, firing signals and guns in celebration, but we had five more hours to wait before the rescue launch arrived. It had to come sixty miles from Felixstowe. We were thirty miles out in the North Sea; our estimate of ten had been highly optimistic.

As the launch took us aboard I felt guilty at having given up hope as soon as I had. It had been thirteen hours — later in the war men would survive for days in a similar state but I believe we were the first crew from 3 Group to be saved from the sea. After we landed at Felixstowe a friendly medical Mess plied us with whisky. We were driven back to Newmarket where we immediately woke and blessed our rescuer, 'Hank' Lines, an outstanding pilot who was sleeping on a camp bed in the Rowley Mile grandstand where we were billeted. Lines, who was killed in action later, said he would never have seen us but for the Verey light. The dinghies were yellow but six men sitting in them masked the colour. I realised this not long afterwards when on a similar search. We saw nothing but quite possibly a dinghy full of men saw us.

The extent of our enormous good fortune was emphasised when squadrons in the group became conscious of dinghy drill and arranged demonstrations, on land of course. I watched two of these but any feeling of smugness, that one knew it all, was swiftly tempered when on neither occasion did the release work.

An escape such as this served to strengthen the illusion that there would be no more mishaps. I recall my father insisting that my mother be told because she would be comforted to know that such rescues were possible. False comfort it proved to be.

One moonlit night in November that year we were trundling back from Berlin, having deposited our little load of bombs which may have mildly inconvenienced a few citizens. All was serene until a German gunner, who had not been taught that it was unsporting to shoot sitting ducks, scored a hit on one engine. An aircraft doing 130 m.p.h. at 12,000 feet looks almost motionless from the ground.

The engine fluttered, as if slightly irritated, but settled down for another hour and more. Then, as we were about to cross the Dutch coast, both engines went completely out of control, alternately cutting and screaming at maximum power. We lurched about the sky like an elderly gull in a hurricane but nothing we tried would work and we lost height rapidly. The only alternative to ditching a mile or so out to sea was to turn back and jump.

There was some confusion over the process of baling out. The flight commander, Pritchard, and I, the second pilot, had different types of parachutes and he was sitting on mine. When he suggested that I might like to depart first we realised that we would have to change. This was not easy with the aircraft reeling all over the place and Pritchard striving to keep it steady. It was well for us that there was no fire aboard.

I dropped through the hatch in the nose of the aircraft with a feeling of despair familiar to thousands. This time I was not going home. For perhaps a second I did not care if the parachute failed to open but this did not prevent me from instantly pulling the release with no thought of counting three before doing so, which I think was the instruction in those days. Then came the tug on the harness and, of course, profound relief that the parachute had opened. Suddenly all was peace. The flat polder land north of Amsterdam lay silver under a brilliant bomber's moon but it seemed that I would never reach it. Hanging there, at about five thousand feet, I distinctly remember feeling foolish and hoping that no one was watching. Later I discovered that others had felt the same.

Judging distance can be difficult enough on a golf course in daylight. It is much harder when making a vertical descent by moonlight. Aware that I was falling towards one of the canals that make a chequerboard of that part of Holland I tried to sideslip but was far too late. Without any warning I was immersed. Luckily the parachute did not fall on me but drifted laterally and helped my floundering scramble up the steep sides of the dyke.

I sat on the bank tearing up various documents that should not have been with me. All was silence, not a soul was abroad in a desolate scene, but a quarter of a mile away I saw a faint light in a small farmhouse. The only course seemed to seek shelter there and dry myself. A dog barked angrily as I approached, dragging the parachute behind me; a suspicious eye peered through a hole in the door before it opened. I was beckoned inside, given tea and bread and cheese while the family sat round the table staring. My clothes were taken to be dried and I was given a pair of pyjama pants and clogs in their stead, but kept my uniform jacket as a means of identity.

My hosts, humble smallholders, spoke only Dutch of which I had not a single word, but I conveyed that I wanted to sleep. The morning could take care of itself. I was put in a vast bed, which several warm bodies had recently left, within a sort of cupboard, and had been asleep for an hour or so when awoken by a light in my face and a German saying in English that I must go with him. I remember telling him I was very tired and could he not wait until the morning. Politely, but unreasonably I thought, he insisted, saying that my comrades were in the police station. All had landed safely but the noise of the aircraft crashing in the deserted countryside must have alerted the police who could have had no difficulty in rounding us up. There were no woods, no shelter of any kind save scattered dwellings and that early in the war we had no escape equipment or advice in the event of being shot down.

The Germans in the police station were quite amiable, gave us beer and insisted that for us 'Der Krieg ist fertig', as if we needed reminding. You will be home by August they said, but they were almost five years adrift in their estimate. We were taken to Amsterdam, where I was hardly at my best clattering in clogs and pyjama trousers across the lobby of the old Carlton Hotel, then the Luftwaffe headquarters. We were taken towards a room whence emerged a screeching little German major. Behind him we could see a party in progress, women, drinks and cigar smoke, but we were not invited to join. Eventually the major stopped showing off; we were taken into a room and left until a minibus took us across Holland to Dulag Luft, a reception centre for air force prisoners near Frankfurt.

Awakening the next morning, refreshed after a long sleep, and realising what had happened remains the worst single moment of my life. I looked round the plainly furnished single room and faced the full impact of my plight, thinking how, in God's name, can I stand living in a room like this for years to come, little dreaming that it was the equivalent of a first-class hotel compared with what was to follow.

Eventually a German in civilian clothes wandered in, speaking flawless English. We chatted in friendly fashion and discovered that we had lived within a few hundred yards of one another in London for a while before the war. At such moments most people are dying to talk and the interrogators hoped that one would reveal details of squadron, aircraft and so on. When I said that I could only give him name, rank and number he remarked that it would then take much longer for my family to be informed that I was safe. In the event it was two or three weeks before my parents heard. The Germans, who were about four up and five to play in the war at that point, could afford to be patronising towards prisoners. Later, when the Allies had won several holes back, they were less than welcoming.

Fortunately, perhaps, I was twenty-seven, older than the average prisoner and not readily susceptible to the optimistic belief that, for all manner of nonsensical reasons, the war would be over by Christmas. From the outset I expected to be a prisoner for at least two years and when they had gone was so accustomed to the existence that time hardly seemed to matter. Four and a half years were to pass before I saw England again, a formidable slice from the most active period of a man's life, but when it was over I had no lasting cause for regret. Having flown on twenty-four operations I felt the odds against me were lengthening. Had I survived I might have been offered a permanent commission and would have accepted, mainly because there was no more attractive alternative. If so I would have been retired at about the time when a career as a golf correspondent was approaching its most fruitful period. On balance being a prisoner of war was a lucky break because in my youth I could never have anticipated a more rewarding life than that which has been my fortunate lot these past thirty years.

As a small boy I had no real interest in cricket, golf or football, all of which had been something of a passion with my father. Once, as a punishment for some childish misdemeanour, he made me write out fifty times some such phrase as 'I must bowl a length' or 'I must keep a straight bat'. Little did he realise that he was sowing seeds of an addiction that would prove almost lethal to any form of academic advancement. At preparatory school and at Wellingborough my thoughts were rarely far from games. Latin was one of the few subjects that came easily and without undue stress I usually had high marks, but my father was not amused when the Latin master wrote in a term report that ability was marred by visions of green fields.

This was probably true of the years after leaving school when I had no clear idea of what I wanted to make of life. One day during this period I happened to play golf with Fred Tomlinson, who was then golf correspondent of the *Manchester Guardian,* and later an editor with the *Observer.* After our round he talked of his plans for the coming season, of the famous courses he would visit and the tournaments he would cover. I was almost sick with envy, never dreaming that some fifteen years later I would be one of his successors, and that my horizons would be far broader than his could ever have been in the thirties.

Shortly before the war I took a short service commission in the RAF, mainly as an escape from a training scheme for young executives with London Transport, which I soon realised was leading nowhere. Knowing of my problem the head of the department, who had served in the regular army in peacetime, suggested the RAF as a career. I recall him saying that there would be plentiful leave and opportunity for cricket and golf. I had no romantic illusion about being in the vanguard of the fight for democracy. I was more interested in Walter Hammond than Hitler.

Soon after I started training as a pilot, war was declared and short service commissions were abandoned. I was fortunate to be in the last group. Training at Derby and Kinloss, where I first became aware of the beauty of Scotland when flying over the Cairngorms with dawn sunlight crimson on the snow, passed agreeably enough. So did the night operations which two or three times a week interfered with a delightful social life in Newmarket and thereabouts. Many families with large houses, among them the Fishers of Kilverstone and the Homes at Cavenham, were uncommonly welcoming and kind to us.

Save for the operations the war seemed unbelievably remote in that peaceful place, never more so than one morning when we returned late from a raid over Germany. There was no point in going to bed, and two of us played golf on the Newmarket course across the road from the Heath within a few hours of dodging flak and searchlights. Those golden months of 1940 were among the happiest of my life to that point, and then with shattering abruptness they came to an end.

Much has been written and filmed about life in prisoner of war camps, particularly concerning the stories of escape. These remarkable examples of courage, endurance and ingenuity compel attention for their inherent dramatic qualities, but there were other aspects of this strange existence. They lacked the appeal of adventure but revealed the balance of mind and resilience of men in adversity, and the sardonic sense of humour, incomprehensible to most Germans, which laughed at disaster without disregarding it and derided the faintest possibility of defeat.

It was a life often noisy, dirty and afflicted with extremes of heat and cold. Food frequently was inadequate and accommodation grossly overcrowded. It was a life of nostalgia and dreams which at times demanded all the reserves of patience and tolerance that a man could muster. In all the dragging days the only solitude was in sleep, unless one was fortunate enough to be sentenced to a few days in the cooler. This was the German prison for various offences ranging from escape attempts to failure to appear on the morning check parade. One was locked in a not uncomfortable little room maybe for five or ten days, with brief interludes for exercise. Twice I was sentenced and recall the relief of being alone in a single room with no one's snoring or stirring to disturb me. One could settle peacefully to reading or writing and I managed the greater part of *The Forsyte Saga*. Five days in the cooler was pure holiday, ten a shade too long.

In general the lack of privacy was probably a blessing. To endure an indeterminate sentence alone in such conditions would have been harder to bear. As it was no one could remain angry or depressed for long when others were there to jolly him out of his mood, and incipient quarrels were stifled before becoming violent. Spells of depression were unavoidable but of all the several thousand men with whom I was imprisoned at various times I know of perhaps half a dozen suicide attempts and not all succeeded.

Many of us did not speak to a woman, even to the point of saying 'Good morning' for over four years. Fortunately women were rarely visible; no beauties swayed enticingly beyond the wire. Occasionally a huddled peasant might pass but they hardly caused any pawing of the ground. Gradually one was able to think of women as creatures of dreams. At the same time it was interesting to observe how, after some while, one became aware of the attractions of other young men. Weary eyes would scan new intakes of prisoners, much as they might a group of girls suddenly appearing in a bar, but this was light-hearted enough.

The camp had its little theatre where plays were produced. The Germans allowed clothes and costumes to be hired, on parole of course, from agencies. Some of the female parts were most convincingly played, stirring thoughts of other times. One young man took a large camp by storm with his seductive rendering of a popular song. People talked about it for days but in ordinary garb he was quite inconspicuous. Erotic illusions swiftly melted once make-up and dresses had been discarded.

When men are totally deprived for years of even the minutest contact with women, homosexual inclinations are inevitable. At best there were never less than eight, and later ten, people sharing a room about twenty-five feet by fifteen, sleeping on two-tiered bunks. Nowhere in Stalag Luft

111 were there private places for assignations and amatory tendencies had no opportunity for physical expression.

Close, sometimes intense, friendships would develop but a severely limited diet, while providing enough energy for games, study and other activities, helped to sublimate thoughts of secret pastimes, even on Christmas Day in 1943. In the autumn of that year ardent spirits fashioned a still, mostly from food tins, with typical prisoner ingenuity and enthusiasm. For months we saved dried fruit and sugar from Red Cross parcels. Night after night the still, zealously watched, would bubble away in an alcove at the end of our hut. I cannot remember whether it only operated in the small hours after the Germans had made their final check, but it did its potent work nonetheless.

Then came the great day when what amounted to near raw alcohol began to circulate round the camp. Within hours the place was alight and scores were drunk, some incapably so. Most of us had not tasted alcohol for years and the effect of that near-lethal stuff can be imagined, but I well recall the joy of the first drink or two. Maybe a certain amount of fondling took place as inhibitions vanished. Certainly there was sickness and if the victim or culprit, according to one's view, happened to be on a top bunk the plight of the man beneath was not enviable. Men were reeling or wandering all over the camp and although no one was supposed to leave his hut after the lights were out one or two unconscious bodies were found outside in the snow the next morning.

The Germans were remarkably understanding. The Stalag Luft camps were run by the Luftwaffe who seemed to pursue a velvet glove policy in their treatment of British, Commonwealth and American prisoners. Their determination to prevent escape was no less evident but rarely were there instances of the petty nastiness, arrogant stupidity and hysterical screaming sometimes encountered at camps controlled by the army. Possibly someone in the Luftwaffe realised that such behaviour usually produced an adverse reaction from the prisoners, and that if they were not harassed they would give less trouble. However, that Christmas German tolerance had been strained. When the still was set up in readiness for the next year they confiscated it. This was as well for all concerned.

I often wondered whether the Germans knew we had a secret radio as, I believe, did other camps. Occasionally there were sudden searches but they never found it and we had fairly regular news from London and elsewhere. Bulletins would be prepared and dictated to readers of whom I was one for a while. With watchers to warn of approaching guards, we would read them in the various huts. I remember the joy of reading some of Churchill's speeches which invariably inspired us without giving false hope of an early release. On reflection thank heaven it was Churchill and not some of his successors.

As the opportunity to escape might occur at any time a paramount duty was to keep as fit, mentally and physically, as possible. Any attempt to gain freedom imposed severe demands on a man's resources. Also there was the future to be considered. Faith in ultimate victory for the Allies, which few ever doubted even in the darkest years, and eventual return to family, friends and a career were a powerful incentive to remain healthy. The food, if memory serves, never included fresh milk or fruit but, thanks to the Red Cross parcels, was adequate for maintaining reasonable fitness. Soon after being taken prisoner I lost about eight pounds and remained at a constant weight for the rest of the war and, apart from colds, never had a day's illness.

Hundreds of men endured four, and in some instances five, years of prison camp life. One of my staunch friends there, Colin Maclachlan, was shot down on 1 October 1939 and returned home on 26 May 1945, possibly the longest term served by any Allied prisoner in the European war. Soon after returning home the great majority of men were fit for flying. This and the fact that they resumed normal life without any serious abnormality was a great testimony to their spirit and health.

For young men, most of whom had led individual, active lives before captivity, to be suddenly confined with hundreds of others in harsh conditions was a great strain. An outlet for their energies was essential and the playing of games provided it. Sorely cramped space within barbed wire and in the early years lack of proper equipment acted as a spur rather than a deterrent to their efforts.

In the first year of the war few prisoners were taken and the Germans guarded them zealously. Opportunities for physical activity were strictly limited and not until 1942 when Stalag Luft 111, the main camp for Air Force officers, was opened did the prisoners' lives become more stable. Prior to that time there were always moves and parties of us were shunted round Germany.

After two weeks at Dulag Luft my Grand Tour began at Barth on the Baltic coast where conditions were not too unpleasant except for the shortage of food. Dried vegetables and potatoes were available and when soaked they would expand so we made huge pies in the mistaken belief that our hunger would be eased. For an hour or so it was but the only lasting effect was to expand the stomach and qualify us for exercises in ptomaine. Thereafter there was a sojourn in an old castle at Spangenburg near Kassel and from there, early in 1941, about two hundred of us were sent to an evil-smelling old fort in Poland.

This was a reprisal for what the Germans alleged to be ill-treatment of their prisoners in Canada. It took the ludicrous form of binding our wrists together with string which we undid within moments. The Germans had made their gesture. But the worst period of the whole time I was a prisoner had begun. We were shut in underground rooms for the greater part of each day and there were no Red Cross parcels. They did not begin to arrive regularly until late that year. For several months in Poland we existed each day on half a litre of soup, a fifth of a medium-size loaf of bread, a little ersatz jam or margarine and foul coffee probably made from acorns.

Anyone wishing to lose weight should try this diet. Very soon you are aware of decline in mind and body. I recall the shock when I first noticed that my thighs were thinner than usual, and when we played bridge it became increasingly hard to concentrate on the most elementary aspects of the game. Very few people in the Western world ever know what real hunger, near to starvation level, is like. Even the most impoverished can find something, somewhere, to eat but there was no way on earth that we could get anything beyond the daily ration.

Reaction to such deprivation was interesting to observe. Some men would cut their bread with a razor blade until they had perhaps twelve paper-thin slices, four for lunch, four for supper and four for breakfast, creating the illusion, for such it almost was, that food was in store. Others would devour their ration straightaway and to hell with the morrow.

It was a salutary experience which, having survived without harm, I was glad to have known. A few days of hunger are quite sufficient to bring a man face to face with the ultimate realities of life. Everything else becomes totally insignificant beyond the desire to eat. It was a lesson I have never forgotten. Whatever misfortunes may beset one it is consoling to remember that nothing, short of serious illness or accident, could ever be as bad as that time in Poland. On occasion the memory of it has helped me when something has gone amiss. However angry, sad or disappointed one might be there is always somewhere warm and comfortable to sleep and something to eat.

I have often thought that many young would profit and learn from an indeterminate, not necessarily long, sentence in conditions of deprivation such as millions suffered during the war. It would teach them the value of everything they take for granted; they would be forced to tolerate and respect those with whom they were confined and, as prisoners of war were well aware, any inclination to bad behaviour would be self-defeating.

Mercifully, that first spell in Poland ended before our constitutions were damaged. The second, a winter later, was not as restricted and there was more food but we lived in large stone buildings with scarcely any heat at all. Morning after morning one wakened with frost on the blankets. In the evenings we would play bridge wearing every garment we possessed including gloves; but better times were coming, relatively that is, and thoughts could turn to the playing of games.

CHAPTER 2
OVER THE WIRE IS OUT OF BOUNDS

The first real opportunity for many of us to play games was late in 1941 when some four hundred RAF officers were sent to Warburg, near Kassel, where for almost a year they were together with two and a half thousand Army officers and men, most of whom had been captured in Normandy. Although the camp was a swamp of mud and cinders there was at least space.

The Red Cross and YMCA had now become aware that prisoners needed books and sports equipment as well as food, and supplies were forthcoming. A football pitch, almost full-size, was levelled and a League of six clubs, five Army and one RAF, with second elevens, was formed. The matches were intensely competitive, and the standard of play quite high, especially by the NCOs' team. The atmosphere was akin to a Cup tie at home and playing in front of a highly critical and wildly excited crowd of a thousand or more was a unique experience for all of us. Betting was rife and large amounts changed hands, either in the well-nigh valueless German Lager Marks or cheques to be settled after the war.

We were so remote from real money that it soon ceased to have much significance. I never took part in the gambling schools, preferring the quieter and more predictable pastures of bridge; not so a friend of mine who could not resist baccarat or chemin de fer. At one point he was sixteen hundred pounds ahead and I begged him to hang on to half of it, a considerable sum in the forties, but within days he had lost the lot.

The Warburg camp was closed late in 1942. Some went to open Stalag Luft 111 but I and others returned to winter resorts in Poland. Those journeys across Germany were ghastly. We were packed into ancient wooden third-class carriages often for two days and more. At night two would try to sleep on the luggage racks, two on the floor and the rest curled on the seats. I have often been reminded of those dark days when incarcerated in a huge modern aircraft, the quintessence of travel discomfort, but at

26

least your destination usually is known, the food is better and you can get a drink.

Eventually I reached Stalag Luft 111 which housed the great majority of British, American and Commonwealth Air Force officers. In 1943 there were three compounds, strictly separated; two more were added later to accommodate the growing numbers of Americans. From the sport viewpoint the east compound, where I resided, was the most remarkable in that, in spite of it being the smallest, 330 by 130 yards, games were more highly organised there than in the others.

We were fortunate in having several gifted games players in our midst. Ted Edwards, a New Zealander, was an All Black trialist; Derek Heaton-Nichols, whose father was South African High Commissioner in London at the time, had played cricket and rugby for Natal, and Colin Maclachlan, a Midlands county rugby player, was also an Association footballer of League standard. These men were a strong influence in quickening the interest and raising the standard of our games. They were all taken prisoner within a few weeks of the war beginning. Edwards was shot down on 6 September, the very first officer to be imprisoned from either side. Later others of above-average or even first-class ability in various games, notably cricket and golf, appeared.

The camp was in a clearing within a pine forest, its surface loose sand blackened with pine loam. A constant battle was waged to try to make level pitches but they soon became loose and rough again. Football and rugby were extremely strenuous, especially as the normal seasons were ignored and games were often played in temperatures approaching ninety, literally in a bath of sand and sweat.

Rugby was comparatively short-lived. The games became too violent as people unleashed their frustrations, and the Germans did not take kindly to an increasing number of injured players in their sick quarters, but before rugby was abandoned it did help a spectacular rescue of a man from a tunnel.

The Germans held their check parades in the morning and afternoon on the football pitch where the prisoners were assembled in companies of five ranks deep. One such fell in daily within a few yards of the wire and as the parades usually lasted about twenty minutes a tunnel was begun, the sand being dispersed among members of the company. Eventually the hole was big enough for a man to be put down and sealed in during a morning parade after the company had been checked, and brought up in the afternoon before the counting officer reached that company.

On one occasion the Germans did not hold an afternoon parade but the man had to be extricated from the tunnel. He could not have lived through the night. The football pitch was in full view of two guard towers and any group suddenly gathering for no apparent purpose would arouse suspicion. A rugby match of about twenty a side was organised and after a while a huge scrum formed over the entrance to the tunnel. The sand was scraped away, the trap lifted and the man safely rescued. The tunnel was then sealed again. Fortunately the German guards knew nothing of the rules of rugby, though the ingenious attempt to escape eventually failed.

Soccer continued with unabated fervour. A League was formed with eight clubs, each bearing a famous name — Aston Villa, Wolves, Arsenal, (for whom I kept goal) and so on. The size of the pitch, eighty by forty yards, restricted the teams to seven players, but as each club had four sides some two hundred or more people had at least a game a week. As at Warburg the competition was intense. League matches were usually played in the evenings and hundreds would look forward to it as eagerly as they do at home.

Sports equipment of various kinds gradually began to arrive and the choice of games to expand. Under the Canadian influence softball soon became popular and when ice-hockey sticks appeared a rink was levelled and banked. When flooded it swiftly froze in the harsh winter and a good supply of skates enabled many to learn to skate to the amusement of the less intrepid. The hockey sticks, often made of hickory, were soon at risk as a source of shafts for home-made golf clubs.

Each summer an athletics meeting was held, involving prodigious labour in levelling a track of two hundred and twenty yards. The sand was harder near the wire where people constantly walked and inch by inch a five-lane track was made. On the great day of the meeting the camp almost had a gala appearance. For weeks the athletes, of whom I certainly was not one, trained and considered their diet and some fine performances were recorded.

When coconut matting came from England our hosts were persuaded to lay a concrete cricket pitch: this was in two sections with a gap of some six yards in the middle so the bowling of bouncers was frustrated. The ball would hit the soft sand short of the concrete and trickle tamely towards the batsman. Perhaps it was as well for the balls were hard.

For six weeks cricket was played for about eight hours a day, then the matting went to another compound for its turn. The boundary on one side was a hut within thirty yards and many a tea party was rudely interrupted. Somewhat naturally windows were left open. We had among us an Australian, Leslie Dixon, who had played Sheffield Shield cricket for Queensland not least, I believe, when Bradman scored 452 not out. Leslie was far too lively for us and rarely slipped himself. Aidan Crawley gave us glimpses of the talent that had made him an outstanding England class batsman for Kent and the Gentlemen. All in all we had some reasonable cricket, a wonderful boon to those who had been starved of it for so long.

Other games such as basketball and deck tennis also had their enthusiasts and I have not the slightest doubt that during the summers of 1943 and 1944 in the east compound at Sagan there was more concentrated and varied sport taking place in a small area than anywhere else in the world, or for that matter at any time in history.

To an outsider the camp on a high summer day would have presented an astonishing spectacle. Everywhere men, as scantily clad as was decent, were throwing, hitting or kicking balls from morning until sunset. Many of us became almost totally immersed in playing, thinking or talking about games. However humorous or trivial they might appear in retrospect the activity involved was healthy, amusing and above all a distraction, an escape from the ever lurking threat of anxiety, foreboding and depression.

From my viewpoint, and that of many others, the most significant happening during this period was the appearance of a hickory-shafted lady's mashie. It came into the possession of Sydney Smith, a journalist of repute with the *Daily Express*. I came upon him one day as he was chipping a peculiar-looking ball back and forth. He had made it by winding wool and cotton round a carved piece of pine and covering it with a laboriously sewn bit of cloth. Although the ball bore no resemblance to a real one, and would travel only about sixty yards, it gave us a wonderful echo of golf. Hour after hour we would play, objects of incredulous stares. When others wanted to take part Sydney would say, 'make a ball and then you can'. His words heralded a revolution beyond our imagining.

In almost no time men were making much improved balls, more durable and tighter-wound than the original. Then one crafty fellow wound strands of rubber round his ball and straightaway was the longest hitter in the camp. Within a few weeks a score of people were involved, including several good players. The best of these were Danny O'Brien, a Scottish schoolboy international, and Ronnie Morgan, a Worcestershire county player who reached the last eight of the first English Championship after the war. George Murray Frame, who had a low handicap at Troon, and Oliver Green, now Director of the Woburn Country Club, probably were next in the ranking.

The Sagan golf club was born but we needed a course. To say that we laid out one is something of an overstatement. All we did was choose places for tees and suitable objects to hit for holes. These included tree stumps, poles, an incinerator door and a tiny fir tree about eighteen inches high. As the poles were quite high many a hole in one was recorded a dozen feet or more from the ground.

When the membership had grown to twelve we had our first competition, a knockout, and Hugh Falkus, well known after the war for his nature broadcasts, and I reached the final. Falkus, no golfer then but gifted with strong hands and a deadly aim, was expert at hitting the 'holes', such as they were. The fir tree caused some discussion because we thought that its little trunk had to be hit, whereas Falkus would claim to have holed out if his shot whistled yards past the tree but grazed a leaf in passing. Fortunately Falkus was not as deadly as usual in our match and I became the first Open champion of Sagan.

As interest grew evolution was swift. An eighteen-hole course was planned and in such a confined space involved some dangerous if fascinating shots. One blind shot over the kitchen hut, controlled by the Germans, had its perils and the fire pool made a splendid hazard for the 18th. It was deep and filthy but this did not deter two madmen from diving in to retrieve a ball on a freezing winter day. The air was alive with balls of all manner and shapes whistling about the camp. Our activities were watched with interest, scorn and at first tolerance, but it was soon obvious that the course would have to be smaller. Hole after hole was played over tiny gardens, a few yards square, where it was possible to coax vegetables into life. The horticulturists were far from amused when a golf ball decapitated a cherished tomato plant. Sunbathers were also in danger. One man was hit on the bare body with a full shot from no great range and was furious when the striker exploded with laughter. One unfortunate creature's peaceful morning shave in front of his window was interrupted when a half-topped tee shot crashed through the glass. On another occasion a German *Unteroffizier's* morning constitutional in the abort at the end of the kitchen buildings was disturbed by the crash of glass all around him accompanied by the inevitable mirth. Someone had shanked. No action was taken save we were asked to move the tee. Such incidents were fairly frequent and we feared that a serious complaint might be laid against us.

Meanwhile the first green or rather 'brown' had been fashioned by Norman Thomas. With the loan of a spade from the Germans this did not take long. An area of about eight by ten yards was cleared of stones, stumps and roots and the ground levelled, covered with good yellow sand and kept smooth with a home-made squeegee. The surfaces were fairly true and quite fast after rain. Eventually we had browns for all nine holes of the new and shorter course which measured some 850 yards. The longest hole was 140 and the par 29. The course record still stands at 57 and is unlikely to be broken.

At first the Germans regarded the shaping of little banks and bunkers with suspicion until they realised that there was nothing ulterior in our motives. Mistakenly, they thought otherwise after Eric Williams and his two companions had achieved the only successful escape from our camp by means of the famous Wooden Horse. The tunnel was discovered later the same might but the German attempt to hold an identity check was frustrated by deliberate fusing of the lights in one hut. This made them more angry than usual and clearly they decided on a show of strength. The next day the whole camp was assembled and surrounded by some 200 soldiers with machine guns at the ready. Had there been further signs of insurrection I think they would have fired. Fortunately they calmed down and the only victim was the golf course which seemed an obvious means of dispersing sand from the tunnel. This was understandable because for months the Wooden Horse had stood between the wire and our sixth 'brown', the one visible in the picture facing page 48. The course was flattened but a few weeks later the Germans were persuaded that it was innocent, which it was, and head brownkeeper Timmy Biden and his helpers restored the course. The excavation of yellow sand was forbidden; the browns became almost blacks and their surfaces not so true.

The planning of the course was a natural development, the evolution of ball manufacture truly remarkable. Once rubber had been introduced it became one of the most precious commodities in the camp and the fervent golfers would make all manner of sacrifices to get it. Prisoners were allowed quarterly clothing parcels from home and many was the plea for gym shoes, air cushions, tobacco pouches and the like which were ripped to shreds on arrival. The man with rubber to spare or to exchange was every golfer's friend. The effect on our golf was no less than the Haskell banishing the gutty forever. The age of the string ball was dead.

Within no time ball-making had become almost an art form. The Scottish craftsmen of old would have nodded approvingly at the ingenuity, skill and patience we devoted to the task. Most of the balls had a solid rubber core, some hollowed to hold a small bit of lead. Several feet of rubber were necessary. This was stretched and cut with razor blades or scissors into very narrow strips which were wound round the core as in an ordinary ball. Experience alone taught one the correct tension. Too tight a winding produced a wooden effect when the ball was struck or would cause the rubber to snap. If too slack the ball was like a pudding. At the same time we strove to make the ball 1.62 inches in diameter and 1.62 ounces in weight. Delicate experiment usually made this possible.

The earlier balls of string and wood were covered with cloth, or Elastoplast coaxed from the officer in charge of medical supplies, but this process was soon abandoned. The new covers were made of leather cut into two figures of eight, similar to those covering a baseball. These were carefully sewn with thread or twine, which was not readily available, or strands of cotton strengthened with wax or German boot polish.

The leather, often obtained by cutting good shoes into pieces, varied in thickness and quality. It was usually advisable to soak and stretch it before cutting the figures of eight according to tin patterns, cut to a fraction of a millimetre of the right size. These had been shaped by one of the experts, possibly Norman Ryder who produced a detailed thesis on ball-making for the benefit of the embryo practitioners. Very soon balls of astonishing quality were appearing from the, so to speak, benches of Ryder and others. An Australian, Samson, was highly skilled and one example of his work is in the Royal and Ancient museum at St Andrews. It is precisely the same weight and size as a real golf ball, perfectly symmetrical, with cover stitching that would do credit to a machine.

I did not rank with Ryder, Samson, Graham Hogg and others as a ball-maker but mine were fairly close to the true mark. Shortly after the war Reginald Whitcombe and Alfred Perry played an exhibition match at Stockport, then my home club. I asked them to hit the balls I had brought back; they did so with drivers and both flew some 200 yards. Years later I asked Nicklaus to try one. He refused for fear that it might burst, but to this day the one I have still bounces well. The other is in the Museum of the United States Golf Association in New Jersey.

Such is my incompetence in matters domestic that my wife Jean still finds it hard to believe that the balls really were my own work. As far as I can recall making one took me about six hours as against Ryder's estimate of four. Many a man laboured long over his ball and sometimes, within moments of going on to the course, saw it soar out of bounds over the wire. If he were lucky a passing guard might throw it back, and the guards on the watch towers occasionally used their field glasses to aid the search, but if the ball were lost there was ample time to make another.

The perimeter of the camp was protected by a high double-stage barbed wire fence. Any attempt to climb this could be met with a bullet but inside the main fence was a strip of no man's land bordered by a low tripwire. Entering this area was forbidden but so many balls from the incessant games went in that the Germans provided a few white jackets. Donning one of these was tantamount to giving parole that no attempt to escape would be made and the balls could be retrieved.

During these early months of golf the little mashie, often in the hands of strong, unskilled players, must have hit several hundred thousand shots. That it survived was a rare tribute to the quality of the hickory and the firm of Patrick of Leven who, I think, were the makers. In the confusion when we were suddenly evacuated as the Russians advanced early in 1945 someone may have taken it with him. I hope so: it deserved a place of honour in a museum. I brought back the first steel-shafted club to reach the camp. It bore the name of Gilbert Heron of Oslo and mighty useful it proved as an aid during our march in the snow, lasting a week, to

Luckenwalde, the final camp for most of us.

As the golfers wrote to various countries pleading for clubs a good supply was forthcoming. Norman Thomas and I had been adopted, in a manner of speaking, by a most attractive Danish girl, Doreen Wessel, who wrote to us and sent parcels. One of these consisted of ten clubs. Sadly, I never met the angelic Doreen, who married an American and went to live in Grosse Pointe, Michigan.

Our joy at the arrival of these clubs can be imagined. All were hickory but in good condition and the pressure on the little mashie was greatly eased. Such had been the demand for clubs as the golfing fever spread that home-made affairs began to appear. Some were extraordinary contraptions fit for a museum but their creation revealed remarkable skill and patience. The shafts usually were carved from ice-hockey sticks and the heads fashioned from sections of water jugs or stovepipes melted down. The latter were found to be strong enough without being too heavy, and were not constantly breaking, but the Germans objected to their use and that source was abandoned. Of the clubs that survived regular use one was the work of a Canadian, Don Elliott, a useful golfer and of necessity a powerful one. His club, known as 'Abort Annie,' weighed about twenty ounces but the best of these efforts was made by Lee Usher, an American from Iowa. As I recall his club was well balanced and strong.

In the autumn of 1943 I wrote to the Royal and Ancient at St Andrews, giving a brief account of our golf and asking if they could spare a few clubs and balls. A copy of the letter was sent to Bernard Darwin who wrote of our efforts in one of his *Country Life* commentaries. He mentioned instances of golf in unusual places in the First War including a prison camp where young airmen were armed with cleeks. 'So erratic were their shots that on one occasion the German commandant, a portly and pompous old colonel, advanced to the middle of the playground, possibly to protest, and was driven into highly undignified flight. The airmen were no respecters of persons and pursued him relentlessly with a creeping barrage of cleek shots. He did not apparently bear any malice; so there must have been one German colonel for whom something good could be said'. We ventured no such liberties at Sagan, at least not intentionally.

Darwin ended his article by assuring readers that arrangements had been made by the R. and A. to send clubs and balls through the Red Cross. They arrived and among them was the steel-shafted driver. Naturally its use was forbidden except for practise swinging but I used to feel it longingly and wonder whether I would ever hit a shot with it. The chance came one bitter winter day when everyone was inside and the camp deserted. I went to a far corner, almost trembling with anticipation, and teed one of the real golf balls which had come with the clubs from St Andrews.

The driver had an extremely whippy shaft like those which Bing Crosby used and was quite unsuitable for me. However, I made a good contact with the ball which soared away out of sight in a great slice over the kitchen building. Anxiously I waited for any indication that it might have hit something and then came the inevitable plonk and tinkle of broken glass. The ball had crashed full pitch through a window and so startled the people in the room that they flung themselves to the floor. In the deep winter silence they thought that a bullet was responsible. Greatly embarrassed I went to apologise, prepared to face any anger if I could reclaim the precious ball. It was given back to me but my stroke was the first and last ever hit with a driver at Sagan.

By 1944 pleas for clubs had borne rich fruit. They came from many countries, mostly neutral. One man received several new steel-shafted irons and eventually we had about a 100 clubs. Real golf balls were considered too dangerous to use except on special occasions such as an exhibition match when the course was cleared and the camp warned. And so in the naive belief that the balls would be less hurtful leather was substituted for the gutta-percha covers. Miraculously, no one was seriously hurt even though it was quite common for people to hit shots back and forth to one another, within a few yards of passers-by on their circuits of the camp.

Within a few months of the golf starting over 300 people had played the course. Although the number on it at any one time had to be controlled the fever did not abate. All day long men were swinging clubs, practising or talking golf. O'Brien and Morgan particularly, and other lesser experts, were much in demand for giving lessons and several prisoners, who had never previously touched a club, were quite competent golfers when they returned home. After all they had reasonable tuition in the basics of grip, stance and arc of swing and opportunity for practice. It was amusing to hear embryo golfers talking of draw and fade, weight transference, backspin and so on, within a few weeks of starting to play.

Hitting approaches of up to 100 yards or more to the minute browns was splendid training and I remember my first round or two on a proper course after the war. The greens looked enormous and I wondered how anyone could possibly miss them, but that illusion did not last long. Nevertheless many learned a great deal about the game and had also grown accustomed to playing in front of crowds. Quiet and well-behaved though they were when an important match was in progress one was always aware of critical eyes and that, as most golfers will agree, is a great aid to concentration.

Competitions of all kinds and challenge matches were frequent. In one such O'Brien and Samson challenged any pair in the camp to a 36-hole foursome and two 36-hole singles for a stake of fifty pounds. The backers chose Morgan and Frame to play for them but after winning the foursome they lost both singles.

In writing an account of this match for the camp newspaper, (a few sheets pinned to a notice board), I began to think that reporting games was the profession for me. Later that summer I wrote the story of the golf in our camp. Several of us thought it might be of interest at home but had no idea where to send it, then someone suggested Henry Longhurst.

Everyone enjoyed his book, *It Was Good while It Lasted* and he looked an amiable soul from his pictures. First it had to be censored by the Germans and some unfortunate fellow had to plough through 14,000 words. Only one part, where I had made an oblique reference to the Wooden Horse, was deleted. The Germans probably thought the story reflected a contented life for the prisoners; it may have done. There was no point in my being critical of the conditions if the story was to reach England. It was duly mailed to Longhurst care of his publishers but little did I imagine that it would be a step towards fulfilling a dream.

The winters in East Germany were too harsh for the regular playing of outside games but most people found pursuits enough to pass the time. Many plunged into serious studies because by then it was possible to take exams in numerous subjects, not least law. I have no doubt that many a career was founded in those dark years. Study was not easy in densely crowded quarters and needed exceptional determination and concentration if it were to be worthwhile.

Neither of these gifts was my strong point but I did pass a Royal Society of Arts examination in Spanish of about O level standard. The exams were as strictly invigilated as any at home and I was quite proud of my certificate, small achievement though it was. My teacher was John Tilsley, a prisoner since 1939, who had taught himself Spanish while in Germany. He started a class and bravely contrived to pass on his knowledge but there were no Spanish speakers in the camp and we lacked practise in conversation.

For many of us bridge was an enormous boon, indeed a salvation in the winter. I had little idea of the game when taken prisoner although both my parents were good players. At first our bridge in the camps was pretty moderate to say the best of it but after a while many of us studied in earnest. The works of Ely Culbertson duly arrived and became our bibles. Day after day we would play from early afternoon until midnight when the lights went out. There were various regular schools, some more earnest than others, but those in which I was involved played with all the thought and concentration we could muster. Difficult hands were analysed, often long after the session had ended, and gradually several of us became above-average players as I realised after the war.

For a long while George Murray Frame was my most frequent partner, his bridge as steady as his golf, and given a reasonable balance of the cards we were usually victorious. We mastered Culbertson's system of asking bids, long since supplanted by cue bids, but we found it invaluable not only for bidding slams but for stopping short when they were not safely makable. Heaton Nichols and Jim Margrie were two other devotees. For two years I kept a record of my bridge, which is of interest regarding slams. In just over 2000 rubbers with various partners I made 24 grand slams and 238 small slams. Obviously we missed some which were makable and bid others which were not, but over so long a period the average is probably a true guide. Every other form of cards was played in the camp but I always preferred bridge. Ultimately the superior player will prevail even if the margin between him and the others is only slight.

One winter five of us played almost every day, cutting for partners after each rubber. One man was less reliable than the rest and inevitably was the only loser. We played for what now would be 10p a hundred, a considerable stake then but enough to prevent careless play. I think I won about £70 paid by cheques written on scraps of paper, all of which were honoured after the war.

Early in 1945 we were happily involved in a game when the Germans came rushing in and told us that we had until dawn to leave the camp. The longed-for Russian advance had reached the Oder not far to the east of us. The next morning we trailed off into the snow, not knowing where we were going and carrying what we could on our backs or on rapidly-made sleds. A vast amount of stuff including, someone estimated, over two million cigarettes was left in the camp. The journey was not pleasant but had its diverting moments.

The second night out hundreds sought refuge in a church and I remember the mad scramble for a space to sleep. I managed a choir stall but one enterprising fellow made straight for the altar, knowing that it offered space for only one. He moved the cross to one end, hung his things on it and slumbered in peace. Little fires were alight in the churchyard as people heated tins but when we left the next morning there was no mess, nothing out of place, no trace that the old church had truly been a sanctuary.

We spent another night in a glass factory which at least was warm, and the last of the journey in a stable on the Graf von Arnim's estate. The next morning brought a rare surprise in the shape of the Grafin. From notes made at the time and forgotten until I ventured upon this book I recall that she was attractive, in her thirties, petite with light wavy hair and clear grey eyes. She was wearing a sports shirt, a brown tweed coat and short riding boots. Years of enforced abstinence had not entirely dulled my awareness of feminine appeal and she was the first woman I had spoken to in over four years.

German guards were at hand but I chatted to her for quite a long while. She spoke freely of the Nazis, of the war and of their estate, and of how they would have to leave it soon in an Alfa Romeo towed by two horses because they had no petrol. One of the mares in the loosebox where we were talking was about to foal and as she crooned to it in German I realised that it was a different language to the coarse tongue I had been hearing for so long. She was apprehensive of the Russians, the local Communists and the Nazis; we are between three stools she said.

The war seemed utterly remote in the morning stillness with the park, wintry and bleak, the lake and the great old trees all suggesting peace. On the top of the castle was a figure holding a spear which to me seemed a brave symbol of the dying world beneath. The incident depressed me and I wondered what would become of her, but soon we were in cattle trucks on the way to Luckenwalde. It is strange how memory can reject the unpleasant and until reading my brief notes I had forgotten that the conditions were 'the bloodiest I have ever seen — two hundred in a room with only two fires and three-decker beds. Many people with dysentery, sickness and exhaustion. Felt OK myself; in fact the worse the conditions the better mentally I have usually been.' Food was desperately short, a greater hardship for recent prisoners than for us, and I cannot remember any games but we could see the fires of Berlin, a dreadful, awesome sight.

Although the end of the war was near we became increasingly uneasy when the Germans tried to evacuate us to the south. We were taken to the station and loaded into cattle trucks, (*hommes* 40, *chevaux* 8). The corridor between Russians and Americans was narrow and under constant bombardment; our chances of passing through unscathed were remote but fortunately no engine was available and the journey was abandoned. I cannot recommend a cattle truck for sleeping quarters. We were packed in and the doors locked throughout the night. Tins were the only means of catering for calls of nature and once I was wakened by a warm stream on my face. A friend, as it happened, was stumbling past me intending to pour the contents of his tin through the window, but in the darkness had failed to notice that the bottom of the tin was punctured.

During the lovely spring days we heard that President Roosevelt had died and then to our relief came the order to return to the camp. The guards by then mostly were elderly *Volksturm*, Dad's Army types, and several times on the walk back to the camp we stopped so that they might rest. There was nothing aggressive or unpleasant about them and we pitied their immediate future. The Russians were very near and the only course for the old guards was to flee — which they did soon afterwards, leaving the camp unprotected. This was an eerie time for it seemed possible that some bloody-minded character might take it upon himself to have a go at us. One night a fighter aircraft screamed low over the camp, cannons blasting, and I well remember the crashes as men toppled out of the top bunks, but the shells fell far away.

A few mornings later we were woken by the sound of Russian tanks and armoured vehicles roaring into the camp and had a first sight of their formidable fighting females. The Russian attitude was not unreasonable. We were allowed to wander freely outside the camp but soon learned to identify ourselves quickly as British or American; there were several instances of others being shot. When we heard that the war in Europe was over a few of us gathered in what had been a German officer's house to hear Churchill's V-E Day speech. Most of the group had been prisoners for four years and more and had become thoroughly cynical and jaded in their outlook. As the great voice died away there was no excitement, no explosion of joy and relief. As I recall it the silence was broken by a harsh voice saying 'Well that rat fuck's over!'

For millions it was but not quite for us. Days and weeks passed without sign of repatriation. An American convoy of 100 trucks came from the Elbe hoping to take the British and Americans away. Maybe they neglected to ask permission from the Russians; we were in their territory. Whatever the reason the Russians posted armed guards by the trucks to prevent anyone boarding them. No one did but many left the camp and made their own way to the Elbe about 100 miles away. As far as I know most of them arrived safely, but I and other old lags were taking no such chances. We might have done had we known, as I heard after reaching England, that the Russians were considering repatriating us by way of Odessa or, worse, making us work because apparently Russian prisoners had been made to work in France or somewhere. Happily we knew nothing of this and the early summer dragged on.

Every day civilian refugees of numerous nationalities streamed into the camp. Many from Berlin were striving to get to the south, among them an English girl named Thomas who had married a German before the war and had survived the final bombardment of Berlin. If I remember rightly she had children with her; and I have often wondered how she fared.

At last the Russians relented and took us to the Elbe in trucks. We were handed over to the Americans who, as I recall the week we spent with them, were kind enough without being over-welcoming. Many of us looked pretty scruffy and to some Americans must have appeared as a bunch of 'Goddam Limeys'. We were very browned off by then and one heard remarks such as 'We've been prisoners of the Germans, the Russians and the Americans but wait till the British get hold of us!' As it proved we need have had no fears; the reception centre at Cosford was splendidly organised. The Americans flew us to Brussels where we expected to wait for a night, but just as some of us were planning to celebrate our first glimpse of civilisation we were hastened on our way home.

One memory of those strange times which will never fade was of the flight back to England. For years one had longed for the day when the English coast came into view again, never doubting that it would. As we crossed the North Sea on a perfect evening late in May, I stood behind the pilots of the Dakota waiting for the coast to appear and feeling nothing but a massive anticlimax.

For years one had lived a cocooned sort of existence, completely screened from all the normal problems of everyday life. Short of escaping one had no control over one's destiny. One never had to think of taxes, rates, bills, transport of any kind, looking after a family, pursuing a career or tending a garden. If the Germans wanted to shuttle you round the country there was nothing you could do about it.

Gradually one came dangerously close to being so conditioned to life as a prisoner that any interruption was resented. I became sharply aware of this one day in 1944. Very occasionally the Germans organised walks outside the camp; the prisoners signed a parole that they would not attempt to escape and little parties with a guard would go out into the country for two or three hours. I went only once because it disturbed life's trivial routine and I was relieved to be back in the camp again.

That evening in the aircraft I knew there was no retreat from reality and that I had to face whatever lay ahead, to make decisions and to accept responsibility. The prospect was disturbing yet, emotional though I am, there were no tears, no lump in the throat as we crossed the coast.

We landed at Dunsfold in Surrey, and almost before I trod at last on English soil a WAAF armed with a flit gun or some such weapon squirted powder up my trouser legs and jacket sleeves. We may have looked odd but we were not lousy. Neither did a long night train journey to Cosford quicken a joyous sense of return but, as I have said, the reception was most efficient. Within twelve hours I was released on six months' leave and a cousin, who lived in Wolverhampton, collected me. I stayed the night with him but not until I joined my parents the next morning was I fully sensitive to the impact of homecoming.

In writing about prison camp life I have dwelt on the lighter side because the games had a decisive influence on my future. I have said little of the frustration, the horror of the unknown sentence, the awful loneliness of spirit which could lead to despair and the anxiety about family, particularly for those who married shortly before being taken prisoner and scarcely knew their wives. There were no visits from friends or relations and no journalists or reformers eager to record complaints. I sometimes wonder what those who show far greater concern for the welfare of vicious criminals than for their innocent victims would think of the conditions endured by prisoners of war.

CHAPTER 3
IT'S NOT WHAT YOU KNOW ...

A prisoner once declared that when he got home he would find a naked woman, cover her in condensed milk and slowly lick it away. Such visions, and even less exotic ones like the enormous rich meals one planned to eat, swiftly vanished. Some may have found a woman willing to enjoy or endure such an experiment, but for the majority of us it was sufficient to know that food and feminine companionship were available. For years I had longed for bacon and eggs, a simple enough repast, but on the first day back I could not finish a modest portion. The stomach had shrunk and I had no real appetite I was always wanting little snacks — probably as an assurance that I never need be lastingly hungry again. After years of sleeping on a straw palliasse, which soon lost its resilience, I could not sleep on a mattress and used a hard camp bed instead. Relatives had been warned that their loved one might behave oddly for a while and I remember my mother's impassive face when, unaware that she was nearby, I swore as I never would have done normally.

Aside from such lapses and quirks it was remarkable how easily most prisoners settled to the ordinary ways of life. Driving was no problem and after a brief refresher course I was flying again. Physically all was well but I came to realise that the confinement had left more lasting effects, restlessness and increasing impatience. My remaining spell in the RAF and thereafter all the travelling involved in covering golf and other games appeased the restless side but not the impatience.

For most of my life impatience, often with myself, has been the root cause of almost every stupid thing I have said and done, including the hitting of bad golf shots. I have an unreasoning horror of queues, traffic jams, even the most trivial delays. I am told that not so long ago when an anonymous professional was taking an age over three putts I said with some feeling, 'Doesn't he realise that my life is ebbing away?' Dread of boredom is a symptom of gathering years and a golfer who goes through his dreary routine of marking, cleaning, often unnecessarily, and lining the ball maker's name towards the hole is a supreme instance of the modern games-playing bore.

At the outset of the war I had no thought of middle age; regrets had not taken the place of dreams. Then, all too swiftly afterwards, one was forty and no birthday since, even fifty or sixty, has depressed me more. Many others who had lived the curiously suspended, detached, almost timeless existence of the prisoner of war must have wondered where their youth had gone. Naturally one was anxious to compensate for the lost time.

Within days of arriving home I was wondering if I could find a job writing about games, preferably cricket or golf. I wrote to Henry Longhurst, then a Member of Parliament, who invited me to dine with his wife Claudine and himself in the House. Straightaway I was fascinated by the sharpness of his mind and the wonderfully quick wit which delighted people the world over for a generation and more.

Henry could not have received a stranger more kindly. He explained how he had tried to interest the Red Cross in publishing the story of the prison camp golf in booklet form. He had thought, and I am sure he was right, that it could have been a profitable venture for them but they refused. I stressed my anxiety to become a golf correspondent and Henry said that the prospects might be good later. Little did I think then that he and I would spend many enjoyable times together in many different places in the years to come.

Soon afterwards Henry arranged for me to meet Henry Cotton who had long been a distant hero. He was living in the Dorchester, was immediately sympathetic and later wrote an article about the Sagan golf in the old *Sport and Country* magazine. These meetings were exciting for one who previously had no contact with the golfing establishment, and further encouragement was at hand.

My father had received a letter from an old friend, William Renison, an eminent Scottish artist well known for his etchings. He did one of Glamis Castle as a personal Christmas card for the Duchess of York shortly before she became Queen. Renison had read an article in the *Glasgow Herald* by Sam McKinlay who asked if any of his readers had played golf in curious places during the war.

I wrote to McKinlay telling him of my experiences and he asked me to write a short account of the golf at Sagan. I did so and we arranged to meet. He was still serving in the RAF at Medmenham and after lunch we played at Beaconsfield. I was much impressed by his golf; he was still one of the foremost Scottish amateurs, had played in the 1934 Walker Cup match and in 1947 reached the semifinal of the Amateur championship at Carnoustie. Later McKinlay gave me an introduction to Robert Browning, who edited *Golfing* for some forty years. The kindness on McKinlay's part led to a happy association with the magazine lasting many years. Browning, a delightful, cultured man and one of the game's most distinguished historians, published my prison golf story in five consecutive issues. I was heartened, but Browning could hold out no prospects of a job. Of necessity staffs on periodicals and newspapers were small and at that time there was no room for inexperienced beginners.

In the event I decided to extend my short service commission for another four years. Having completed various courses I was posted to 31 Squadron on the old Hendon airfield. We existed as a communications service for the Air Ministry as it was then. Either we would provide an aircraft for someone to use himself or, if he were not a pilot, one of us would chauffeur him. We were a small friendly group, mostly flight lieutenants, could fly when we wished and the West End was only twenty minutes away by tube. Quite often I would fly to Ringway, the nearest airport to my home, for the weekend. In all it was a pleasant life which suited me admirably. Now the field has almost vanished beneath buildings and often when passing I can hardly believe that I took off from there 150 times or more. Even in the late forties the field was surrounded by buildings, but we hardly gave a thought as to what might happen if the single engines of our little Procters were to cut before we were high enough to turn back. Happily no such emergency befell us.

Many people's lives are changed as a result of chance meetings and one such probably had a decisive effect on mine. The Hendon Golf Club had generously given the courtesy of their course to the squadron. One day our adjutant, Ken Brabner, and I were playing there and I mishit my approach to the first green. I dropped another ball which finished through the green and when we were halfway up the second fairway I remembered that I had not recovered the ball. I hurried back, passing two girls who were playing behind us. Thereafter some chatter, carefully contrived on our part, ensued and we invited them for a drink in the clubhouse. The parents of one of the girls, Gillian Long, a lively attractive person, joined us and this led to a lasting friendship with the family. They were most kind to me during my time at Hendon and Gillian Prentice, as she became not long afterwards, and her husband John are among our closest friends.

Kingsley Long, Gill's father, was on the staff of *The People* and for many years wrote the 'Man of the People' feature. He was a gentle, retiring man and I would never have suspected that he was the author of 'No Mean City', a story set in the Glasgow slums and told to Long by Alexander McArthur who had lived there. The book was far more outspoken than was fashionable in the thirties and became a sensational best seller. It was reprinted numerous times and many years afterwards Long's daughter was still receiving royalties.

Perhaps because I had settled back into the RAF and had some domestic problems besides I had almost forgotten about writing. A year and more must have passed when I asked Long if he would introduce me to John Addison, sports editor of *The People*. A lunch was arranged and Addison agreed that I could report a rugby match for the paper on Saturdays. This was a beginning but there were other matters to be resolved.

A few months after arriving at Hendon I was promoted to squadron leader. My immediate reaction was one of dismay because it meant that I would have to be posted. There was no vacancy at Hendon for a squadron leader and I was anxious to remain near London. Neither Group nor Command headquarters could help and it seemed that I was destined for Yorkshire. Channels had failed; the last chance was a direct approach.

Many officers of high rank used our aircraft. Group Captain 'Gus' Walker, now Air Chief Marshall Sir Augustus, was a regular customer. By strange coincidence when we moved to Norfolk twenty years later we found that the Walkers had a house at Brancaster and we became firm friends. One of the famous Atcherley twins also used our aircraft and I ventured to ask him if he had a vacancy in his department at the Ministry. He did not but said he would do what he could. His kindness in taking immediate action was typical of that I always encountered in my few dealings with very senior RAF officers.

A few days later the head of the Air Historical Branch, then based in a house in Cadogan Gardens, telephoned to say that he could make use of me. For the three remaining years of my service I led what amounted to a civilian life in Chelsea, while still being able to fly quite often. I was occupied mostly with writing a monograph on the airborne landings in Europe and had an office to myself until another man came to share the room. He was Mervyn Mills, eventually author of several novels and a much more gifted historian than I was. Later he told me that I did not warmly welcome his intrusion on my solitude, but I soon had the sense to recognise a kindred spirit and another enduring friendship was born.

Researches for my task involved a trip to Normandy to examine the dropping zones used in the D-day operations. One afternoon as I was about to take off from Carpiquet I recalled my mother having spoken of a holiday she had spent at Dinard. I suggested to my companions, Johnny Bailey, another pilot, and Dick Davies, a historian, that we take a look at Mont St Michel. In doing so we greatly increased our flying time to Rouen where we planned to stay the night, but we arrived there and landed at Madrillet, then a little private field.

On enquiring whether we could refuel I was told that as a military aircraft we would have to get written permission from the British Consul. I remember that Bailey and I both thought that this would be rather a bore.

Surely we had enough petrol to reach Paris? But common sense prevailed and thank God it did in the light of what was to happen the next day. We went to the consulate and found the consul, normally an amiable soul, in testy mood. It was a Sunday and he was having trouble struggling out of his consular uniform after attending an official ceremony.

However, he gave us a chit for the petrol and, as an afterthought, suggested that we go to a cocktail party that afternoon in the Ecole des Beaux Arts. We arrived and two girls, secretaries at the consulate, were detailed to look after us. They were attractive and one, I thought, was particularly fetching. Jean Stewart was born in Rouen, one of two daughters of a Scottish father who had lived in France since the First War, and a French mother.

As a British citizen her father was interned in Saint Denis near Paris until the Germans left France. Her mother suffered the same fate for several months, thus Jean and her elder sister, Gladys, were alone. Because of their age Madame Stewart was released but not allowed to return to Rouen which was considered a military zone. For a while they lived in Paris and thereafter Chaumont, suffering the privations and dangers shared by millions under the German occupation.

I was soon aware that she had a lively, perceptive mind and an ironic sense of humour, qualities she was to need in full measure in the years ahead. Her English was stronger than my French, not that any language problems would have arrested my pursuit which continued that year by way of the packet from Newhaven to Dieppe.

As we had decided to stay a second night in Rouen, I wanted to see if the aircraft was safely bedded down and to check the refuelling. Hoping to confirm what I hoped was a favourable impression I asked Jean if she would like a flight. Somewhat to my surprise she agreed; we took a taxi to the airfield and I made a careful circuit of the city. She had flown before and I am sure my tactic did not influence her to consider marriage, but it was amusing to have taken one's intended for a flight within an hour or so of having met her for the first time.

We were married in January in the Holy Trinity Church in Sloane Street. As the bride had no convenient male relative Mervyn Mills gave her away, possibly with reluctance because he had not then met the charming Frenchwoman who was to become a splendid wife to him. We settled in a mews flat which was where the Carlton Tower Hotel now stands and began to wonder what the future held. I had little more than a year before my commission expired and my application for a permanent one had been turned down. This was not surprising. Although I passed the medical tests for flying, at 35 I was getting on from a General Duties viewpoint and my service record showed a complete blank for five years. As I

45

have said before an apparent disappointment proved to be an enormous blessing.

Three days before our marriage I had covered my first rugby match for *The People* and I remember the feverish search through the sports pages to see if it had been used. Suddenly, there it was, about 150 words on a London Welsh match at Herne Hill. Thereafter I covered several more matches and when the summer came the sports editor was good enough to let me do some cricket. During a match at Lord's, notable for a pleasing innings by Cyril Washbrook, I met Denys Rowbotham, cricket correspondent of the *Manchester Guardian* as in those days it was called. A week or so later I spent an evening with Charles Burton, long a familiar Fleet Street figure, who wrote regularly for the *Guardian.* He arranged for me to cover a match at Bournemouth, where Jack Robertson and Bill Edrich scored centuries, and subsequently regular soccer matches, but the most significant event was to come.

The 1949 Ryder Cup match was at Ganton and I was to cover it for *The People*. A friend at Hendon flew me to Driffield whence I made my way by bus. The days at Ganton were wonderfully exciting for me. Hogan was there as nonplaying captain, still recovering from the accident that almost killed him earlier that year and only able to walk a short distance. The British played splendidly in winning three of the four foursomes and Charles Whitcombe, the captain, was pardonably optimistic afterwards. But I have no doubt that Hogan had some cool plain words for his team that evening. They tore from the gate the next morning in the singles, produced some devastating golf and only Dai Rees and Jimmy Adams could win for Britain. I had seen a great deal that I wanted to get off my chest and the space in *The People* was nowhere near enough so I decided to write a full account for my own benefit. It was mightily fortunate that I did so, as I discovered months later.

The week after the Ryder Cup I was due to cover the final of the *News of the World* matchplay championship for *The People*. The *Guardian* had also asked me to report a football match at Charlton on the same day. So desperately keen was I not to imperil any contact that I decided to try to do both. Walton Heath is no mean distance from Charlton and I did not have a car. The old Standard that I had bought for £12.50 from a breaker's yard in Cambridge in 1940 had been cherished through the war by my parents but when Jean and I were living in the heart of London we decided to sell. It fetched £135. Thus, on that awful Saturday I was tied to public transport.

We lived near Lingfield and having travelled to Walton Heath I watched the morning round between Cotton and Rees, raced across London and arrived at Charlton in time for the kickoff. Luckily Middlesbrough were the visitors and the quicksilver genius of Mannion gave me the basis of an article, and inspired an easy win for his team. I left at half time and was back at Walton Heath as the final holes were being played. Again I was lucky. The match went to the 36th where Rees won, and gave me the climax for *The People* piece. Having telephoned this I hastened back to the *Guardian* office in Fleet Street, completed my football piece with the aid of evening newspapers and left it to be wired the next day to Manchester where all the printing was then done. Not for years did anyone save Jean, who greeted an exhausted husband some time after midnight know of my absurd double act, but it sufficed, and I was quietly pleased with myself.

In the following weeks I covered several more matches for the *Guardian*. As these were always on Saturdays they did not conflict with my work in the Historical Branch. It was then arranged that I should meet Larry Montague, the sports editor, for the first time. The headquarters of the paper, until 1961, was in Manchester and I shall never forget the dark winter afternoon as we talked over tea in the Old Rectory Club.

My first impression of Montague was of a genial and yet slightly forbidding person, as I was to discover he could be when the occasion demanded. Denys Rowbotham was also there and after some general chat I asked Montague if I could possibly write golf for the paper. Fortunately I had brought the long piece I had written about the Ryder Cup match the previous autumn. I passed it to Montague remarking as I did so that I had brought my music. The phrase was typical of the trite remarks that leap to the tongue when one is as apprehensive as I was, but Montague said nothing and swiftly skimmed through the article. I remember thinking that he was not giving it his full attention but learned later that he was an uncommonly fast reader. He handed it back and simply said 'I like golf written like that.' Not long afterwards he made the decision that transformed my life.

CHAPTER 4
UNDER MONTAGUE

Early in 1950 Montague planned the events I was to report during the coming season, even to the approximate length I would have to write. What magic reading the names of the places made to one who had never visited any of them before — Deal, Newcastle, County Down, St Andrews, Troon, Birkdale, Formby and Carnoustie. A whole new world was unfolding, a wonderful summer world fulfilling the dreams of youth. I was to cover cricket as well during the weeks after the Open, when there was less important golf than there is nowadays. I knew that unless I failed the greater part of my working life thereafter would be spent in the good air and in beautiful places, and that never again would I be lastingly confined in an office, save for occasional spells in the winter.

I was exceptionally fortunate in starting and remaining for almost thirty years with a serious and in the early days even austere paper. I wanted no part of sensational journalism with its magnification of the trivial, but simply to write about the games themselves, the way they were played and their settings. Never had I thought of myself as a journalist in the complete sense of the term. I did not have the essential curiosity or persistence to any great degree, or the desire to intrude upon people's private lives.

Neither did I have the breadth of interests that make a good reporter and as such I would not have been considered for a job with the *Guardian*. My only claim was as a specialist writer and so Montague was prepared to give me a chance. Long afterwards I asked him whether he had not taken a risk. He said that he had not, that he could see I was passionate about certain games, reasonably able to express myself and that, where necessary, my writing could be schooled to the *Guardian* style which was more strictly observed then than it is now.

It did not take long to realise how lucky I had been mainly because of being, through coincidence rather than contrivance, in the right place at the right time. When I appeared the *Guardian* did not have a regular golf correspondent. Eric Prain had covered the 1948 season and the *Manchester*

Evening News writer had done both jobs the following year, too great a burden for him. Had the *Guardian* had their own man there would have been no opening for me.

The first golf tournament I covered for the *Guardian* was the Assistants championship at Worsley. Happily it coincided with my terminal leave from the RAF. Memories of those days still linger, not least the kindness shown to a newcomer by other writers; Freddie Pignon of the *Daily Mail*, Bill Guild of the *Yorkshire Post* and Geoffrey Cousins of the old *Star* immediately come to mind. For many years Cousins, as secretary, did sterling work in founding excellent relations between the Golf Writers Association and the various governing bodies and, at this writing, is as active an octogenarian as anyone I know.

The late Harry Weetman won the championship with much to spare and completed the process by holing in one with his last stroke. When he saw his seven-iron shot roll into the hole Weetman strolled to the clubhouse without going to the green nearby. I have never heard of another instance of a man finishing a 72-hole event, or any other for that matter, in such spectacular fashion. Weetman's massive strength and beautiful putting were the basis of a notable career, but of the others who competed at Worsley only Peter Butler and Bernard Hunt reached the game's highest places and remained there for many years.

Although obviously on trial I do not recall feeling anxious; it seemed to me that reporting a golf tournament, when given the ample space of those days, was simply a matter of producing comment about certain players, some run of play, and of never forgetting to tell the reader about the weather and its effect on the course, and what the setting was like. There is little point in praising an eagle if the player reaches the green with a drive and a medium iron, without saying that the fairway was fast and the wind helping, but even today such facts are often ignored.

I was confident that I could become a golf correspondent; nonetheless I was hoping for a word from Montague that he was satisfied. None came for several weeks. I realised later that he spared praise and did not criticise unless strongly moved to do so and that his silence implied confidence in me. Montague never interfered with his correspondents. Once he had appointed me, inexperienced though I was, I never felt that he was looking over my shoulder. Gradually I knew that I was trusted as the man on the spot, best able to judge what was happening. Obviously he and his successors as sports editors would make suggestions for articles and would ask for comment on topical affairs or items of news but in thirty years I was never told how to approach or deal with a daily report. No one ever said 'That must be your angle, get quotes from so and so, or build up someone else.' Never were one's articles rewritten, save in the cause of grammar.

There was always a feeling of freedom and no newspaper writer could expect more.

Before I started Montague told me never to strive to write an exceptional piece every day, advice which was often a comfort when I knew that at best my article was moderate. He also said that if ever I felt tired or stale to let him know, and take a day off. I never did. Although there were no Continental events which involved much travelling or planning, my schedule was demanding. Week after week I travelled about Britain, loving the feeling of exploration and completely absorbed in the golf.

Jean meanwhile spent some time in France during which I had been to Newcastle, County Down and seen the Vicomtesse de Saint-Sauveur, as she then was, win the British championship. So taken was I with the dark grace and beauty of her golf, against a setting in all its Maytime glory, that Denys Rowbotham threatened to send my wife a wire saying that it was high time she returned.

When we did reunite, while I was at a tournament in Worthing, we had been apart for eight weeks. For a while we felt like strangers to one another. I determined that this would not happen again and it never has. Unlike his cricketing counterpart, who might be on tour for months, the golf correspondent rarely has to be away from home for as much as a month. Two or three weeks would usually suffice even for trips to America.

Before that first summer was over Jean was undergoing what must have been an alarming readjustment. Never having lived in Britain before, her contact with sport had been confined to a little gentle lawn tennis. Golf, cricket and the football games were total mysteries and she had married a man whose life, by force of circumstance and inclination, was to be possessed by them. In those early days she must have needed all her reserves of loyalty and patience to survive. Fortunately, as it proved, after a few lessons she decided not to play golf. Our lives therefore have not been totally submerged by the game but she was quick to appreciate its fascination while regarding it objectively. In time she came to know the famous players — Palmer, Nicklaus, Thomson and others — socially, and as human beings rather than as golfing gods. She was quick to detect feet of clay and if I were to become too emotional about someone she could provide an essential tempering effect and still does. Discussions with her have often been more valuable than with someone greatly experienced in playing the game.

As a freelance that first year I was paid five guineas a day including all expenses except travelling; it seems a minute figure now but we managed and Montague saw to it that, with the odd cricket match, I hardly had a spare moment. Winter was a different matter. A weekly soccer match and an occasional article brought in very little. By then we had moved to

Stockport where we shared my mother's largish house. She had been living alone since my father's death in 1945, only a few months after my return from Germany. This was a great sadness; he was a singularly fine character and an uncommonly gentle person for all that he was not without temper. I have always wished that he could have lived until the *Guardian* days began; he would have loved the association with the games.

One day during 1951 a friend, Tom Gribbin, who was news editor of the *Daily Express* in Manchester, suggested that I write rugby league for the *Sunday Express* who would pay double the fees I was getting from the *Guardian* for soccer matches. I could not afford to refuse the kindly offer, but this time I was apprehensive. My previous experience of the game was confined to watching two matches.

I liked Archie Freedman, the editor of the *Scottish Sunday Express*, and begged him to let me go to several matches unannounced so that I could get the feel of the game, but they jumped the gun. In no time there were posters round the grounds bearing my somewhat sickly-looking countenance and signature. I was terrified but could not protest further and remember arriving for matches at places like Wigan, Castleford or St Helens with a handkerchief to my face hoping that no one would recognise me. My reports duly appeared in the paper but exposure of my ignorance was inevitable, and I quote from a letter which began 'my many friends and myself have been wondering what qualifications, if any, you have to cover Rugby League ... if there was a bar at least we could possibly understand your account' and so on. An article in the *Rugby League Review* was more damning. Referring to one story which I had been told in good faith but did not have time to check, the writer remarked 'It is a long while since R. L. followers enjoyed a joke such as a certain PWT (careful with that hyphen, Mr Printer) perpetuated in the august columns of the SE the other week', and there was more.

I was also, and rightly, taken sharply to task in a rugby league paper for a story headed 'Irish star turns down "pick your club" offer', in which I wrote that a leading rugby union player had been approached to turn professional. I vaguely remember that my information came through the *Sunday Express* and that I had no time to check the original source. Had I done so it would not have appeared under my name. I was more careful thereafter.

One winter day I was making my way over the snowy Pennines to a match in Yorkshire when I had to seek comfort in a wayside café, where to greet me in the loo were squares of newspaper ready for use. The first to hand was one containing my article for the previous week. This seemed a fitting epitaph to a career as a rugby league correspondent which, although I did not know it at the time, was to end at Wigan early the following season. To my boundless relief Montague told me that there was a vacancy on the *Guardian* sports staff. I bid farewell to the *Sunday Express* who had been very kind but as far as rugby league was concerned I was not their man.

Montague said that the *Manchester Guardian* offered £700 a year, I think it was, but that if I liked to ask for £750 I would get it. One afternoon he sat at his desk writing a letter offering the £700 while simultaneously at another desk I wrote to him saying I would appreciate £750. This was my first experience of Montague's preference for writing notes to his staff, even though they might only be a few feet away.

Soon after joining the staff I came to regard Larry Montague with increasing admiration and affection. He was a son of C. E. Montague, a distinguished writer on the *Guardian*, author and critic, who had married a daughter of C. P. Scott. He was educated at St Edward's School in Oxford and at Balliol and his love for the paper, its nature and traditions can rarely have been equalled and were imbued in his staff. His writing had a classic simplicity; his mind was remarkably swift and lucid and he had a rare gift for organisation.

I doubt that a keener intelligence ever directed the sports pages of a newspaper, and I used to think that the task was hardly worthy of his gifts. Certainly, I cannot believe that any sports editor ever had a broader knowledge of games. Athletics, at which he had excelled, and rugby football were his great passions but he was almost equally conversant with all the other games, including real tennis, fives squash, billiards and even pigeon racing. When he had time to spare he was an avid golfer using what was once described as 'a Basque wood-chopper's grip'.

The standards Larry Montague expected of his staff could be exacting, even spartan, but he never asked anything of anyone that he would not do himself. His enthusiasm for whatever task was at hand was boundless and above all he was considerate and kind, but he could be ruthless. I recall a contributor who wrote appealing accounts of London football matches. Everyone, including Montague, liked them but, like everyone else's copy, they sometimes had to be cut. The writer sent a message to Montague in Manchester complaining of this even though he was warned by a member of the London staff not to do so. Within moments a wire fizzed back from Montague saying that the writer's contributions would no longer be required and they were not. Montague would not tolerate criticism from someone who was not on the staff and had no idea of the problems of producing a page, but such was his capacity for blending command and friendship that he and the writer still kept in touch. His reprimands were fair but however irritating they might sometimes be any resentment would be stifled at birth. The next moment he would be as cheerful and amiable as ever.

Another of the paper's correspondents would testify that it was impossible to deceive Montague on questions of sport. One rugby contributor was asked to take particular notice of the point to which an England scrum-half passed and whether the stand-off was able to take the ball on the burst. The report arrived saying that he could do so. Montague and Rowbotham were suspicious, checked with reliable sources who had watched the match and discovered the contrary. The correspondent was asked if he were sure of the facts, asserted that he was and never covered another international match for the *Guardian*. He had tried to bluff his way out of a mistake and that was fatal.

The upshot of this was that I was sent to Paris two or three times to cover internationals. Montague knew of my 'French Connection' and although my experience of rugby was slender he thought I could cope after receiving a thorough briefing. Watching my first match when Scotland were playing France I little realised that twenty years later Norman Mair in the Scottish front row that day would become a friend and fellow-writer.

The sports staff in those days was a select little company. In addition to Montague, the athletics and rugby union correspondent as well as sports editor, there was Rowbotham who wrote the cricket and rugby union, Harold Mather, who covered rugby league and sundry other games, and then myself. We had an office all to ourselves at the end of a long corridor in the Cross Street building. It was so quiet that our visitors could be forgiven for thinking that they were in a rest home, a far cry from the open-plan offices which I have never liked.

Between us we wrote most of the copy and did all the sub-editing. This was not as remarkable as it sounds for the paper carried no racing, except special articles on great occasions like the Derby and the National. This custom was a legacy of C. P. Scott, the great editor who made the paper famous throughout the world. Because gambling was involved he would not have racing in the paper. Boxing likewise was banned, although Alistair Cooke, the chief correspondent in the United States, would enlighten us with a colourful piece on a heavyweight championship fight. Lesser contests had no part in our reckoning. Sub-editing was largely a matter of reading through well-written copy from most reliable people such as David Gray, who joined the paper in the early fifties and became probably the finest lawn tennis correspondent of his time.

The main soccer was written by a gifted, delightful little man, Donny Davies, whose pieces appeared under the by-line of 'Old International'. Donny was a man of abundant good nature and kindness. He had great sympathy with human frailty and a blessed sense of the ridiculous. The freshness of his mind brought the settings, the moods of the crowds and the temper and humour of the game vividly alive in his pieces for the *Guardian* and radio. As a schoolmaster he could not attend midweek matches, and I had the good fortune to report some of those at Wembley, notably the one in 1953 when Hungary demolished the pride of England, and began a revolution in British football. When he retired from teaching Davies was looking forward eagerly to covering matches in Europe. It was cruelly ironic that one of his first should be in Munich where he died in an aircraft accident.

For three years after going to Manchester I enjoyed covering soccer matches and never more so than when I was sent to watch Preston North End. They were blessed with Tom Finney who personified the finest virtues of a professional footballer. With his unawareness of the beauty he was creating, his delicate changes of pace, superb control, rare balance which often enabled him to slip past his markers on the unexpected side, and capacity for scoring goals, he enchanted me on many a grey Lancashire afternoon.

Inevitably a player of Finney's talent, who could transform a match by himself, was often harshly marked but whenever he was fouled he never showed the faintest sign of resentment or retaliation. Neither did he, or the great majority of players, indulge in the puerile histrionics and exhibitionism which have become a tedious feature of the modern game. And Finney remained loyal to one club throughout his career.

In the early fifties Matt Busby's first fine Manchester United team were in full swing and men like Carey, Rowley, Pearson, Cockburn and company became familiar figures. I saw many memorable matches and did not mind the travelling. There was no fear in those days of being molested or even irritated by vicious thugs. Violence among the crowds did not exist whereas now it seems likely to be a continuing menace as long as punishment fails to fit the crime.

Another advantage of reporting soccer from my viewpoint was that I need only be concerned with the game itself. Montague had no use for gossip, quarrels behind the scenes and inside stories so there was no call for me to interview players and managers. Occasionally one was invited into boardrooms for tea or a drink after a match but this was rarely stimulating. I usually slipped away after the final whistle. Few, if any, contemporary newspapers would allow such a detached approach but that was the way of the *Guardian* and part of its strength. The readers knew that the writer had striven to give an objective account not coloured by opinions which could be heavily biased.

The function of the critic was zealously preserved on the sports pages of the *Guardian, The Times* and one or two other newspapers. When the Open championship was at Portrush in 1951 a room was set aside for the writers to work in comparative peace. After Max Faulkner had won he was brought into this room to be interviewed by some members of the press. Understandably Max was excited and during the hubbub Bernard Darwin stumped testily out of the room. As he passed me he muttered, 'It's what we think about him that matters, not what he thinks.' Few would share his view nowadays when many writers, particularly in the United States, rely on the player coming into the Press tent to tell them about his round. Once when a writer who had watched nothing of the play asked Ben Hogan an ill-advised question Hogan remarked, 'One day a deaf mute will win a golf tournament and no one would know what happened.'

One or two *Guardian* writers in my early days made a point of not getting to know the players well. They reasoned that to do so made it all the harder to criticise, however justly. This is probably why many modern commentators on television often temper criticism with remarks such as 'He won't like that one', referring to a dreadful shot; or 'That was not one of his usual superb shots' when the ball has been hoicked straight down long leg's throat.

As far as a writer is concerned there is something to be said for remaining remote. It certainly made life more comfortable for me. I shrank from having to approach a player of any game, who was a complete stranger, and introduce myself. Occasionally, of course, the writer who views from afar so to speak can be wrong when a word with someone involved would have set him to rights.

On one occasion I remember rushing back to the Manchester office and writing of how Middlesex had been unlucky not to beat Lancashire in a hockey match. A headline to that effect and my copy had been set in type when, shortly before edition time, John Woodcock, then on the *Guardian* staff before joining *The Times*, appeared with his report of another match.

I mentioned what I thought was Middlesex's misfortune whereupon Woodcock, who had happened to meet one of their team, said they had won. I had seen John Conroy, that beautiful player, fail to score from a penalty bully but had not noticed that a penalty goal was awarded because Conroy had been obstructed. But for Woodcock the *Guardian* would have carried the wrong result in a headline. Montague was in the office at the time and gave me a decidedly old-fashioned look; carelessness such as mine was a real black and there was another instance when he was very far from amused.

One day during a Pakistan cricket tour of England, possibly the first, two of the team made hundreds but the headline, written by me, which appeared in the paper read 'Two Indian centuries at Lords'. Letters arrived, justly complaining and one said that the headline might as well have been 'Two Chinese centuries' . . . Coals were heaped on my head for that one but I survived.

Until the early summer of 1953 *Guardian* sports writers were anonymous. The only clue to their identity was that a staff writer's initials appeared at the foot of his article. As I was not on the staff until late in 1951 mine did not appear after my golf pieces until the following season. In a manner of speaking I had been given my 'colours' by the captain of the eleven, but only for golf. This troubled me slightly because I had written numerous pieces on soccer and had covered other games.

Enlightenment came one day in a letter from Montague which he handed to me in the office. To use a phrase, which lately has become a joke, it was a 'short, sharp shock'. Montague was not satisfied with the way I planned, or failed to plan, my reports as to the blending of comment and run of play. The letter continued 'When you are annoyed do not let your anger make your writing visibly angry as well as critical. Calm condemnation in simple words is more effective'. Also I was found guilty of criticising referees and rightly he would not stand for that. His comment that 'all Football League referees certainly know the rules better than 100 per cent of the press box' may still hold true today. For these reasons my initials had not appeared. You earned your colours on the *Guardian* in those days.

Every point Montague made was valid and the letter, which I kept, is a reminder of the valuable training I had during those Manchester days. Standards were strict and writers were expected to observe the dictates of the style book. It gave numerous examples of clichés, jargon, superfluous adverbs and adjectives, words that were banned and those wrongly used. A. P. Wadsworth, editor of the paper, was not interested in sport but he spared a moment to send Montague a note pressing him to bang into Ward-Thomas's head that alibi does not mean excuse.

Christian names were forbidden on the sports pages except when players like the Langridges of Sussex had the same initials. Occasionally the rule was observed to an absurd degree. At the height of Sir Leonard Hutton's career he appeared in the *Guardian* once as 'L. Hutton, a Yorkshire opening batsman'. I loved the 'a' but it was a true statement. Few words in the language have suffered greater misuse than the definite and indefinite articles.

A year or so after I had been awarded my colours for football it was decided that everyone was to have a personal by-line. I objected as firmly as my junior position allowed. I was proud of being The Golf Correspondent of the *Manchester Guardian*. It was a title I did not want to lose. I could not foresee then that the name rather than anonymity could be an advantage in the future, particularly in being offered work for publications and a few television ventures in the United States.

If I did not like the personal by-line I was more strongly opposed to my picture accompanying an article. This seemed an unnecessary concession to possible public curiosity. The writing not the appearance was what mattered. When my turn came to be photographed for these pictures I scowled so at the camera that I had to be ordered to have them taken again. I pointed out that the golf correspondent was exposed to the public to a much greater extent than were writers on most other games. The danger of being recognised and interrupted or bored when trying to concentrate on the golf was increased. Fortunately, perhaps out of sympathy for my feelings, the picture was rarely used.

Much to my surprise early in 1960 Larry Montague said that I would go to Rome with him for the Olympic Games. He was probably the best athletics correspondent of his time, and while he concentrated on this and other important issues I was to cover hockey, association football and sundry bits and pieces. Montague had a passion for trains and planned the journey to the last detail. We would travel by way of Harwich and the Hook to Lucerne where we would relax awhile before going on to Rome.

Three weeks before we were due to leave London Montague was stricken by an aneurism. It was soon clear that he would not recover in time and his deputy, John Rodda, took his place. I was about to begin the journey from home in Weybridge when we heard that Montague, who was only 50, had died. This was a stunning shock and as we crossed to Holland Rodda and I spent one of the saddest nights in all the years. We could not believe that the man who had been such an influence in our lives had gone. My debt to him was beyond reckoning.

After reaching Lucerne neither Rodda nor I was in much of a mood to relax. He went to an athletics meeting elsewhere in Switzerland and I continued to Rome, little suspecting that I was plunging into a maelstrom of bureaucracy. Although we were fully accredited long before leaving England I became involved in a seemingly endless paper chase and hours of mostly futile talk before the documentation was complete. Rage often bubbled near the surface and at times the stoicism and patience of the charming girl interpreters seemed the only lifeline to sanity. I was exhausted on the threshold of the hardest two weeks' work of my life and would cheerfully have torn up my passport and cast the bits into the Tiber rather than lose the precious Olympic passes. One writer did lose his and had a ghastly time getting another.

The days of the Games were stimulating but frenetic. Rodda and I rarely saw each other from early morning until late at night. Hockey was usually played in the mornings, football in the evenings. The intervals were filled with glimpses of basketball, fencing, wrestling, gymnastics, swimming and rowing. Rodda was at home from the outset, revelling in the challenge.

For me it was a fascinating new experience but, demanding though the task was, I loved it.

Wherever possible the Italians made use of their ancient buildings and it was impossible not to be moved by watching contests in settings two thousand years old. Athletes competed in the Terme di Caracalla, once the greatest baths in the world, and in the Basilica di Massenzio; they raced along the Cristoforo Colombo and rode in the Villa Borghese; the Olympic torch burned in the Piazza di Campidoglio, and the marathon runners toiled along the old Appian Way towards the Arch of Constantine. Every event was held in a place of beauty from the Bay of Naples to Lake Albano in its volcanic basin high in the hills where I watched the rowing one day. Even in the magnificent modern settings such as the Stadio del Nueto, where I saw Anita Lonsbrough win her gold medal for the 200 metres breaststroke, and the Palazzo dei Congressi, the theatre of the occasions was beautifully emphasised.

The whole affair was symbolic of man's ageless need for contest. It made stirring and varied watching as well as a challenge for a writer whose technical knowledge of some of the sports was negligible to say the best of it. No Games this century has been held against such wonderful backgrounds and in this I was lucky. Ignorance of finer points could be cloaked with basic observation and description of the places and people. The most rewarding writing was that of a general nature, the opening and closing ceremonies and the odd feature article.

The hockey was interesting for the struggles of the British team, notably in a match against Kenya. Almost an hour of extra time was needed before C.J. Saunders-Griffiths scored the goal which gave his team a place in the semifinal against India. This must have been the longest match ever played in first-class hockey and my report one of the longest ever written on the game. The British gave a brave account of themselves in losing to India by the only goal of the match, but Spain beat them in the match for third place. Following the fortunes of British hockey in those days could be an exasperating exercise.

The British football team were dismissed from the qualifying competition by Italy. The other matches made little impression but I remember one Hungarian player, F. Albert, a beautiful mover, always poised and effortless. Under floodlights he made a wraithlike figure all in white, gliding into position and then streaking on to a pass like a darting flame. For all his genius Hungary lost to a gallant Denmark who could not quite hold Yugoslavia in the final. Only once was I able to watch the track events and the victory of Herb Elliott in the 1500 metres was unforgettable. Few men can have commanded a race of that stature to the extent that he did. It was, I thought, a gesture of supremacy as ruthless in its efficiency as those of Bradman or Hogan.

After twenty years impressions of the various sports I saw have faded somewhat but fragments of those days still linger: the glory of *Aida* on a summer night within the vast walls of the Caracalla and, judging by their scanty applause, the apathy of the audience until one realised that the majority were tourists whose great moment came when the horses thundered on stage; and walking out afterwards still under the spell of the music and the colour, and being asked by a young Australian if Aida was the pretty girl in a green dress. That evening was a rare interval in my labours.

I recall trying to write a basketball story on a foreign typewriter in the pressroom of a football stadium with a television set two feet away screaming athletics. One distinguished journalist was almost clutching the ceiling in desperation. In trying to phone the Olympic stadium he was given four wrong numbers ending with his own which the operator said was engaged. The press headquarters seemed as if specially designed to magnify the incessant noise. The temptation to sabotage the loudspeaker system with its idiot but necessary repetition of *attenzione*, smash one of the blaring television sets and shoot one of the moon-haunted dogs that tortured our sleep was almost overwhelming.

Noise was a frequent hazard but there were quiet moments: gliding through narrow, brown streets in a *carozzella* on a still Sunday afternoon, the sound of the horse's hooves echoing softly back from the sleeping walls; innumerable policemen, handsome in white, always polite yet rarely seeming to know very much; the city lying like a mirage in the haze of noonday heat over the plain as one came down from the hills; St Peter's, etched sharp and black against a sky of gold and flame, and the towers of Radio Vatican blinking in the darkness; the hot dusty hinterland, olive green and brown, glowing in the sunshine; the Forum bathed in floodlight; the massive incongruity of the Vittoriana, like a royal wedding cake in a transport café; the Castel St Angelo outlined against the night above the Tiber, green and slow and tired.

All these things made indelible memories and how fortunate we were that the Games were not afflicted with the tiresome, sometimes vicious, political overtones and the racial issues which have beset many Olympic occasions since. In later years I realised that if I only attended one Games in a lifetime I was extremely lucky that it should have been in Rome.

CHAPTER 5
THE YEAR OF HOGAN

Coincidence, I imagine, rather than destiny decreed that the first year of Queen Elizabeth's reign, in so far as golf was concerned, should be one of the most enthralling of the generation. Even without the aid of aging scrapbooks many of the events of 1953 are still sharp in the memory and will remain so long after those of far more recent origin have vanished.

No single occasion in the watching of golf made a more lasting impression upon me than Hogan's victory in the Open championship at Carnoustie. Apart from the impact of his peerless skill and compelling personality Hogan became the only golfer thus far to have won the Opens of Britain and the United States, and the Masters, in the same summer. His triumph was the peak of a season when championship after championship, tournament after tournament produced an achievement or a climax of absorbing interest.

It was the year when Joe Carr beat Harvie Ward, then the world's finest amateur, on the last green of an unforgettable final in the Amateur championship at Hoylake; when Gerald Micklem enjoyed the greatest triumph of his career by defeating Ronnie White for the English title at Birkdale; when Henry Cotton won a masterful victory, one of his last, at Wentworth.

There were many other occasions which gave great pleasure to watchers and writers, such as the victory of Charles Stowe in the Brabazon Trophy at Sunningdale, and I shall always remember the rosy beaming face of Harry Bradshaw after he had won the Dunlop Masters, his first important victory outside Ireland and on his fortieth birthday. It was the year when a boy named Nicklaus was beginning to break 80, and a young man named Palmer reached the fifth round of the American amateur championship, only for an eminent British observer to declare that he was far too wild to be any good. Above all it was the year of Hogan.

Although my first visit to America was still some while ahead I was fascinated by what I knew of Hogan. An American professional in one of the prison camps had talked of a hard little man from Texas who, after years of unavailing struggle, had fought his way to the peaks. By 1953 Hogan was supreme and his survival in 1949 of a serious car accident which had made him something of a legend in British minds. When it was known that he had yielded to the persuasion of men like Hagen and Armour, who said that if he were to achieve lasting greatness he had to win the British Open, his appearance at Carnoustie was awaited with an expectancy the like of which I have never known since.

Thousands headed for Carnoustie and swarmed over the Burnside links to follow Hogan's first qualifying round. In their anxiety to see him they became an uncontrolled mob; the stewards were helpless and Bill Branch, a very good golfer, was given no real chance to play. The morning after, Leonard Crawley introduced me to Hogan and I remarked on the dreadful crowd control. He looked straight at me with his disturbingly chill gaze and said that he thought the control had been all right. I was amazed, and the conversation almost ended there and then but I realised that he was not about to risk making critical comments to a stranger which might be quoted against him.

I shall never forget the first morning of the championship and the sight of his opening strokes piercing the cold, grey wind. I was convinced that he would win, a feeling which he, for all his implacable determination and thoroughness of preparation, did not share. Be that as it may his scores — 73, 71, 70, 68 — made a ruthless downward progression and he finished four strokes ahead of Rees, Thomson, Stranahan and Cerda. Each day John Derr, an American who was broadcasting radio reports to the States, followed Hogan round. There were no scoreboards on the course in those days and occasionally in the last round Hogan would ask Derr how others were faring. Years later Derr told me that as Hogan left the 15th green he asked about Cerda, the only possible challenger left. When Derr told him that Cerda was no longer a threat Hogan said, 'You can set up your broadcast, this tournament's over.' In no sense was such a remark boastful but simply a cool statement from a golfer so certain of his technique that he was not going to throw away four strokes even on the last challenging holes. Some measure of the superb quality of his golf through the green on a course of 7200 yards was that of his total of 282 no fewer than 130 were putts, a high proportion by today's standards.

On the last day when two rounds were played Hogan was paired with Hector Thomson who, before turning professional, had been one of the finest amateurs between the wars. Although leaders did not go out last Hogan was fairly late. Long after I should have been writing I was still out on the course, unable to tear myself away, thinking that I would just see one more hole, rather as the cricket watcher lingers for just one more over.

In those days there was no television and no hole by hole information pouring into the press tent. The urge to stay on the course and see what was happening was all the stronger.

When the lateness of the hour forced me to retreat to the press tent I was too excited to settle down and write upwards of a thousand words. The only alternative was to try to dictate the piece from notes, which I had never done before. This gave a little more time and I watched Hogan and Thomson come to the last green. There were no stands then and some 12,000 people lined the fairway amid a resounding silence as Hogan struck a perfect second shot and holed out for his four. As the crowd roared its tribute to the greatest golfer most of them had seen, or were ever likely to see, Hogan stood quietly, almost humbly so it seemed, and bowed his appreciation.

Hogan has said that he was surprised that so many people obviously wanted him to win. At the time he would not realise that the most knowledgeable crowds on earth saw his victory as the only fitting outcome to the championship, and that this transcended all partisan loyalties. After watching Hogan check his card with scrupulous care, clearly playing every shot over again in his mind, I rushed to one of the public telephones behind a shelter near the 18th green.

I have never been a methodical note-taker and that afternoon was no exception. Various facts and thoughts had been jotted on slips of paper. As there was no room to arrange these properly I sat on the floor of the box with my bits arrayed around me and hoped for the best. Concentration was not helped by the shuffle of feet on the roof of the boxes where people had gathered to watch the presentation. The copy-taker in Manchester was most efficient and patient and I finished in time for the edition, but with an uneasy feeling that I had failed the paper on a historic occasion. I could hardly wait to call the office for a verdict, and offer to rewrite for the next edition. To my great relief Denys Rowbotham said the piece was all right and that I could relax. To my surprise it was included in *The Bedside Guardian,* the paper's annual anthology, the following year, but I have never forgotten the near panic that accompanied its production.

A year or so later play was running late in the *News of the World* championship at St Andrews and match after match went to the last green. This frequently seems to happen when one has made arrangements for the evening. I had accepted an invitation to dinner and anxiety not to be late, allied to the difficulty of describing the day's play, again frustrated attempts to start writing. This time I did not panic but went back to the Scores Hotel, had a quick bath and changed. By then I had calmed down, went to a telephone and with the copy-taker warning me when a paragraph was too long, or when I had used the same adjective too often, managed an adequate piece. Except in North America when the time difference often compels one to ad-lib part of an article I have rarely used this method. It is much safer to have the piece written out, however roughly, and if necessary change it during dictation.

To a great extent success in golf is the reward of patient endeavour. No matter how many disappointments a man may suffer, if he has the character to bear them and if his golf is of sufficient quality, he will usually prevail, but not always in the expected manner. For many years Joe Carr, the greatest of all Irish amateurs, had played with distinction in the Amateur championship but had been frustrated, often in the quarter or semifinals. In the first such championship that I covered, at St Andrews in 1950, Carr lost at the 20th to Cyril Tolley who had won his first Amateur in 1920 before Carr was born. The years seemed to have taken little from Tolley's majestic, effortless swing. He played beautifully, strolling through round after round, a splendid sight, with pipe contentedly in his mouth and a boy carrying a light bag. After beating Carr he made Stranahan work hard for his place in the final.

In each of the next two years Carr lost in the semifinal to the eventual champions, Charles Coe and Harvie Ward. Then at last the gods decided that his turn had come, and bestowed much fortune upon him at Hoylake. In three successive matches before the final he faced almost certain defeat, but failures by his opponents allowed him to escape. In his semifinal Carr was two down on the 16th tee to Cecil Beamish, an admirable Irish golfer and member of a famous games-playing family. Luckily for Carr, Beamish drove out of bounds into the Field and at the 19th, when Carr was unlikely to get a four, Beamish, perfectly placed from the tee on that menacing hole, cut his wooden-club second out of bounds. Blessing though this was for Carr the tragic lapse possibly cost Beamish a place in the Walker Cup team that year.

During all these agonies Carr had been like a great greyhound straining at the leash. Now he was free and armed to meet Harvie Ward over 36 holes. From the outset he was in command, and when after 29 holes Ward squared the match it was he and not Carr who faltered slightly in the cold gusting wind. Even then Carr had to get down in two from 40 yards at the 17th to remain one up after Ward had hit a noble long iron to the green. Ward drove into the rough at the last and was never in sight of the three which might have saved him.

During the week I must have implied unintentionally that Carr was British. This provoked letters to the paper and I was surprised to see the following paragraph added by Montague to my account of the final. 'For the benefit of those who wonder why Carr has been spoken of as a British player this was because he played for the British side in the Walker Cup match. [It was then entitled "Great Britain" — Great Britain and Ireland came later.] Golf, like Rugby Football, is not politically minded.' Would that the same principle were true of games today.

Carr's victory was a triumph of rare character. Ward, who was to win successive American championships a few years later, was among the most accomplished golfers in the world, professional or amateur. His swing was a model of orthodoxy and smoothness but after the United States Golf Association had suspended him for a year for infringement of amateur status over a matter of expenses, he was never the same force again. Doubtless the punishment was meant as an example to others but it was sad nonetheless. Ward, a delightful, carefree person, seemed an innocent abroad, and the circumstances which led to the suspension could have been avoided had others acted more thoughtfully.

As for Carr his enormous power and remarkably sensitive touch around the greens had come into their own. Until Michael Bonallack's reign was firmly under way some ten years later Carr remained the foremost amateur, and possibly the most striking personality to have emerged on his side of the Atlantic since the war. He became the most popular citizen in all Ireland not only because of his golf but because of an appealingly uninhibited outlook, gentleness of spirit and charming manners to everyone with whom he was in contact. In victory he was always modest and chivalrous towards opponents; while defeat was accepted with good humour and grace.

For many years Carr was capable of holding his own with the finest professionals. An abiding memory is of the weekend when Jean and I stayed with the Carr family at Sutton, across the estuary from Portmarnock where the Dunlop Masters was being played. After 54 holes Joe was leading the field by four strokes. Our excitement was intense. Could an amateur beat the strongest professional company in these islands? In the end it was an Irishman who denied him. Christy O'Connor played a great last round of 66 and Carr tied second with Norman Drew. That was in 1959 and I am getting ahead of my story.

Soon after the championship at Hoylake the Home Internationals were played at Killarney, a good reason for Jean and me to visit that delightful place. It was her first experience of Irish hospitality. One evening a party was given in the clubhouse by the lake. We were staying in a hotel some distance from the course and one of our hosts said he would collect us about 9.30. Two hours later he had not appeared and my wife was threatening to go to bed when he arrived. We might have realised that in Ireland the party was only just beginning. Memories of that night are clouded but I was told that Henry Longhurst and I were dancing together on the lawn shortly before dawn. Meanwhile a policeman, presumably there to see that the licensing rule was obeyed, had stuck to his post with such devotion to duty, fortifying himself the while, that he became unconscious, was lifted into a truck and borne away.

After surfacing the next day some of us were strolling by the lake when Tony Goodridge, who later joined the *Guardian* from the *Irish Times*, appeared with a telegram for me. It read, 'Copy required. Take waters instead. Montague.' I had written nothing the previous day and we all concluded that Montague was annoyed and expected an article from me. With throbbing head I toiled to produce a substantial piece and then had a problem, I cannot remember what, about telephoning it to Manchester. Eventually the local postmaster let me use a phone in his office. Having dictated the piece I spoke to the sports room and my feelings were decidedly mixed when I was told that nothing was expected from me and that there was no room for the piece I had sent. It was discovered that some ass had omitted the word 'No' from the beginning of the telegram. Its meaning was transformed. It then read as a thoughtful suggestion and not as a reprimand.

As if Joe Carr's victory at Hoylake were not enough to set a writer's pulses racing there was another contest that year which also revealed match play at its finest pitch. Had it been necessary at that time to examine an amateur golfer's character to the limit he would have been sent to play Ronnie White over 36 holes on his own course at Birkdale with much at stake. I still think that White was one of the finest amateurs ever to emerge in Britain, certainly as a striker of the ball. His swing was so solid and true that there was a sense of the inevitable about his shots. The ball flew from the clubface with an unerring flight that few professionals, apart from Cotton, and no amateur could consistently match, and what is more in any conditions.

I recall a dark evening at Formby during a Brabazon Trophy tournament when savage rain was lashed by a gale-force wind. It was difficult for spectators to stand still, umbrellas were impossible to control but White's golf through the green was steady as a rock. Whatever the angle of the wind his shots arrowed through it with almost implacable certainty. Few golfers could have controlled the ball as he did that day. Some months earlier he had won a magnificent match against Charles Coe, one of the greatest of all American amateurs, in the Walker Cup at Birkdale. White's record in this match then was remarkable, and not a few professionals must have been relieved that he remained a solicitor and did not join their ranks.

The outlook for Gerald Micklem as he prepared to meet White in the final of the English championship on a lovely Maytime day was formidable. I was among many who thought that Micklem had precious little chance of winning. The evening before the match the BBC asked me to interview the champion. I asked Ronnie if I could do so in the event that he won and he agreed. More out of politeness than expectation I approached Gerald and he it was who sat with me and a microphone the next evening. His victory was a perfect instance of unyielding character, and also of the truth that there is more to golf than striking the ball superbly.

For all that Micklem was a long-experienced international golfer and, like White, had won the championship previously, he was hardly a match for his opponent through the green. As it proved his driving was equal to the challenge but it was his putting that finally destroyed White.

Frequently he would halve a hole when White seemed likely to win it, but White could not hole the telling putts. Micklem was never more than one down and this was a crucial factor. White told me afterwards that if only he could have become two up he thought he would have won. As it was the frustration probably led to one or two errors towards the end and Micklem had the courage to take toll. For White it was almost an exact reversal of his match against Coe when he came from behind. Micklem ended the match with a perfect spoon to the old 17th green. One of his greatest satisfactions from the victory was in showing that at forty a man's competitive force was not spent, and that he could recover from a lean spell. Seventeen years later Nicklaus must have felt much the same.

The Dunlop tournament, which the company used to run in addition to the Masters, was over ninety holes, a considerable test of endurance. Cotton, who was then forty-six, only played in occasional tournaments and everyone at Wentworth that year looked forward to a contest involving him and Bobby Locke who was at his peak. There was a rivalry between them. In effect the issue was decided on the first hole of the fourth round. Cotton played it in three soon after Locke had taken eight there. He swung his long second out towards extra cover, as was his wont, but extra cover for once failed to curve it back again and the ball vanished in a bush.

In the end Cotton finished five strokes ahead of Rees but not without anxiety. Towards the final turn his lead was slipping away but he recovered in masterful fashion. Drives flew far and straight and iron shots, struck with all the authority of old, hummed to the heart of the greens. This was his last triumph in a major stroke-play event.

Six months later Wentworth was the setting of torturing disappointment for Cotton as nonplaying captain of the Ryder Cup team, for every follower of the game in Britain and for Peter Alliss and Bernard Hunt. I shall never forget crouching behind the 18th green in the October twilight as Alliss and Hunt in the last two matches to finish bore the whole responsibility for the team on their young shoulders. We watched in an agony of suspense. Someone, it might have been Sam King, suggested to Cotton that he walk the last fairway with Alliss but, rightly or wrongly, Cotton thought it best to leave him alone. There is no call to dwell on the awful details of how both he and Hunt took sixes after good drives when fives would have won the match for Britain and Ireland. They were unfortunate that all the pressure should descend upon them when others far more experienced had failed.

When Hunt missed the putt that would have halved the whole contest one could almost hear the mocking laughter of the gods mingled with American sighs of relief. Their greatest golfer had been desperately lucky not to have thrown the match away. On the 13th tee Snead was four up on Weetman and at that point an American victory seemed certain. I hurried back down the course, always an awful trail, for what I thought might be a last sight of Snead, little dreaming that twenty years and more later I would still be admiring the finest and most enduring natural swing of the age.

I reached the 15th in time to see Snead slice twice into the woods and repeat the stroke from the next tee. I could scarcely believe my eyes. Weetman had only to keep the ball in play to win these holes as he had the previous two. Bravely he did so, won the mighty 17th with a splendid four and halved the 18th for the match. Had Snead won as had seemed inevitable the British could not have won but his collapse had opened the door for tragic anticlimax. If coronation year drew down on a sad note it had been one of rare vintage and a constant source of rich material for a writer.

CHAPTER 6
A WORLD AWAY FROM GOLF

One day in 1924 my father, with a proper awareness of what was important in a boy's education, took me to a cricket match in Llandudno. It was, I think, the first of any note I had seen and forever afterwards I was able to say that I had watched Sydney Barnes who, in the opinion of many, was the greatest of all bowlers. He was playing for North Wales against the South African touring team and although I was only eleven I still have an image of his stern, commanding figure as he destroyed them by taking five cheap wickets. Years afterwards my father and I played the beautiful little course which used to nestle in a hollow on the top of the Great Orme. Sadly it vanished during the Second War; it was a magic place where one was alone with sea, sky and mountains. Little did I realise that a long while afterwards Llandudno would again be a special place for me.

Until after the war cricket was more important to me than golf. My game, such as it was, made little progress and I began to regret that I had not heeded my mother's advice to take lessons from the professional at Stockport during the school holidays. She herself had benefited from lessons and although not a strong golfer played to her handicap as often as not, and won a host of prizes. In this she was aided by an unshakeable Yorkshire temperament which I did not inherit; the Welsh from my father's side would usually take control, not always with favourable results. My mother was of a generation of indomitable women and lived to eighty-seven. Four of her sisters were at least eighty-five when they died, and another survived to a hundred and six. The family had a distant connection with Harrison Ainsworth, a Victorian writer of historical novels, hence my second name of Ainsworth.

After leaving Wellingborough I did not go back for almost twenty years. Circumstances, and a job which demanded my regular presence, had prevented my returning for Old Boys matches. Later, when one would have been able to go, the incentive had waned as the boys and most of the masters one knew had left.

Furthermore, I have never been keen on organised reunions — the 'what are you doing now' syndrome. When a chapter of life, leaving school, job, service or prison camp, is irrevocably finished there seems little point in deliberately reopening it. Occasionally it is pleasant to run into people from the past but often the common ground which once stimulated mutual interest is no longer there.

Tempting though it sometimes is to revisit the places of one's youth I try to avoid doing so. Whenever I have passed my old home I have always been depressed. The house is divided into flats; a nondescript dwelling stands on the lawn where we had a net and my father taught me to play cricket; others cluster nearby. The old stables where I used to play, although we never had horses, is a ruin and around the neighbourhood the atmosphere is of the dinginess frequently found on the fringe of industrial towns.

During my early years with the *Guardian* I covered many cricket matches. The majority involved Lancashire and one of my first was against Northamptonshire at Wellingborough on the school ground. Straightaway memories of the happier times there quickened. As I have said cricket and, to a much lesser extent, football had occupied most of my waking thoughts. In my first term at the school I was fortunate in becoming a fast bowler for the Under 14 Eleven. Even without reference to the school magazine I can quote the report of the master in charge of the team. 'Thomas,' he wrote, 'is a fast bowler who uses and sometimes loses his head. As a batsman he is a Wild Man of Borneo.' Perhaps it was intended to be funny; its effect was hurtful and led to a good deal of leg-pulling. After all, I reasoned, I had taken more wickets than anyone else. The master, I am sure, was being spiteful because against one rival school, after all our main batsmen had failed, I could have won the match had I not ended my gallant, attacking innings of 11, joint top score, by stupidly running myself out. We lost by five runs.

The previous summer at my preparatory school there was a match which was considered important enough for a prize to be given to the best batsman and a ball to the bowler with the best average. It happened that I took the last three wickets for a very few runs, a performance of no particular merit, but my average was better than that of the boy who had taken more wickets against the better batsmen. He received (and obviously deserved) the prize but it had been said that the best average would win the beautiful shining new ball and I felt seriously wronged. On another occasion at the same school I took nine wickets but we lost the match and I clearly remember hoping for a crumb of praise from the headmaster but he was so annoyed that we had lost that he did not say a word. It is extraordinary how such trivial incidents can linger in the memory for half a century but they were not trivial for me at the time. Who knows if they may

69

not have contributed to such elements of a tail-end complex that may be in my nature?

Provided one showed reasonable form at Wellingborough the path to the first eleven by way of the third and second was fairly clear, and I duly arrived there. One privilege of being in the first was that it afforded escape from a long boring period of chemistry, a subject which then and for evermore found me totally unresponsive. All I can remember of the class was that the master, who had a great booming voice, would occasionally refer to his Plasticine balls. He had several of various colours to demonstrate the components of complicated substances such as water.

The cricketers had to attend the class for a little while until the longed-for moment when we had to change for the match. I can remember the joy of those mornings as we wandered down the long avenue to one of the most beautiful playing fields I have known. I used to pray that we would field first, such was my longing to start bowling. It may sound mildly absurd but one of the pleasantest memories of my life was the feel of a new cricket ball and opening the bowling in the freshness of a summer morning. No matter how many wickets I took or how much stick I suffered, as I often did, nothing could mar those moments.

My lasting regret was that none of the cricket masters then paid enough attention to coaching the bowlers. I was never told about variations of pace, or of the proper grips and body action to swing the ball or indeed any of the refinements. One simply picked up odd hints along the way. The main reason why I was quite successful was because for years I had worshipped Macdonald, the great Australian fast bowler, who was largely responsible for Lancashire being county champions several times during my boyhood. I strove to imitate the smoothness and grace of an action which used to move Neville Cardus to poetic flights; the beauty Macdonald created was worthy of them all.

Macdonald was a tall dark man, somewhat sinister of countenance and always inscrutable. His movements were feline and silent, the coil of his wrist before delivery like a snake about to strike. He fascinated me intensely. Whenever possible I would be at Old Trafford, absorbed for hours, and never more so than one day in 1928 when Macdonald, having taken seven wickets in the first innings, took eight in the second, demolished Kent and won the championship for Lancashire. When he could summon his destroying moods, very few batsmen could play him with confidence. Woolley, Hammond and Sutcliffe were notable exceptions.

During the Lancashire match at Wellingborough, Brian Statham, on the threshold of his great career, bowled splendidly. I see from my account that neither he nor John Deighton could extract any life from a pitch on which I had toiled so often. If they could not what chance could I have had? From the outset the match was doomed to a draw but Nigel Howard, the Lancashire captain, played a fine innings of 75, the only memorable batting of the match. He was a lively, cheerful person, a gifted games player, a solid centre half for Cheshire at hockey and a low-handicap golfer. Soon after being elected to the Championship Committee of the Royal and Ancient he died from a heart attack when seemingly in glowing health.

In time I came to know and admire the Lancashire cricketers and for several weeks on end would be absorbed in a world far removed from golf. Washbrook, then at the height of his powers, Ikin, Grieves, an Australian of rare if mercurial gifts, Tattersall, Hilton, Berry and Statham were the nucleus of a fine side. One of its great strengths was the close catching of Ikin, Grieves and Geoffrey Edrich, who gave splendid support to the spin bowlers. On a helpful wicket they could be deadly. That same summer I saw Lancashire beat Sussex in one day at Old Trafford when Hilton was almost unplayable.

There were many pleasant excursions to other counties — Hampshire, where Desmond Eager, their captain and secretary, was always so kind and helpful, and Roy Marshall's brilliance was worth any long journey to see; the lovely Kentish grounds where a young Cowdrey's batting was beginning to bloom, and Queen's Park at Chesterfield where a damp morning came vividly alight with a masterful century by Washbrook.

I was fortunate too that many distinguished figures — Leonard Hutton, Denis Compton, Alec Bedser, Godfrey Evans and others — were playing in those years. The cricket made a welcome change of setting and subject for writing, but much as I loved the game I realised that the life of a golf correspondent was preferable. I did not think so before the war. How I envied the cricket writers their voyages in wintertime to far sunlit lands, Australia, South Africa, which must have been the most delightful of tours, and the West Indies. I had no thoughts of marriage then and did not realise what it must have meant for men to leave their families for many months. Neither did I think of the other extremes of reporting cricket, rain-broken days and many hours of tedium while moderate performers entrenched themselves. I never covered cricket for long enough periods to be bored.

Every county had spin bowlers. One was never condemned to days of dreary, defensive fast medium. There was always variety. The West Indians in 1980 introduced a massive element of boredom with their endless fast bowling, unthinkable when I was watching cricket regularly. One remembers the pace of Larwood, Macdonald, G.O. Allen and many others with half the run of a Holding, and the life that Tate, Geary, Miller, Hammond and Bedser, as obvious examples, generated with beautifully economical runs while many modern bowlers achieve far less after running absurd distances. Surely the case for limiting bowlers' runs or increasing the average number of overs to be bowled each hour grows apace. All this is no concern of mine, except as a spectator, and one can always turn off the radio or television. The sad thought is that first-class cricket may be destroying itself as an entertainment.

One day in 1926 my father took me to Old Trafford to see my first Test match. England were batting and, as Gregory was about to bowl the first over of the day to Hobbs, apparently I said 'Dad, this is the greatest moment of my life'. I have no recollection of saying anything but my father often recalled the remark, and I do remember Gregory's great bounding run and the effortless ease with which Hobbs played the first ball. He made 70-odd and Ernest Tyldesley, a beautiful batsman, a few more.

Already the seeds of a passion for cricket and a misguided urge to bowl as fast as possible were deeply sown. After leaving school I played club cricket. While living in London in the late thirties my job occasionally involved evening work, leaving days free to go to Lord's or the Oval. They were memorable cricketing times. Some of the great figures who had endured so long were reaching their close of play. Years before I had seen Hobbs and Rhodes play for the last time at Old Trafford; I watched Hendren make a wonderful century at Lord's on what was, I think, his last appearance there, and all over the country in 1938 Woolley was making farewells, batting with an enchanting ease for all that he was 50 or thereabouts. One 50 in an hour at the Oval was the purest joy to watch as he made the Surrey fast bowlers look nondescript, which they were not.

If there was sadness in the departure of these legendary figures the genius of Denis Compton was burning bright and Hutton was on the threshold of an indelible place in history. I saw all but an hour of his monumental 364 at the Oval in 1938. It seemed desperately slow then but he scored at something like 27 runs an hour, comparatively fast by modern reckoning. I was always fascinated by the variables of Wright's bowling and the beauty of Verity's and, commanding the whole scene, the imperial figure of Hammond. I was fortunate in seeing him play many superb innings, including the 240 at Lord's against Australia in 1938. I doubt whether any cricketer of modern times had greater presence on the field than Hammond, even when he was standing at ease in the slips.

Immensely powerful though he was, his every movement as a cricketer was graceful and unhurried. In later years Snead would remind me of his feline strength. Hammond seemed incapable of clumsiness even in falling to take a difficult slip catch. Everything was made to look easy and natural, and his manner, invariably impassive, even remote, hardened the impression of authority. Neither Hammond nor his great contemporaries walked to the wicket swinging their bats over their heads; teams did not trot out like footballers, nor indulge in callisthenics or puerile histrionics. The game had more dignity then but dignity is gradually losing its meaning in sport. And, of course, there is no money in it.

A huge crowd took heart that day at Lord's as, with England about 30 for 3, Hammond descended the pavilion steps. Immediately he imposed a massive command on the proceedings and, with Paynter in gallant support, all sense of panic and impending collapse soon vanished. I think Hammond scored about 70 in each session of play and I left Lord's that evening convinced that I would not see the like of that innings again. There were many hours too of watching Bradman destroy bowling with his merciless efficiency, and too-brief glimpses of the flashing sword of McCabe's bat.

Of all the innings I saw Bradman play, one of the briefest was the one I shall remember longest. In the 1934 test at Lord's in the first over he received he took fourteen off Farnes bowling fast from the pavilion end. Three times he pulled him to the boundary past mid-wicket and none of the balls was that short. Others were plundered as well and I sat there praying it would last, but sadly he played a fraction too soon at a ball from Verity and was caught and bowled. He had made 36 in 20 minutes. I was furious. It mattered not that Verity had taken a precious wicket for England (on the Monday he took fourteen more and won the match). The prospect of seeing a historic innings had gone. As a watcher the quality of the cricket has always been more important to me than the result. What genuine cricket lover in his senses would hope for Vivian Richards to be out for a low score when, if he stayed, he might play an innings of skill and power incomparable nowadays?

CHAPTER 7
AT LAST TO AMERICA

If 1953 was an unforgettable golfing year 1957 was of greater significance from a personal viewpoint. During the winter Frank Whitaker, the editor of *Country Life*, invited me to share the weekly golf commentaries. Bernard Darwin, who had been writing them for half a century, was over 80 and arthritis made travel an increasing burden for him. Except for certain amateur events, which had long been close to his heart, it was agreed that I would cover those which involved travelling, and we would each do 26 commentaries a year. I regarded this as a great privilege and we pursued the arrangement until his death in 1961. Since then I have written the weekly articles save for six by Peter Ryde. Writing for a magazine of *Country Life*'s quality and distinction, with the freedom of expression enjoyed by its writers, has been a continuing pleasure.

As the fifties unfolded the number of golf tournaments increased and I saw little cricket. In the meantime a move to London had come about unexpectedly. John Woodcock had joined the *Guardian* staff as cricket correspondent in place of Denys Rowbotham who had married an Australian and gone to live in Sydney. Within a year he decided to return to England and the *Guardian* agreed to give him his job back. Woodcock, who was to become one of the most accomplished cricket writers of the generation, foresaw no great future with the *Guardian*, but happily was taken on by *The Times*, whose cricket correspondent had just retired. On hearing this I asked Montague if I could go to London, a better base for the golf than Manchester and take over the coverage of hockey from Woodcock who had revived it.

For the next thirteen years hockey was my main winter task, with countless hours on freezing touchlines, but rewarding nevertheless. Hockey was a purely amateur game, the company invariably was agreeable, there was never any talk of money, leagues had not then been introduced and I enjoyed being involved. Except on special occasions, such as the University match or internationals there were never any crowds and frequently Richard Hollands, who wrote for the *Telegraph* and the *Evening Standard*, Woodcock, when he was not on a cricket tour, and I were the only spectators at a midweek match. Surprisingly, for hockey is a splendid often tough game, there was no public interest. I used to wonder whether anyone, except a few players, ever read the reports but I was not complaining. International matches took me several times to Germany, Holland at the peak of tulip time, and other Continental countries which then I had not visited for golf, and to the Olympic Games in Rome.

My only playing experience of hockey had been at my preparatory school. I remember nothing of it save that when we played the local ladies' team one of the masters who came in to strengthen our side caddishly insisted on playing right back, with me on the left, a much more difficult position. Had our positions been reversed his 'groin', as they say, and not mine might have received a fierce hit from close range by one of the opposing amazons.

I had covered the odd match in the north for the *Guardian* but had much to learn when I started in London. In this I was most grateful to Hollands who was a constant source of help and encouragement and always willing to share his knowledge with a novice. He was an exceptional man whose talents were never rewarded as they might have been. Hockey had cause to be lastingly grateful for his loyalty to the game and the integrity and fine style of his writing. For many years he edited a magazine, *Hockey News*, which involved considerable sacrifice of time and effort with precious little reward or appreciation. He was one of those rare people who never resented the fact that frequently his efforts were taken for granted.

Once established as the golf correspondent my next hurdle was to convince the editor that I should go to America. I argued that the experience was essential, but the *Guardian* had little or no money for such ventures. Rowbotham went to Australia for the cricket but none of the rest of us went further afield than Ireland or France. A few impatient years passed until in 1957 it was agreed that I should go to the United States. The main object was to report the Walker Cup match in Minneapolis, but to justify the expense I was to cover a so-called World championship in Chicago; the Canadian Amateur in Winnipeg and the American at The Country Club in Boston.

Even as recently as 1957 flying the Atlantic seemed something of an adventure, at least it did to me. While still in the RAF I had crossed the Channel many times but always took the shortest course, climbing in a Procter to about 5000 feet over the Kent coast. By doing so I calculated that there would only be about three minutes halfway across when if the one engine cut I could not glide to either side. This sounds unduly cautious but the memory of the ditching in 1940 still lingered, and now I was going to cross some two thousand miles of ocean.

The flight in a Stratocruiser left London and called at Manchester, Prestwick and Iceland before the long haul to Montreal. As we left Reykjavik I took two sleeping pills. The aircraft was more comfortable than the modern horrors and I knew no more until waking over the St Lawrence River. I stayed a day or so with relatives of my wife in Toronto before going to Chicago.

The late George May, who promoted the World championship, had kindly made me his guest at a motel near the Tam O'Shanter Club where I arrived after an interminable taxi journey. I was to discover that American ideas of distance bear little relation to the British. Whenever you are told that the club is 'right near' the airport, the hotel or wherever it may be it is usually upwards of ten miles. If someone says it is 'real close' then it may be within a couple of miles, but invariably too far to walk.

The *Guardian* could not then rise to my renting a car and that first evening I was feeling somewhat isolated when a voice hailed me. It was Lois, then Peter Thomson's wife, who suggested that I join them for dinner with Harry Radix, a Chicago jeweller and a great friend to American professional golf. He was a delightful, generous little man who took me under his wing and introduced me to numerous people. I soon ceased to feel that I was a solitary newcomer. His kindness to a stranger was typical of many Americans but of few Europeans. Whenever we met in later years, either in Britain or the United States, he always insisted on giving valuable little presents to his friends.

Peter Thomson had warned me that the George May tournament was a carnival, unlike anything seen in Britain. He was right. To a stranger the atmosphere was like a bank holiday fair with piped music, hot dogs and hamburgers and thousands teeming all over the place. For three dollars May gave the public a straight deal. Car parking and programmes were free and the crowds were unhampered by ropes and only in dire necessity by stewards; they could jostle their heroes and wander about almost at will. The clubhouse was open to all who could eat and drink in half a dozen dining rooms or thirteen bars. The classic British phrases, closed, members only, lunch has finished, tea has not started, the bar is not open and so on, did not exist.

To eyes accustomed to the peaceful pastures of British tournaments this seemed rather vulgar but the golf was fascinating. It was my first sight of heavily watered greens and fiendish pin positions and I marvelled at the accuracy, familiar nowadays, of the players. In the heavy humid heat I rushed around in pursuit of the golfers, most of whom I had never seen before. The American writers in the cloistered cool of the air-conditioned press room must have thought I was crazy. I marvelled too at the composure of the leaders as they competed for the first prize of S50,000, a huge sum in those days. The winner also was given the option of doubling his take by playing fifty exhibitions around the world. Not everyone accepted because several had found that it damaged their tournament careers.

Before I left England it had been arranged that I would wire my copy to the *Winnipeg Free Press*, with whom the *Guardian* had a liaison, and they would re-wire it to Manchester. This was cheaper than sending it direct from the United States. I followed instructions and was startled when on the second evening a cable arrived from Manchester saying that no copy had been received. My feelings can be imagined. After all the pleading that I should go to America there I was on my first assignment and nothing would appear in the paper. An anguished call to Winnipeg revealed that no one had alerted the *Free Press* as to the arrangement and my copy had been spiked, but eventually all was well.

The last hour of the tournament was stirring for one unaccustomed to the manufactured drama now commonplace the world over. Leaders rarely, if ever, played last in European events and there to my wondering gaze was a quiet, slim figure in a white shirt descending into a cauldron of roaring excitement knowing that if he finished with a four the prize probably was his. The difference between first and second was $40,000. I wondered how any man's nerve could survive such a situation but Dick Mayer had won the US Open that year. He played the hole perfectly, Snead and Balding failed with their birdie putts to tie and Mayer was safe. I admired his golf for its graceful simplicity of style, and his modest appearance which contrasted sharply with the vivid garb of others. That autumn he was one of the few Americans who played their game at Lindrick when Dai Rees, with inexhaustible enthusiasm, faith in himself and his players led his team to a famous victory in the Ryder Cup.

I arrived in Winnipeg, another world after Chicago, an hour or so before the Walker Cup team, who were competing in the Canadian championship, and a few other writers appeared from Britain. They were wearied after the endless journey and just as they arrived at the bar in urgent need of sustenance the shutters clanged down and they were thwarted. Bars in Manitoba then closed, and may still do so, for an hour in the early evening to discourage the homeward bound from lingering. The serving of dinner ended dead on a given time. Leonard Crawley and one or two others were only a minute or so late but were refused a meal. Later I asked Crawley where he had eaten. He replied that he had dined at the chemist's (drug store).

One evening we were taken to a football match. None of us understood the subtleties of a game that seemed dreadfully slow, and afterwards we were asked to give our impressions on the radio. Arthur MacWeeney summed up our feelings when he said in his soft, slightly lisping Irish voice that the only time he had seen anyone move fast during the whole affair was when a loudspeaker announced that someone's car was on fire.

MacWeeney was a rare man with a delightful sense of humour. He loved and appreciated the good things of life but not to excess. I greatly enjoyed his company and that of his brother, Paul, for many years. Later on that trip Arthur was due to stay with me at the Beaconsfield Hotel in Boston but was taken ill and returned to Ireland. The following summer he gave some of us dinner at the Royal Dublin Yacht Club and I still have a splendid vision of his impressive figure glowing with good nature at the head of the table. Everyone was grieved when he died not long afterwards.

Most of us were of a mind that a week in Winnipeg was enough, but it had moments. Alan Thirlwell's majestic striking took him to the semifinal of the Canadian championship; Alan Bussell also played admirably as he did in the Walker Cup match a week later. And night after night in the hotel by the station I would listen to the haunting cry of the engine whistles dying away across the prairie.

The Walker Cup match at Minikhada, in the lovely state of ten thousand lakes where all the names seem to sound like running water, will always remain in my mind for the golf of Billy Joe Patton. I doubt that anyone ever swung the club at such a furious speed or based his game more consistently on attack. He was mercurial to a degree but when inspired by adversity or a great occasion he was a tremendous player with a rare flair for the unexpected. In 1954 he failed by a stroke to tie with Hogan and Snead in the Masters at Augusta; at Minikhada he destroyed reasonable British hopes of victory with a lethal exhibition of recovery play against Reid Jack. Patton produced several miraculous strokes in saving holes which Jack, with his beautiful style, had played perfectly. Over the day Patton had been outplayed through the green but as can happen in such matches, he gradually wore down Jack and won on the last green. In other Walker Cup matches Patton was the villain of the piece to British eyes but as a person he was far from villainous. I often enjoyed his swift talk and lively Southern charm.

Wolstenholme and Shepperson gave a brave account of themselves and Sewell and Jack, who played together in the foursomes, lost all three matches on the last green. Gerald Micklem and his team had cause for pride in having given the Americans a real battle.

As the week in Minneapolis had progressed so had my education in things American. My friendship with Herbert Warren Wind, the most distinguished of all American writers on golf, was briefly threatened when I drove his car unaware of the effect of power brakes. I soon learned that

American martinis should be treated with respect; and that when pretty American women approach you at parties do not be deceived into thinking that their charm and interest in you are signs of encouragement. Once your curiosity value has evaporated they have a way of evaporating also. I learned too that television mostly is rendered unwatchable by the incessant commercials. Occasionally I may have ignored early lessons about martinis, but having altogether spent almost two years in North America my aversion to television there, save on a public network, remains. How millions can stand the interruptions every few minutes is beyond me. The man in the Minneapolis hotel was astonished when I asked him to remove the television and bring me a radio instead.

One day Peter Ryde of *The Times*, also on his first trip to America, and I made a pilgrimage to Interlachen and played a few holes. The course is enshrined in history because it was there that Bobby Jones won the United States Open in 1930, the third stage of the quadrilateral which remains impregnable.

A few years earlier Ryde, like myself and others, had become a golf writer by chance. When the editor of *The Times* decided that Bernard Darwin should retire Ryde, then on the paper's staff, was asked to take over. The thought of doing so had never entered his dreams or ambitions, but occasionally he would drift into the office carrying his clubs and doubtless had been spotted as a likely prospect.

His writing graced *The Times* sports pages for another twenty years and more, during which he became famous for absent-mindedness with his own property. Rarely, it seemed, did he leave or arrive at a golfing place with all his equipment and this became a standing joke among his friends. One year a group of us was flown from Miami to see a development in the Bahamas. Peter, of course, had forgotten his swimming trunks but the ocean was so tempting that he wrapped his loins in a copy of *The Times*. To his evident surprise, even that august journal could not withstand the warm waves and Peter soon had to keep his back to the beach.

There were no heavy hearts as we left Minneapolis on a private aircraft for Philadelphia and a first acquaintance with the glory of Pine Valley. Very few courses in the world make as great and lasting an impact on the golfer. At first he may be fearful of the awesome punishment that can await the erring shot, and he will hear tales of men taking an unconscionable number of strokes, but will gradually realise that the course is absolutely fair and his fears will subside. I know that mine began to fade a little after the first round. Some years later when playing with Warner Shelly, a delightful man who with other Pine Valley stalwarts is a faithful attender at St Andrews for Royal and Ancient meetings, I managed to break 90 with a few disasters on the way and was not displeased with myself.

79

No great length or uncommon accuracy are needed to survive the challenge, only a reasonable degree of striking, but I know of no course where the golfer must ever be aware of his limitations and play to them accordingly. Woe betide the man who attempts otherwise. Nowhere is the true stroke rewarded so splendidly by comparison with the weak or timid. The fairways are not menacing gun barrels and the greens are spacious. Only on the tee of the mighty 15th is one aware that nothing less than a good drive will suffice. There is no alternative to carrying some 150 yards across a lake. The short 5th, which in fact is far from short, may strike fear to those attempting to reach the green cloistered in a neck of woods, but the wary can always play short and be in sight of a comfortable four.

The course, which was completed shortly after the First War, was the inspiration of George Crump whose life work it became. He spent $250,000 of his own money on bringing his dream to life. Sadly, he died when only fourteen holes had been finished but he had founded a monument to the beauty and challenge of golf which has few peers in the world. The host during our stay there was the late John Arthur Brown, a legendary figure, who was president for over forty years. He was a most impressive man and a benign yet stern preserver of the traditions of the club.

Pine Valley is a very special place, secluded and majestic, and one of the last bastions of golfing masculinity in America. There are no women members and although women may play at certain times they are not permitted in the clubhouse. Provision is made for them nearby. This may seem an unduly conservative attitude but no more so than that of the Royal and Ancient some of whose members are also overseas members of Pine Valley. Some years ago I was proud to accept an invitation to become one of their number, of whom only Henry Longhurst and I were golf correspondents.

As soon as I reached The Country Club at Brookline near Boston, I had the feeling of treading on hallowed ground. It was there in 1913 that Francis Ouimet beat Vardon and Ray in a play-off for the Open championship. In so doing he fired the first shots of the American revolution against British golfing supremacy, then unchallenged. No more significant round has ever been played and we had the pleasure of meeting the great man that week.

It was not a good championship for the visitors. As in Canada Alan Thirlwell survived longest by reaching the fifth round. The rest of the play was academic, if pleasantly so, for a British writer. On the second day I had a first glimpse of Nicklaus, then 17. As I recall, he was somewhat cruel to Sewell on the closing holes. I will not pretend that I then foresaw in him the great golfer he was to become; this became much clearer two years later in the Walker Cup match at Muirfield.

On the way to Boston I had stayed a while in New York where Herb Wind introduced me to aspects of American life far removed from golf. So vivid were those first impressions that I felt compelled to write . . .

We had been looking at golf courses on Long Island all through the warm afternoon and the coolness of evening was welcome and the city enchanted in the twilight as we crossed the East river in search of contrast and baseball.

For many years the desire to watch major league baseball had been strong not only because it is a national game as close to American hearts as cricket is to those of Englishmen but also to confirm the impression, long defended, that it is far more subtle in its tactical variations, more stimulating to watch, and even more beautiful than most foreigners would believe. Disparaging criticisms are sometimes heard in Britain, where comparisons with cricket are made in the ignorant belief that there must be a basis for comparison — where actually there is none. A ball is thrown, struck, and fielded. There any similarity ends. And so on this evening in September we came to the old ground beneath Coogan's Bluff where the first game of polo in the United States was played and where the New York Giants had made their home since far back in the last century.

It is their home no more. No longer will the crowds filter through the teeming streets of Harlem, raw and exciting in their dark fascination; no longer will the sleek cars prowl in search of parking space, and no longer will the subways to 157th Street be crowded on summer evenings. The Giants have gone to San Francisco. For some time the threat that New York might lose two of its three major league teams had stirred uneasily in the minds of the faithful followers of the Giants and the Brooklyn Dodgers. Now the Dodgers also have gone, to Los Angeles, and in all the great city of eight million people only the Yankees remain, proud and powerful in the Bronx, a couple of brassie shots or more across the Harlem river from the Polo Grounds. It is almost as if Tottenham Hotspur and Chelsea had left Arsenal in lonely eminence and is a comment on the strange indifference of New York.

There is always a sadness about last things. We knew that evening that never again would the Dodgers come from that swarming tip of Long Island which is Brooklyn to meet their ancient rivals on the Polo Grounds. Recently both teams had fallen on quieter days or, as one American writer said, albeit with affection, when talking of the Dodgers, "The twilight of the Bums". But to the stranger this did not matter for the setting was infinitely fascinating. The lights, banked high in the dark

81

sky, flooded the ground without shadow and gave a brilliant emerald sheen to the coarse grass; and the diamond with its tracks between the bases was neat, intimate, and clean. Baseball is a game of distinct patterns, of lines, angles and curves, sharp and clear enough to delight the eye of the most exacting geometrician. It is vivid, alive, and swift: it knows not the awful lethargy which can afflict cricket, for there is always motion and change. It is a perfect expression of the American urge for movement, for sudden excitement, slickness and deception and yet withal an awareness of beauty.

There is beauty and rhythm in the coil and sweep of the pitcher's action; there is grace in the flowing power of the hitting, but above all it is the superb fielding and throwing which is so enthralling to those accustomed to the gentler curves of the cricket field. Would that all cricketers would learn to throw with the speed and flat, deadly trajectory which these men achieve from almost any range. Much of baseball depends on running the striker out, for he must run if he makes a fair hit and get to base before the ball. Thus the excitement of the race is constant and in a double play when the ball is fielded and thrown from one base, and then to another, before two men can run thirty yards each there is co-ordination and timing rare and beautiful. This was a quiet game as baseball goes. Young Podres pitched admirably, allowed the Giants few hits and no runs, and the Dodgers scored three. When it was done the floods dimmed for the last time, the crowd poured over the grass and the evening still was young.

My next sight of the game was one evening in 1961, in San Francisco, when the baseball writer of the *Chronicle*, with whom the *Guardian* had an agreement, took me to a game at Candlestick Park. By odd coincidence, the Giants were playing the Dodgers, as they had been four years earlier when I had seen them in New York. Again Johnny Podres was pitching for the Dodgers, then of Los Angeles, but was soon dismissed when the Giants took four runs from him in the first innings. One of these was a majestic home run by Willie Mays that pitched halfway up the stands in left field (the mid-wicket area) a carry of 130 yards or more.

Mays was one of the great baseball players of all time and it was extraordinary to hear boos for him when he made a fractional error in fielding. There is no room for sympathy in baseball parks. The greater the player the louder the jeers for his mistakes. The catching is made to seem so automatic that dropping the kind that cricketers fumble would almost lead to loss of citizenship. High 'flies' would sometimes tower a 100 feet into the night and when wind is swirling about they must be desperately hard to judge.

One impression of that game still endures. Mays, who was paid $80,000 a season, no mean sum then, was at bat. For a few seconds he and the pitcher were motionless, tense, absolutely concentrated upon each other; Mays slightly crouched with bat poised, the pitcher ready to uncoil his wind-up. It was an instant, commonplace perhaps to the watchers, but one that seemed to express part of the game's compulsion. There was an acute sense of expectancy about the two superbly trained athletes, facing each other as if utterly alone, as in their minds they were, even though 30,000 were watching. There was also the certainty that within seconds there would be an explosion of sound and movement.

I wrote my impressions of the game for the *Guardian* and was immoderately pleased when the *San Francisco Chronicle* reprinted the article across seven columns of a sports page. Lack of expert knowledge can be an advantage when making occasional forays into a foreign field.

CHAPTER 8
JONES AND PALMER
AT ST ANDREWS

One chill autumn morning at St Andrews in 1958 I met Bobby Jones for the first time. It was the eve of the first World championship for the Eisenhower Trophy and Jones was captain of the United States team. I had watched the early holes of their practise round on the Old Course and came upon Jones sitting alone in an electric cart near the 5th green. I introduced myself and we chatted for a while as he waited for the Americans to emerge from the Loop.

For Jones the return to St Andrews was a sentimental pilgrimage. His last visit had been in 1936 when he had come to play what he imagined would be a peaceful round on the course where he had won the Open in 1927, and the Amateur championship in 1930, the first step towards a peak where no golfer had stood before. In all probability no one will ever again win the Open and Amateur championships of the United States and Britain in the same year.

To Jones's astonishment the word that he was about to play had spread like fire through the town. Some two thousand people were gathered before he left the first tee with Willie Auchterlonie the Royal and Ancient professional. This was a rare tribute but Jones had endeared himself to the local citizens as no golfer from overseas had ever done. Six years had passed since his retirement from championship golf but, in spite of a five at the short 11th, he was round in 72.

As we talked that morning the head greenkeeper approached and Jones asked him about the little bunker behind the 11th green which had trapped his tee shot. The bunker had long disappeared and the greenkeeper had no knowledge of it, but Jones's memory was clear. There was a wistful note in his voice as he talked of how the character of the course had changed. Where once the fairways had been fawn and sleek they were like pile carpet by comparison. Some years later in replying to a letter I had written mentioning the condition of many seaside courses he said that he had been shocked at the changes at St Andrews. 'If this sort of thing is happening to all British seaside golf then, indeed, progress has been dearly bought.' Jones went on to say. 'Although I did not feel this way in the beginning, I am happy now that I did not miss playing seaside golf when the greens were hard and unwatered and the fairways and putting surfaces like glass. Nothing resulting from man-made design can equal the testing qualities of such conditions.'

During the practise days Jones had moved reminiscently about the course, much as a man would return to an old and beloved garden. Doubtless he recalled the shots he had played, the subtleties of the holes, the slight changes here and there, the moments of triumph and of acute anxiety. He mentioned the beauty of the gentle hills which he had scarcely noticed in the past. 'I guess I was too preoccupied.' How rich and full his memories were, memories of the youth who in 1921 came to conquer and, in his failure, to dislike the Old Course, and of the wiser young man who grew to love and respect it. And all the while the people would come to pay homage, the old who remembered and the young who wished they had known.

When the time came for Jones to follow his players home the cart would not start. I called for help from the telephone box which used to be by the 9th green but none was forthcoming. Jones, who could only walk a few yards with the aid of sticks, was stranded. By then spectators had appeared and several of us pushed the cart until the batteries had regained their breath. In the event of further mishaps I rode with Jones back to Rusacks where he was staying. We arrived safely and he invited me to join him and his wife Mary for lunch. Although, as I have said, he could only walk with difficulty I had not realised the extent of his frailty until, unthinkingly, I asked if he would sign my copy of one of his books. He did so and, although it cost him a great effort, insisted on inscribing a little message as well. This was my first experience of the man's kindness and I shall always treasure the book.

During the summer of 1966 I was myself writing a book about great courses of the world with Alfred Wright, a distinguished member of the *Sports Illustrated* staff. We had progressed far enough to be thinking of the introduction and who should write it. We came to the conclusion that Bobby Jones was the only person in golf whom we would approach. There was no point in having platitudes, probably ghost-written, from famous contemporary players, and we knew that every word that Jones might write would be his own. Somewhat diffidently I wrote asking if he would consider doing it. His reply, I have always thought, was a masterpiece of courtesy and tact; he said, 'Believe me, there is nothing I dislike more than

85

failing to accept enthusiastically any assignment you might give me; now, however, I simply must make some reservations.

'My health has been especially troublesome lately and I have been sorely pressed with personal matters. I am not one of those fortunate persons who can sit down before a typewriter and spill out words that make sense. The act of creation on a blank page costs me no end of pain.

'I honestly see no way I can do what you ask straight out of a clear blue sky. If you might be able to accept the reservation that I shall try once I have seen your proof, then I shall be happy to have a go at it.

'I hope you understand and will on your part act quite freely. If the uncertainty thus imposed is too great, I shall not be sensitive. On the other hand, I hope to be feeling better later on and perhaps may gain some grain of inspiration from the reading of your proof!' In the end there were publishing difficulties, then Alfred Wright died suddenly and the book did not appear until long afterwards.

The one shining fact about Jones the golfer is that he was an amateur in the true meaning of the term, which is rapidly losing significance on the highest levels of sport. He was no product of a college golf factory like the great majority of the leading American golfers today, but spent his formative years to the best possible purpose. He gained degrees in engineering at Georgia Tech; in English at Harvard; and, having decided to follow his father's legal profession, passed his bar exams in 1927 and became an active and most capable partner in a prominent Atlanta law firm. In his spare time he just happened to be the finest golfer in the world.

Every spring Jones would emerge from pursuing the law, play in one or two lesser tournaments to ensure that his swing was in order and then, more often than not, conquer the best players in the game. His record over a period of eight years still makes the mind reel. Only once from 1923 to 1930, in eleven British and American Open championships, did either Hagen or Sarazen, the greatest professionals of the time, finish ahead of him. He competed in twenty-one British and American Open and Amateur championships, won thirteen of them and three times, twice after play-offs, was second in the US Open. He came very close to beating the might of all the professionals seven times in eight years.

It may be claimed that this would be impossible now, such is the depth of competition, but no man can do more than be supreme in his own time. Had Jones appeared forty years later he would have risen to the challenge. He had all the attributes of greatness. The rhythm of his swing was wonderfully smooth and unhurried; he had rare sensitivity of touch, an acutely observant golfing mind and the ability to control what had been a lively temper in youth, and nerve in times of awesome pressure. Occasionally he brought these pressures upon himself and one of his few regrets was that he did not win some championships as comfortably as he knew he should have done. One of my lasting regrets is that I never saw him play. Schooldays interfered without mercy.

It was no wonder that Jones was considered invincible and that in the first booming age of American sport, the age of Ruth, Dempsey, Tilden and company, he should become the greatest of its heroes. He was subjected to a worship probably more intense, uncontrolled and ill-mannered than that heaped upon Arnold Palmer long years afterwards, and yet it is said that Jones was never discourteous, never insulted anyone and never lied to the press. He also knew that millions, not least his friends, expected him to win every time he played. This became an insupportable burden.

When, on a September afternoon at Merion in 1930, he completed the Grand Slam, a conclusive statement of absolute supremacy, there were no more worlds to conquer. Long afterwards Jones wrote 'All at once I felt the wonderful feeling of release from tension, and that on this particular project, at least, there could never at any time in the future be anything else to do.'

Whether Jones was the greatest of all golfers cannot fairly be argued and greatness in a man is not solely the sum of his achievements in a pursuit which is not his career. He had a cultured, lucid and perceptive mind and a wry sense of humour, qualities which were to sustain him during the burden of his later life. And withal he was modest, courteous and handsome. If it seemed that the gods had been too generous in bestowing so many gifts upon him they exacted a terrible toll.

For over twenty years Jones suffered from syringomyelia, a rare spinal disease, and knew that progressive physical decline was inevitable. And yet I never heard him complain. Rather would he mock his incapacity so that visitors were not embarrassed. Miraculously the wasting of the body did not blemish the crystal of his mind. This was vividly clear on the evening when he received the Freedom of St Andrews. The ceremony in the Younger Hall of the university was the most emotional experience of all my years in golf. After the provost had welcomed Jones to the Roll of Honorary Burgesses, (the first American to be honoured thus since Benjamin Franklin), Jones made a moving response. He described the Old Course as 'a wise old lady, whimsically tolerant of my impatience, but ready to reveal the secrets of her complex being, if only I would take the trouble to study and learn'.

As Jones continued he found that he had no need of the notes he had prepared. Supporting himself on the rostrum, he spoke of friendship. 'When I say, with due regard for the meaning of the word, that I am your friend, I have pledged to you the ultimate in loyalty and devotion. In some respects friendship may even transcend love, for in true friendship there is no place for jealousy. When, without more, I say that you are my friends, it is possible that I may be imposing upon you a greater burden than you are willing to assume. But when you have made me aware on many occasions that you have a kindly feeling for me by every means at your command, then when I call you my friends, I am at once affirming my high regard and affection for you and declaring my complete faith in you and trust in the sincerity of your expressions.' Everyone there sensed that he was speaking from the heart when he said 'I could take out of my life everything except my experiences at St Andrews and I would still have a rich full life.'

As Jones departed and rode down the Hall in his cart, the people began to sing 'Will ye No Come Back Again'. They must have known that he could never do so. For a while the sense of finality was almost overwhelming and many people did not trust their voices for several moments afterwards. The love affair, and it seemed no less, between Jones and St Andrews was a phenomenon. I doubt that there has ever been such a depth of affection between a great games-player and a place and its people, although St Andrews must have a warm place in Nicklaus's heart.

The championship that week in 1958, team medal on the highest world level of amateur golf, was a unique experience for everyone at St Andrews. In each round the three best scores from the teams of four counted towards the final total. Exact calculation as to their relative positions at any one point was difficult, indeed almost impossible. On the last day only a stroke or so separated Australia, the United States, and Britain and Ireland and all manner of drama attended the play of the last few holes.

I remember seeing Peter Toogood, a splendid little golfer from Tasmania, take four putts on the 17th when, in trying to tap the ball in from a few inches, he hit it twice. Bob Stevens, the Australian captain, had incurred a penalty of two strokes when a putt hit an unattended flagstick, but Australia still seemed likely to win. Then Arthur Perowne, one of the finest strikers of the time, stirred hope for Britain with a birdie at the 16th and another at the 17th where a superb two-iron finished within six feet. There was no way he could tell what was needed of him at the last, and in going for another birdie he missed the putt back. Finally the issue rested between Guy Wolstenholme and Bill Hyndman, both of whom needed a birdie and a par for their countries to tie with Australia, although Hyndman thought that he needed two birdies.

Before the championship Jones had ordered his team never to play their second shot for the upper level of the 17th green, sound advice in a competition of that kind, but the situation was desperate. Hyndman indicated to Jones sitting in his electric cart that he was going for the forbidden shot. Jones nodded whereupon Hyndman hit as fine and brave a stroke as could be imagined at such a moment. His four-iron shot bored through the greying twilight to within five feet, and he holed the putt while Wolstenholme took five. In the years to come I was to admire Hyndman's swing to an increasing extent as one of the purest I have seen. Both men finished with fours and the United States and Australia had tied, with Britain and Ireland one behind.

Two days later Australia, for whom a young Bruce Devlin was a great spearhead, won the play-off by two strokes. If Bobby Jones's farewell to St Andrews was not attended by victory his memories of the place had been enriched, just as his presence had enriched the memories of everyone who was there.

Within two years of Bobby Jones departing St Andrews Arnold Palmer came for the Centenary Open on the Old Course in 1960. Although Kel Nagle beat him by a stroke the championship, as all the world knows, was never the same thereafter. The first tremors of Palmer's impact on golf in Europe were felt at Portmarnock where, on his way to Scotland, he and Snead had won the Canada Cup for the United States. Already that year Palmer had triumphed in the Masters and the US Open and not since Hogan in 1953 had the appearance of a golfer quickened such anticipation.

Straight away Palmer's golf fulfilled every concept of the American power approach in its remarkable capacity for attack; we had heard of his famous charges under severe pressure and of his consuming desire to succeed. Everything about him suggested strength, the cast of his strong broad features, the powerful sloping shoulders, the lithe quick walk and the massive hands. His grip of the club might have been moulded in bronze and the swing was a controlled fury of attack. He was compelling to watch, especially in contrast to the majestic grace of Snead, and then one day I became aware of the personal magnetism which was to capture the golfing world.

It had been arranged that I would interview Palmer on the radio after the third round at Portmarnock. When I found him in the locker room there was a look of cold anger about him. He had taken 75 and felt that he had let his side down. Snead's superb 67 served to emphasise the failure. I asked him if he was ready to do the broadcast. He said that he must find his wife and strode away with me in pursuit, wondering whether I would capture him for the few crucial minutes. I need not have worried. As I realised on countless occasions afterwards Palmer honoured his commitments. Few professional games-players have behaved more graciously towards the public or the press. After he had spoken to Winnie, his wife, he came to the radio caravan, sat down opposite me and grinned. His face was transformed, all the anger with himself seemed to have melted away and I was made to feel that there was nothing he would rather do than answer my questions. From that moment on I was attracted to him as a person as well as a great golfer.

In the years that followed we became friends. I spent a good deal of time with him in private and on golfing occasions and realised that his charm was natural. It was part of a personal appeal that was unique in contemporary sport. He rapidly became the most marketable symbol in golf which Mark McCormack converted into uncommon wealth. Palmer's name could be used to sell all manner of products unconnected with golf and while he soared to the heights McCormack became the most successful entrepreneur that sport has known. I have sometimes wondered how each would have fared had they never met.

Palmer has always been aware of his public image. A genuine liking of people and anxiety not to offend made him vulnerable to all kinds of pressures but I never saw his patience fail. Jean and I were dining with the Palmers one evening in Scotland when a man, spotting Arnold, weaved across the room after a training session at the bar and more or less demanded audience. Palmer, courteous as ever to strangers, greeted him. The man asked for an autograph which was given and then asked for several more. Not satisfied with having interrupted our dinner he launched forth his views on the coming championship, saying that if X, naming a player who had no chance, did not win he hoped that Palmer would. Most famous games-players have suffered this sort of tactlessness, but none more so than Palmer.

No golfer since Jones, and in recent years Nicklaus, attracted the support that Palmer did and still does in some measure. The very nature of his golf suggested a man fighting to overcome great odds, a man unafraid of challenge. Danger was his inspiration. The fact that he embodied toughness and confidence, and was adventurous besides, made him particularly attractive, especially to those Americans who believe that an ordinary man can achieve anything. To them Palmer was a symbol of heroic struggle and ultimate triumph. His army, as it was called, pursued him with a fanaticism that sometimes betrayed him into thinking that a task was complete, when it was not, and spectacular failure followed. So intent upon their hero and so noisy were his army that playing with Palmer in those years was not always enviable. Occasionally I thought he might have helped silence them when others were putting. His voice would have had more effect than those of marshalls.

Every army has its deserters and occasionally when Palmer was below form there would be comments such as one I heard, 'Aw hell, I ain't gonna watch that guy, he can't play no more.' It was said in a voice plainly audible to Palmer. Anonymous letters would convey the same message, adding that in future the writer would follow 'you know who', meaning Nicklaus. A man less sensitive to other people's impressions of him would ignore such nonsense but each incident probably caused Arnold a twinge. As it happened Nicklaus probably had to endure far more active rudeness from a small minority of spectators than Palmer ever did. Nicklaus was the villain who, after a few years, beat the hero more often than not. Palmer's army sometimes showed their resentment in idiotic fashion but Nicklaus behaved admirably, never once betraying his feelings. I think it took Palmer a long while to come to terms with the fact that by about 1966 Nicklaus had become the stronger and more successful golfer.

Palmer's readiness to be involved with people and innate restlessness must have imposed a burden on his resources of nerve and concentration. This possibly cost him two or three major championships but had he not been the type of person he is and had won more often, he would not have been the Palmer that millions came to worship. And I am sure that Arnold would never have wanted to be anyone but himself.

Before Palmer competed at St Andrews the Open had declined in stature and appeal as a world golfing occasion. Since the Second War Americans had never entered in force. Hogan only appeared once and Bobby Locke and Peter Thomson almost established a permanent lien on the championship. So assured was their golf that year after year the victory of one or the other seemed inevitable. I grew bored with writing preliminary articles on the Open, suggesting for the readers' benefit that there could be hope of a British victory when I knew it was most unlikely.

Thomson was gifted with a beautifully simple style, immense confidence, serene poise and lively intelligence while Locke was the most experienced world golfer of the time. Although the frequency of his victories in the Open and other events became monotonous I was fascinated by his unshakeable calm, wonderfully constant rhythm and putting that few golfers in history can have matched. While everyone admired these two golfers the time for a revival of world interest in the Open was overdue. Palmer's play at St Andrews and victories the next two years injected new life and meaning into the championship. American entries increased forthwith, following Palmer, the Pied Piper.

One evening during the championship at St Andrews I was partly instrumental in persuading Palmer that he should play in the French Open the following week. I said that St Cloud resembled an American course, ideal for the big ball, and would serve as practice for the PGA championship soon after he returned home. Winnie was also keen to see Paris and finally Arnold gave way. Frank Pennink phoned the French Federation who agreed to accept the entries of Palmer and Gary Player who also wanted to go.

Three days later I arrived at the hotel in Paris and ran straight into an enraged Palmer about to leave for the airport. On arriving at St Cloud he had been told that neither he nor Player could compete as their entries were too late. Maybe they were but the French should have stuck by the original decision and given their golfers a first sight of the great man at his peak. I was most embarrassed but Palmer was readily forgiving.

Among my most vivid memories of watching golf are those of Palmer drilling shots through a gale at Birkdale in 1961, and of mastering totally different conditions the following summer on a fast, burnished course at Troon. Palmer then was king but already the foundations of his throne were beginning to tremble, as one suspected they might. The shadow of Nicklaus had already darkened his horizon.

CHAPTER 9
A JOURNEY OF DISCOVERY

At no time when I was on the *Guardian* staff did I consider moving elsewhere. For many years the pay did not match that on some other leading newspapers but there were many compensations. There was always freedom of opinion; never once was I fussed or hectored by a sports editor, and until space restrictions were imposed on everyone a few years ago one usually had about 700 words or considerably more on important occasions. There was room for general description and very rarely was this challenged.

After Montague had become one of the paper's assistant editors Bill Taylor, a most able journalist, took over as sports editor for a while until David Gray succeeded him. Gray was one of the most gifted writers on the staff. Apart from covering the lawn tennis his talents were often borrowed for political reporting at election times in Britain and the United States. It was not easy for him to write as much as he did and be sports editor and I am sure he was relieved when he could hand over to John Samuel, the present incumbent. Samuel's lively mind, knowledge of all games and enthusiasm for the job greatly contributed to the increased breadth and variety of the sports pages.

I was fortunate in having editors who became personal friends and with whom there was always a sympathetic relationship. Differences of opinion never stretched beyond the bounds of amiable, if firm discussion. For one who sought a settled existence and loathed personal conflict my position on the *Guardian* was ideal and not one to be surrendered lightly, but opportunities to do so did arise.

In the summer of 1960 when the *Sunday Telegraph* had been conceived Jim Swanton, cricket correspondent of the *Daily Telegraph*, asked if I would like to join the new paper. Eventually I met Brian Roberts, the managing editor, who made me a handsome offer to be golf correspondent of the Sunday, second string, so to speak, on the daily and to help out in other respects during the winter.

The offer more than covered what I was earning from the *Guardian* and *Country Life*. While I appreciated the invitation the decision to decline it did not take long. In a letter to Brian Roberts I said that I was loth to give up *Country Life* and that difficulties would arise regarding the golf I would be expected to do for the *Daily Telegraph*. With the increasing number of clashing dates of important events there would be times when Leonard Crawley and I wanted to go to the same one. This would apply particularly to foreign travel and I said that it would be unreasonable for the *Telegraph* to send both correspondents to the United States, as on occasion has proved to be the case. Had I joined the Sunday paper it is most unlikely that I would have gone to the west coast of the United States the following summer, Crawley would have covered for both papers, as indeed he did, and I would have missed the most memorable of all American journeys I ever took.

The Walker Cup match that year was in Seattle and the beauty of going to that remote corner of the country was that one could make a huge diversion on the homeward journey at no great extra cost. We made the most of our opportunity. Having deposited Jean with her family in Canada I went on to Tacoma where the US Women's championship was being played the week before the Walker Cup. I had been booked in a motel there but the next day a Doctor Cameron, a member of the club, insisted that I stay with him and his wife and that I have one of his cars, an enormous Thunderbird, for the week, yet another instance of spontaneous American kindness.

The course, possibly the oldest west of the Mississippi, was delightfully sited amid oak and Douglas fir on the edge of American Lake with Mount Rainier like a white mirage, rising above the early morning mists. The weather was perfect and so was the golf of Anne Quast Decker, now Mrs Sander, who played through the championship with a ruthless consistency, the like of which I have hardly, if ever, seen since from a woman golfer. Nineteen years later Anne Sander won the British championship at Woodhall Spa and spent the weekend with us in Norfolk afterwards. As I write Mount Rainier still looks down upon me from the picture she brought, a beautiful reminder of a delightful week.

As far as the golf was concerned there was little to delight the British gathering in Seattle. The Americans, headed by Nicklaus and Deane Beman, were far too strong for the late Charles Lawrie's team and Martin Christmas alone won a point. Before leaving England Gerald Micklem and I had planned to drive from Seattle to San Francisco, something over a thousand miles. Brian Chapman, who had played in the match, came with us.

It was a wonderful trip; Gerald did most of the driving and I was able to relax and enjoy the beauty of Oregon, the noble woods and the rockbound shores, and be amused by the warning road signs one of which read 'Drowsy? — just remember — pard — that doggone marble slab is awful hard'. I longed for my first sight of the Pacific itself and became rather a bore on the subject until, I think it was at Gearhart, my impatience was stilled. We lingered awhile in the redwoods in northern California, humbled to silence in the presence of so many ancient, living things. Towards evening on the third day we came to the Golden Gate and San Francisco, its towers gleaming in the late sunshine on their hills across the bay. I was profoundly moved, as millions must have been by their first sight of that enchanting city.

Gerald and I stayed in the Bohemian Club, which could easily have been in Whitehall, a pleasant privilege. On our first evening, after drinks at the Top of the Mark, we dined with Frank D. (Sandy) Tatum who, in the years ahead, was to be a valued friend. One day Sandy and Gerald played at Olympic while I wandered round a course which has taken its place in history as the setting of two of the most dramatic and unexpected turns of fortune in all championship golf. I looked down from the clubhouse to the tiny 18th green in its amphitheatre and thought of the day six years before when Jack Fleck holed from eight feet to tie with Hogan in the US Open. The next day he won the play-off and the whole golfing world was stunned into disbelief for Fleck was unknown and the master had seemed certain of a fifth victory. When the Open returned to Olympic in 1966 Palmer also lost a play-off, after Casper had gained seven strokes on him over the last nine holes of the fourth round. Few people then agreed with me that, after this crushing blow to his confidence, Palmer would probably not win another major championship. Sadly he did not.

While in San Francisco Micklem and I sent a cable to Bernard Darwin for his 85th birthday, unaware that he was failing and had written his last commentary for *Country Life*. Later I drove alone towards the fulfilment of another dream. Again travelling hopefully was not the better part. As I came down through the woods to Pebble Beach, and glimpsed the red flag on the 18th green with the Pacific softly surging beyond, I knew there could be no disappointment. The majestic creation of Douglas Grant and Jack Neville has become familiar to golfers the world over through television, films and innumerable articles. Several of the ocean holes, notably the 9th and 18th, are amongst the finest and most beautiful in the world. It is a great pity that considerations of commerce seem to prevail on one of the noblest of courses. From dawn until dusk the four-balls grind their dreary way round. The last time I was there in 1977 we waited for every shot. After 5¼ hours we had only played sixteen holes and darkness drove us in, but Cypress Point a few miles away is another matter altogether.

Whenever I am asked to name my favourite courses Cypress Point always comes first to mind. No other that I have seen anywhere in the world fulfils more precisely all that I would hope to find in a golfing place. The clubhouse, a serene and secluded plantation-style building, is minute by American standards and as usual all the more soothing to British eyes. The main sitting room could well have come from an English country house; the dining room is far from large and the bar tiny by comparison. Upstairs there are four bedrooms giving on to a balcony running round the house from where one can look down across a sloping lawn and groves of ancient gnarled and writhing cypress, some centuries dead but seemingly still alive, to the most famous hole in America, the menacingly beautiful 16th. In the years to come I was to enjoy other visits to Cypress but my introduction was in 1961 when Elizabeth Price Fisher and I played the course. I recall little of our round save that when we came to the 16th there was a damp wind from the ocean, and no question of my attempting to carry the inlet of surging ocean between tee and green. Elizabeth and I took the safe route, pitched on and she holed for a three.

Meanwhile at Pebble four miles away Nicklaus was making his final massive impact on the amateur scene and Joe Carr was striving his utmost to meet him in the final. I watched most of his 36-hole semifinal with Charles and Margaret Lawrie and Joe put us through the wringer before losing at the 36th to Dudley Wysong. On that magnificent last hole, Carr was some way short of the green in two when Nicklaus, who had long since won his match, appeared beside me. He remarked that Carr was 116 yards from the flag and when I looked surprised at such a specific figure he produced a card with exact distances of various shots on every hole. That was my first experience of the measuring which has become commonplace throughout first-class golf. Needing a birdie to prolong the match Carr overhit on to the rocks fringing the green. The next day Nicklaus, who was about 20 under par for the championship, murdered Wysong. At the prize-giving he said that he was not intending to turn professional. He still wanted to try to match Jones's record as an amateur, but inevitably the financial temptations were too great and he changed his mind a couple of months later.

From Monterey I took the California coast road to Los Angeles, pausing for the night at Big Sur. I had been advised to dine at a restaurant called Nepenthe and while at the bar fell into conversation with a young American and his wife. They invited me to join them for dinner and insisted that I be their guest. The next day I was tempted to visit San Simeon but time was pressing, and years later Jean and I did see that bizarre monument to man's acquisitiveness. I loved cruising quietly along the beautiful winding road above the ocean and by then was taking a

Sagan golf course 1944. The famous wooden horse from which three prisoners escaped was close to the furthest 'brown'. In the distance are the outlines of our home-made skating-rink.

One of the camp's leather-covered golf balls. On average each took six hours to make.

Above left: The incomparable Bobby Jones. Above right: Larry Montague who, as Sports Editor of the *Guardian,* had a rare capacity for blending command and friendship.

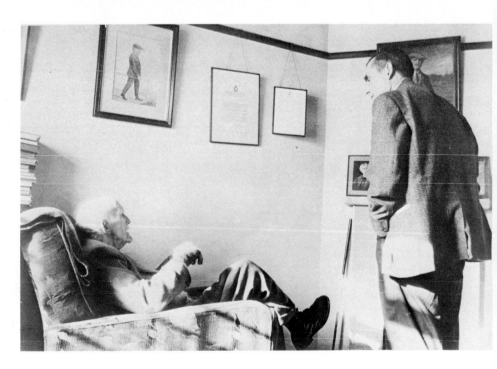

John Henry Taylor in his house overlooking the links at Westward Ho! I went down to interview him on the eve of his ninetieth birthday.

Left. The 'infamous' Rugby League poster. My coverage of the sport lasted for less than a season. Above: The real beginning. Jean and I leave Holy Trinity Church, Chelsea, in January 1949.

A '60s-version Jack Nicklaus stresses a point. George Simms, Press Officer for the Open, bears the rosette.

Above: Wentworth, 1956. Jean studies Hogan, while others follow the flight of the ball. Right: Arnold Palmer and I take off for the links at Muirfield, 1966.

Above: West Runton, Norfolk, 1979. My effort with his ten-pound
club amuses Gary Player.
Below: A companionable moment at the U.S. Amateur Championship at Pebble Beach with Leonard Crawley and Henry Longhurst,
1961.

A contented foursome at Cypress Point with Donald Steel, Bing and Dick Snideman, 1971.

Rita Hayworth and two lucky men.

Moor Park, 1938. No wonder the Don remains a fine golfer. I played against him at Royal Adelaide during my trip to Australia in 1972.

'Suffering' in the Bahamas. From left to right: Ben Wright, Peter Dobereiner, Jean and I, Truman Connell and Peter Ryde.

An unfamiliar sight at Pinehurst — making a tribute to Lady
Heathcoat Amory during 1975.

highly contented view of the United States.

During the week at Pebble I had met a son of Ethel Barrymore who arranged for me to visit Universal Studios, and I would happily have lingered a few more days, succumbing to the fascination of Hollywood, Sunset Boulevard and so on. I was reluctant to leave California, but Jean and I had planned to meet in New Orleans three days later. I could have gone by air but a deal of writing had to be done and the *Sunset Streamliner* offered the seclusion essential for unburdening. As the famous names gradually vanished from American railroads and train travel became more of an endurance than a pleasure I was happy to have taken that journey. The train ambled along for some forty hours while I thrilled at my first sight of the desert lands that I would come to love, and to a true sense, impossible by air, of the vastness of the country.

Leaving the train at New Orleans I felt deep humid heat for the first time, a startling change from the weeks on the west coast and even more so for Jean who came from autumn in Toronto. We stayed in a charming little hotel, La Motte House, on the edge of the French quarter, recommended to us by W. J. Weatherby, one of the *Guardian* writers on theatre and the arts. Later he followed the civil rights cause with considerable courage in the southern states. The only air conditioning was a fan in our bedroom and after each day's exploration we would lie beneath it before braving the short walk to a restaurant for dinner. For a long while afterwards Jean would recall the Rockefeller oysters at Antoine's. We did all the standard things, eating at Brennans and the Courtyard of the Three Sisters, a trip on the Mississippi, and listening to the jazz, not least that of Al Hirt to whom Palmer had given us an introduction. We found Preservation Hall, where the old jazzman played night after night, almost irresistible. The Hall then was, and may still be, a bare room with wooden benches. People of all kinds drifted in and out, giving a dollar or so when the hat came round. Jean was determined not to leave New Orleans without something truly indicative of the place. After some searching in the little galleries that abound there she found a crayon drawing of three old jazz players in the Hall. It still hangs in our dining room. We loved the whole atmosphere of New Orleans, foreign to anything we had known before, not least the soothing influence of sazerac in shaded courtyards.

Golf was far from my mind for several days but the Palmers had told us to call the Bronson Ingrams, close friends of theirs, who then lived in the Garden District. They were most hospitable and Bronson suggested golf at the New Orleans Country Club. Before starting he asked if I would like a cart. I refused, saying rather loftily that we did not use them in Britain. Long before we finished nine holes I was exhausted and dripping from the humidity. Needless to say Bronson insisted on a cart for the second nine and I collapsed gratefully into it. Let no one scorn the use of carts until they know what it is like to play golf when humidity and temperature are in the nineties.

Soon after leaving New Orleans we crossed Lake Pontchartrain. The bridge is low to the water but is about twenty miles long and for some time there was no sight of land at either end. It gave us an eerie feeling of total isolation. We drove along the Gulf of Mexico for a while and as we passed through Louisiana and Alabama, with its interminable pines, we had glimpses of the life which many of the black people were forced to endure.

Before leaving England I had written to Bobby Jones who said that he would take us to East Lake, the course where as a small boy his genius began to flower. He collected us from the motel and only later did I learn that he had been suffering from a virus and that this was his first day abroad. It was typical that he should not disappoint his visitors. Harold Sargent, then the professional at East Lake, joined us for lunch in the clubhouse which enshrined so much evidence of Jones's triumphs. Later the club moved to new headquarters and when the US Open was there in 1976 I saw the room with its beautifully arranged collection of trophies, books, pictures and clubs which the USGA had determined should be a permanent tribute to his memory.

After lunch Sargent and I played the course. Jones did not linger and was spared the sight of the ghastly quick hook with which I started the round. That evening Harold entertained us in his home where we met his father George Sargent, who had won the US Open at his first attempt in 1909 after arriving from England. Within moments of a long talk beginning the generations had melted away and I felt a humbling awareness of all that had happened in his lifetime.

Sargent's early days had been spent at Epsom Downs as assistant to one McWatt, who had actually played with young Tom Morris. McWatt told the youthful Sargent that Morris kept his head so still that his Glengarry used to be jerked off by the impact of his swing. Eventually Sargent realised that there was little chance for a young player to reach the top in Edwardian Britain, when Vardon, Braid and Taylor were supreme and so, like many another young golfer, he emigrated to North America. The profession had little status in those days and, as he said, 'we were struggling for recognition, and then came Walter Hagen.'

There was a glow in the old man's voice as he spoke of Joyce Wethered (Lady Heathcoat Amory) and the way she 'hit from the inside'. He learned that the Wethered family used to take notes separately when watching Jones play, and Sargent himself was sent to England with a special high-speed camera to photograph her swing and those of Jones and Vardon. All this made vintage listening and one envied the richness of his memories.

The next morning we visited Peachtree where Harold's brother Jack, a delightful man, was the professional. He showed us one of the most beautiful of American courses, its design an expression of the combined talents of Robert Tyre Jones the golfer and Robert Trent Jones the architect. I would love to have played it but Augusta was calling and time pressing.

Before we left Atlanta Jones had arranged for us to be shown the Augusta National course. Driving down the long avenue of magnolias towards the serene old plantation clubhouse I felt something of the excitement which must have stirred Jones when he first saw the land in 1930. It seemed to him that it had been lying there for years just waiting for someone to lay a course upon it. It was closed that September day, as it had been for the summer. Only pyrocanthas glowed amid the trees, but it was easy to imagine the beauty of the setting in spring when azaleas, camellias, dogwood, wisteria and other shrubs, legacy of the nursery that once had been there, were in bloom.

Our hosts, Julian Roberts and Jerome Franklin who, as I write, is the only surviving original member of the club, showed us all the famous holes lovingly designed by Jones and Alister Mackenzie. We walked where the stuff of legends had been made by men like Sarazen, Hogan, Nelson, Snead, Demaret, Middlecoff and Palmer, men whose greatness spanned a generation. I stood in the bunker by the 18th green and understood Palmer's feelings as that very spring he had cast away a Masters that he seemed certain to win. Needing a four to beat Gary Player, his second with a seven iron was struck without sufficient care, his bunker shot was too strong and he took six.

At last Augusta was a known place. Now I was conscious of its atmosphere and of the traditions that, remarkably, had grown in less than thirty years. When I did see the Masters for the first time in 1964 I was so excited on the opening morning that I could not begin to write. Sheet after sheet was wrenched from the typewriter and hurled away in an increasing fury of frustration. I could not, as I believe Neville Cardus did once from a cricket match, send a wire to the *Guardian* saying, 'Take PA (Press Association) cannot get started'. There were no such resources at Augusta. Finally, when I was becoming desperate, Herb Wind told me to forget it for an hour and go and watch the golf with him. This was wise counsel. When I returned all was well.

From Augusta we headed north through the Carolinas, took the Blue Ridge Parkway, paused in Virginia and Washington and thence to Palmer's dwelling in Latrobe. When the visit had been arranged he had mentioned that we might play golf but for two days rain lashed down and by then it was too late. Our journey home, and to the Ryder Cup match at

Lytham, could not be postponed. Nonetheless we had enjoyed seeing the Palmers as private people.

Their home stood, as it does today, on a wooded hillside above what then was the nine-hole course where Palmer's father had been the professional since he had helped to create it before the war. Although by 1961 he had reached a peak and prosperity was growing fast there was nothing ostentatious about his house. It was comfortable and attractive, as one had expected it would be with Winnie Palmer in charge. Arnold had indeed been fortunate in marrying an exceptional person. The demands upon him were enormous, and the more so because of his outgoing nature and reluctance to say 'No'. Many a man would have been sorely harassed but his wife's cool intelligence, poise and devotion to the cause were ever there as barriers against the bombardment of mail and telephone, the needs of two little daughters, guests, callers and an abundance of detail.

One did not have to know Palmer long to appreciate that there was nothing contrived or false about his manner, that he was always true to himself, and that he had a trusting nature. Some years later I was in his house when he suddenly sounded off to me in no gentle terms about someone who had upset him. His remarks would have made a startling story in print but it never occurred to him to say that he was speaking off the record. I was a guest in his home and therefore was trusted. Such belief in people is no small part of his appeal.

Palmer was blessed with a strong heritage. His father, known as Deacon, was a man of an older fashion, moulded from strength and simple beliefs, with a tough independent mind of his own. He was Arnold's only teacher and a stern parent. Even after his son had become a national figure and very rich Deacon never boasted about him and always stayed in the background whenever he watched tournaments. There was never any danger of Arnold being spoiled. Deacon was a reserved man, not at first easy to know, but once accepted as a friend, a friend you remained. I played golf with him occasionally at his beloved Latrobe, the last time a few months before he died. As my partner he holed an enormous, swinging putt on the last green to win our match, to the chagrin of Michael Williams of the *Daily Telegraph* and a member of the club. It made a happy memory of an uncommon man.

Palmer has always had a vigorous appetite for the active life. Not for him quiet reflective hours with a book, or hobbies distinct from golf. His refuge was in his workshop where he would work with clubs for hours. When I was last at Latrobe it was equipped with all the machine tools he could possibly want, and the collection of clubs had grown to a thousand or more from the few hundred he had in 1961. Aside from golf flying has always been a consuming interest. That year he had bought a twin-engine aircraft in which he flew us to Pittsburgh on our way home. I saw then, as on occasions later when he had jets, that he was an extremely capable pilot.

We stayed in New York for a night or so, went to a cocktail party for the United States team on the eve of their departure for Britain, and a wonderful voyage of discovery was over. I had travelled on land through all the peripheral states, save those in New England, a privilege that many Americans never enjoy, and much knowledge of the country, previously gained from books and films, was now based on personal experience. It was all made possible because the *Guardian* had sent me to the Walker Cup match in Seattle.

CHAPTER 10
AMERICA THROUGH THE SIXTIES

Whenever I recall the sixties it seems that journeys abroad rather than golf come first to mind. Summer after summer I travelled all over Britain and in many Continental countries to such an extent that memories of all but exceptional events have become blurred. Until the appearance of Jacklin little of historic moment involved British golfers. Inevitably, the sharpest recollections of that period are of the American scene. A dozen or more visits between 1965 and 1969 took me to many fascinating places — California, Mexico, Hawaii, Las Vegas, the eastern cities — and every year to Augusta, Georgia. I had seen my first Masters in 1964 but could not go the following spring. Later that summer, during the Walker Cup match at Baltimore, Charles Yates, one of the most engaging of men and an imperishable figure at Augusta, asked Peter Ryde and me if we would be at the Masters in 1966.

I said that I was doubtful because of the cost; one American trip each year was the most I could expect from the *Guardian* at that time. Eventually, Yates wrote and said that if I and others could get across the Atlantic the rest of our problems would be solved. And they were, in remarkable fashion. We were told to be at La Guardia airport by a certain time and we would be flown to Augusta in one of the private jets belonging to Jackson T. Stephens, a member of Augusta National. He lived in Arkansas and his aircraft had to come all the way from Little Rock to collect us in New York.

This was privilege indeed. I had not flown in a small jet and taking off gave one the sense of being in a rocket. For several years Jack Stephens sent his aircraft and on one occasion Ronald Heager, then of the *Daily Express*, now of the Sunday, and I were the only passengers. As we settled in our seats, a bottle of bourbon between us, we had one common thought, that this was the life, but Augustan hospitality extended to the point where we were housed and fed at no cost to our papers. All this was vastly more than we could have expected but for a while made the difference between my going or not.

I never discovered the precise reason for this kindness but Clifford Roberts, the tournament chairman and possibly the last great dictator in golf, and Bobby Jones were anxious that the Masters should have an international flavour. To this end many foreign players were invited to compete and coverage by the British press was welcomed. Furthermore, the club had close associations with the Royal and Ancient several of whose members are members of Augusta.

1966 was a significant year. Nicklaus became the first and thus far the only man to defend the Masters successfully, surviving a wearisome five-hour play-off with Gay Brewer and Tommy Jacobs. No fewer than ten British players competed and after two rounds Peter Butler, who always played Augusta well, shared the lead but the rest melted into oblivion. Nicklaus then won a memorable Open at Muirfield. As he strode purposefully from the 17th tee in the last round he said with a smile 'Interesting, isn't it?' I asked if he knew how interesting — there were not many scoreboards then — and he said 'Two fours to win'. He mastered the long 17th with a three-iron and a five-iron; hit a one-iron from the last tee, then a three-iron, holding the right-hand breeze perfectly, and beat David Thomas and Doug Sanders by a stroke.

A few months later I was looking down on the wonder of Mexico City by night, a myriad jewels in a vast black bowl within a seemingly impenetrable embrace of mountains. I was on my way to cover the World team championships for the Santo Espirito and Eisenhower trophies. The women's affair was at the Club Campestre, the oldest course in Mexico, and the flattest I have ever seen. A cricket pitch could have been laid almost anywhere on the fairways and the course was too long for most of the players, but Belle Robertson did return a 69, the lowest score of the whole event. I remember the superb golf of Marlene Streit, one of the smallest and yet for years one of the finest players in the world. She had the best individual total of all and was largely responsible for Canada finishing second to the United States. Apart from Mrs Robertson the British did not have the guns for a demanding course, but there were high hopes for the men's team the following week at the Club de Golf.

Two years earlier under gloomy, storm-haunted Roman skies, I had seen the British win the Eisenhower Trophy for the first time at Olgiata. Michael Bonallack and Ronnie Shade, who were in that team, were playing in Mexico with Peter Townsend and Gordon Cosh, but frustration was to be their lot. The course was a pretty formidable test; some holes, enclosed within a mighty uprush of firs, were like a cathedral nave, a menacing sight from the tees. From the outset the British were struggling: Townsend, until then a brilliant attacking golfer, unaccountably lost confidence and early in the third round Bonallack, who was in good form, tore muscles in his back. He played on courageously but the burden lay heavily on the others. Shade played supremely well, was easily the outstanding golfer of the championship and with gallant support from Cosh enabled the British to finish third. A remarkably consistent Australian team won.

Even to those accustomed to clubhouses in the United States the one at the Club de Golf was a rare experience. The dining room seated some 700, there were more than 900 lockers and the whole affair resembled a liner rather than a clubhouse. But once the day's golf was done I could explore one of the most fascinating cities I have known. In common with most others in the Latin world there was no escaping the contrast between poverty and riches, beauty and ugliness. An immediate awareness of progress was tempered by ever-present signs of fecundity.

There was much of beauty in the city: the handsome parks, the sweep of the Reforma, a street which compares with the Champs Elysées in its restless surge and grace, the castle of Chapultepec, rising on its green hill, the splendour of abundant statues, the soft glow of the cathedral square by night, the incomparable Museo de Antropologia, the matchless colour of the Ballet Folklorico, the still, warm days and the cool of the nights. Rarely have I known such a feeling of wellbeing as in Mexico.

The golf confined me to the policies of the city for a while and then Jean joined me from England. One day we drove to the Pyramids of Teotihuacán and glimpsed the other world of Mexico. The massive remains of the great Toltec city are impressive enough but so too in another way was the journey home. We paused at villages where progress had made no mark and once, after turning aside down a rough earth road towards a church, were surprised to see weeds and cactus leaves hurtling over the old churchyard walls. Within was a fury of activity, cleaning and tending graves and adorning them with the bright orange zempazochitl flowers. This was the eve of the Day of the Dead when people, with appropriate sustenance to fortify them, hold vigil by the graves. To watch seemed an intrusion; this was far from the tourist beat and we hastened away into the twilight.

By then the urge to see more of Mexico was growing. The season of the rains, not as threatening as it sounds for they mostly fall at night, was over; the great tourist invasion from the north was not yet under way and a quiet hotel in Acapulco, only 260 miles distant, sounded inviting. The road climbs from the city over mountains to 10,000 ft before the almost imperceptible descent to the ocean begins. It was a relief to escape the furious challenge of driving in the city, with its minimum of signs and numerous police awaiting private subsidies, and roll at peace into the gathering warmth, down through the Sierra Madre, a western rampart of green, folding mountains.

A first sight of Acapulco should be towards evening when the land enclosing the beautiful bay turns black against a Pacific sunset that even motion pictures cannot exaggerate; the lights begin to sparkle on the hills, and the outlines of the big hotels, incongruous cubic horrors by day (wherein Americans having escaped from the United States can escape from Mexico) mercifully are softened. But development was nothing like as alarming as we had feared.

Day followed flawless day, with the certainty that there would be no rain until May; that the water temperature in the seventies varies but a few degrees in the whole year; that there will be a rich abundance of fruit for breakfast; that a sweet ocean breeze, albeit deceitfully, will temper the sun's heat; that if one wants only sea, sky and solitude, mile upon mile of beach, where long rollers ride, await up and down the coast but, just possibly, there might be an earth tremor. During breakfast one morning in a covered restaurant by the hotel swimming pool we felt our world beginning to tremble. I leaped to my feet and rushed outside dragging my wife behind me but within seconds all was still. We returned to our table, feeling rather foolish, to the amusement of a group of German residents who said that such moments were not uncommon. Years later, high in a Los Angeles hotel, we were woken by another tremor. It did not last long but gave us a hint of how terrifying a large earthquake must be.

To linger in Acapulco was tempting but the call of Yucatan was insistent and the days were running out. Returning to the city we took the ever-winding, beautiful road to Taxco, old and enchanted, clinging to a mountainside a mile above the level of the sea. We longed to spend much money on the silver jewellery, ate *ceviche* high above wild plunging green valleys, and hated the leaving. It was wellnigh impossible to believe that Acapulco was only a morning's drive away.

Another hour or so and there was Cuernavaca, city of expatriates, where Cortes had a summer palace, on a wall of which Ribera, great master of the murals beloved of Mexico, had painted a disturbing impression of slavery under Spanish rule. For a moment the sunshine lost its warmth. This is a city where African tulip is an eternal flame, bougainvillea blooms for ever, and there are no seasons as Europeans know them; where you can breakfast on an open terrace every day of the year, within sight of Popocatépetl, its peak a shining cap of snow; where the police used to park your car in the main square and you could lunch in a garden where crane and flamingo wandered and margheritas tasted divine; a place where the air is so pure that you feel like living for ever.

Not long ago Yucatan was one of the remote places, little known or even imagined by the peoples of Europe. Now Merida, its principal city on the site of the old Mayan capital, is only a short flight from Miami or Mexico

105

City, and the fascination of a lost and beautiful world is familiar to legions of visitors.

One warm noon our aircraft came to rest on the strip at Chichen Itzá, a thin white ribbon in the interminable green. As it taxied to the tiny palm-covered shelter that served as a terminal the great El Castillo pyramid could be seen towering above the jungle. This is one of several massive structures: the vast ball court, with its remarkable acoustics, where a single game would last for months with death awaiting the captain of the losing team; the observatory, where Mayan astronomers took sight upon the stars, a strangely moving place when seen under the moon with fireflies glowing in the darkness.

Thence we travelled to Uxmal, where the evidence of faith was even more impressive in its immense simple beauty, with the theme of a serpent ever recurring in the carvings on the stone; and all dedicated to worship of the rain god. Had the Mayans but realised that water in plenty lay beneath the ground, the cities might never have been abandoned to the jungle seven centuries and more ago.

The appeal of Mexico is infinite and we were sad to leave but Jean had to return to England while I, after a few more days looking at preparations for the 1968 Olympic Games, began my homeward journey by way of Houston. It was a good opportunity to see Champions, the beautiful creation of Jack Burke and Jimmy Demaret, where the Ryder Cup match was to be played a year later. I was delighted to see that the surrounds of the greens were sleek and smooth, unlike so many in America with their coarse, thick fringes. I thought then that the British players would enjoy Champions; as it was Hogan's team gave them an awful hiding.

While in Houston I called on a remarkable old golfer, Ike Handy, author of *It's the Damned Ball*. He was a lively eighty, had beaten his age every year, except twice, since he was 68, had holed in one fourteen times and had extremely positive ideas about golf. His theory that mass times velocity equals power had a particularly good example in the Nicklaus of those days.

I had been told that Handy was an authority on shanking, a disease with which I was only too familiar, and on the practise ground of the Houston Country Club he gave a convincing demonstration of how to shank and how to avoid it. He was absolutely right in saying that if the left hand does not supinate you cannot shank; in other words make sure the hand does not roll over. Having absorbed this comforting advice I declined an invitation to accompany him on a duck shoot and sought a peaceful room on the Gulf coast for a last feel of summer.

All too soon I had undergone one of those startling temperature changes common in the United States, and was in the snows of western

106

Pennsylvania. Log fires glowed and all was peace in the house of Palmer. One afternoon we drove into the wooded hills above Ligonier, remote in deep winter silence, and a long escape from mundane realities was almost over. There remained only a day at Baltusrol, where preparations for the next US Open were well under way, and another with Alistair Cooke whose passion for golf was such that his eyes and talk sparkled like those of a man enraptured by a new mistress whose charms he is convinced can never fade. Every golfer knows what an enviable state that can be.

Late in 1966 it seemed that I would not be seeing any more of Augusta for quite a while. Cooke had warned me that the *Guardian* was facing something of a crisis. I soon learned that there had been a threat of the paper being taken over and losing its splendid independence under the ownership of a private trust. Mercifully the danger was averted but the prospect of overseas trips was not bright.

I had little hope of going to the Masters but during the winter Cooke had been in correspondence with Bobby Jones, whose latest book he had reviewed in an American journal. Unknown to me he must have mentioned that I would probably not be at Augusta the following April. The outcome of this was that Jones acting out of pure kindness arranged through a friend of his, who owned several newspapers, that I should write a daily piece on the Masters which would be syndicated. For this I would be paid a fee which, as it proved, covered my expenses.

I was exceedingly grateful to Jones because as it happened that Masters was the last in which Hogan played. It was also Alistair's baptism at Augusta. His addiction to golf had become a serious case by then. He had never played until in his fifties but the application of an uncommonly keen mind and diligent practice were making him into the competent golfer he is. His visit to Augusta, now a springtime habit, was an absorbing experience for him. We had talks with Jones, an evening with the Palmers, meetings with hosts of others and the joy of seeing Hogan play the homeward nine in 30, as he did in the third round. What more could anyone newly wedded to the game have wished for?

One of Cooke's proudest moments was when he played in the Autumn Medal at St Andrews for the first time. Although nothing may be at stake except personal pride the moment when one stands below the great windows of the Clubhouse can be alarming. I remember being unreasonably fearful when I first played in a Medal but Cooke hit an absolutely solid shot and was almost prepared to walk in there and then.

Often we would watch Hogan practise. Michael Bonallack, who had the enviable privilege of playing with him in one round, and I would sit on the grass by his bag and watch the shots stream into the morning sunshine. On one occasion Hogan was alone on the practise ground and was disposed to chat at intervals in the hitting of shots. Most of these had been straight or fractionally right to left and I asked him to fade one. Without any apparent alteration in stance or angle of clubface a three-iron shot rifled away. For an instant it seemed that the ball would not fade but as it reached the peak of its flight it leaked slightly to the right, only a few feet from the original line.

When I asked how this was done and what was in his mind Hogan looked straight at me and said 'You are too old'; there was a pause and he added 'So am I; it would take too long to explain.' I think he meant that he shaped his shots by feel rather than by any physical adjustment. This was fascinating, for he had brought the science of hitting a golf ball nearer to mechanical precision than anyone had and yet the abstract quality of feel still played an important part.

When his practise ended, the caddie gathered the balls, never moving far to do so, and Hogan said, 'Now for the bloodbank'. As we walked to the putting green I remarked on the constant frustration putting must have been to him, and of how the balance of the game seemed amiss, and he said that it was out of kilter, golf was two games, one in the air, the other on the ground. At times in his later years, it was agony watching Hogan on the greens but on the Saturday that year all was well. In his 30 he holed only three putts of any length and was round in 66, the finest round ever played in the Masters by a man of his age.

I still have vivid impressions of his golf in a PGA championship one year at Laurel Valley in Pennsylvania, a long and searching test, and notably of how drives would gently draw or fade away from hazards and finish in the dead centre of the fairway. During the week I asked if Ken Bowden, then editor of a British magazine and a most able writer who later helped Nicklaus with the production of several of his books, and I could have a quiet talk with him. We did so at a tournament the following week and Hogan talked of his early life and of how he had never achieved the standard (which was wellnigh inhuman) that he had set himself. One could imagine the kind of thing he had in mind when he said, 'I dreamt one night that I had seventeen holes in one, and a two, and when I woke I was so *goddam* mad.'

Hogan's manner could be disturbingly direct, especially to those whom he thought were seeking a cheap story or quote. It was said that he could express more in fewer words than anyone. If a monosyllable sufficed he would not embellish it. But once he knew a writer was sincerely interested he was polite and patient and would give his full attention to the subject. There was nothing of hypocrisy or false modesty about him, nothing superficial in a land where the superficial abounds. The intensity of his quest for perfection in golf can rarely, if ever, have been matched and it was a lonely pursuit. As he said that day 'I must be alone, way to hell out there by myself, I just love it.' He seemed to have no need of people, of cheering crowds, finding complete fulfilment in the hitting of perfect golf shots. There is no way of disproving his assertion that 'I know that I have had greater satisfaction than anyone who ever lived out of the hitting of golf shots' but he must have been very close to the mark.

Even when Hogan was in his middle fifties it was generally agreed that from tee to green he had no peer. One year we were at a tournament in the Napa Valley and Nicklaus and Deane Beman called on us for a game of bridge. Knowing that Nicklaus liked iced tea my wife had prepared some but he had to show her his way, the proper way of making it. At one point I asked their views of Hogan's golf, whereupon Beman described him as the greatest misser of all time and Nicklaus agreed. When, without thinking, I leaped to argue they laughed and I realised that they, who were not prone to overpraise other golfers, had paid him an unusual compliment. On the rare occasions when Hogan did mishit the effect on the shot was so slight that the fault would probably be imperceptible to the watcher.

During one of our talks Hogan had said that he would prefer the 1.62 ball if it were legal in the United States but that he would make it to American specifications. This surprised me somewhat but on arriving at Houston for the Ryder Cup match in 1967 I heard that Hogan, captain of the American team, had insisted that they all use the small ball which was permissible for the match. A day or so before the contest several survivors of the American team who had played in the first match in 1927 gave an exhibition. Among them was the indestructible figure of Gene Sarazen. He had recently been to the funeral of Francis Ouimet, a man he greatly admired. While telling me of this he said that as the coffin passed him he tapped on it and said, 'Make sure the greens are fast up there, Francis!'

As in 1963 after the match in Atlanta it had been arranged that the British team be flown to Las Vegas for the Sahara tournament. As far as I can recall Robert Hudson of Portland, Oregon, a generous patron of the Ryder Cup, took care of the flight and Del Webb, who then owned the Sahara Hotel, provided the accommodation for the visitors. Towards the end of the week at Houston, Palmer offered to take Lincoln Werden of the *New York Times* and myself to Vegas in his aircraft. For a while over the arid vastness of New Mexico he let me take the controls. It was the only time I have handled a jet, a rare pleasure for a pilot from the relative dark ages of flying. We were at about 30,000 feet and I remember how terribly sensitive the controls were at that height. Delicate though I thought my touch was, Palmer was soon warning me that I was off course.

The visitor, descending from cool skies and the presence of mountains, may find the first impact of Las Vegas overwhelming. He may wonder at the cynicism which makes untold wealth out of a human weakness, the belief that there is a short cut to prosperity; the philosophy of the jackpot, just one more dollar, one more quarter. For the vast majority there is no fortune around the corner and never will be, yet they go on hoping. The descendants of those who toiled across the western wastes of America in search of gold now seek it across merciless wastes of green baize.

Nowhere proclaims its mission as blatantly. The temptation to appease the dollar hunger is maniacal in its persistence. Nothing ever closes. Twenty-four hours a day, every day for ever, the muttering roar of the slot machines, the rattle of dice, the whisper of dealt cards and the cries of the wheelers and dealers never cease. All night the pretty waitresses flounce through the vast lobbies. At the hour when the abnormal (by Vegas standards) appear for breakfast people are still draped across the bars and tables, and attractive girls in evening dress, their predatory purposes accomplished, depart into the brilliant sunlight.

And yet rare is the visitor who, for a day or so, cannot resist the spell of Vegas. Leave the tables alone or stay within your limits and you start two up. Nowhere is there such a spread of entertainment. Where else could one see, as I did on various nights, Harry Belafonte, Ella Fitzgerald, Tony Bennett, Victor Borge and so on for the modest cost of a dinner, or listen to famous live bands and entertainers in place after place for the price of a few drinks?

Eventually, of course, unless one is a fanatical gambler or a very lucky one the whole atmosphere begins to pall. In 1963 when Peter Ryde also was there we yearned for escape, rented a car and drove through the desert into Death Valley. It was autumn, not unbearably hot and peaceful beyond belief. Nicklaus won the tournament that year and did so again when I returned four years later. Afterwards I had planned to see the Grand Canyon and then one day a journalist I knew named Hal Wood, sports editor of the *Honolulu Advertiser*, suggested that I go to Honolulu for the Hawaian Open. He arranged a flight and a room in the Ilikai Hotel at Waikiki. I could not resist this and have still not seen the Grand Canyon.

I found Honolulu fascinating on several counts, not least for a touching act of kindness. While waiting for my flight in Los Angeles I had chatted, but only for a moment or so, to a Hawaian couple. Two evenings later a bellboy brought a large basket of fruit to my room. I told him that it could not possibly be for me but he insisted and a card revealed that a Doctor and Mrs Kushi who lived on Maui, one of the other islands, had sent it with their wishes. As it proved the doctor was about to undergo an operation but they still thought of a stranger they had known for a couple of minutes.

After a day or so I realised that Hawaii was not to be judged by Honolulu, which is on Oahu, the third largest of the group of islands. Hawaii itself is

110

the biggest and it was there that Captain Cook was killed. Although I did not have time to visit the other islands there was contrast and beauty enough on Oahu to enrich my stay. From downtown Honolulu to the north side of the island is no more than fifteen minutes' drive through the mountains and the scene there is as different from Waikiki as Argyllshire is from Brighton. The mountains, ever caressed by gentle rain clouds, plunge to the ocean and but for the deep blue water and the temperature one might be on the western coasts of Britain. Here and there enchanting bays break the rugged coast and in the exquisite curve of Hanauma palm trees stand hard by the beach.

I learned that the headquarters of the Pacific defence system were on Oahu, and that Pearl Harbor, the navy's most important base in the Pacific, was the largest industrial organisation in Hawaii, a far cry from the small coaling station of the nineteenth century. By 1967 more than a million people had visited Pearl Harbor to see the setting of that December morning in 1941 when more than two thousand American servicemen were killed. Almost half of them were aboard the Arizona, one of seven battleships moored together, and over 1000 are still inside the sunken ship. She remains upright in 35 feet of water, her main deck only eight feet below the surface. Parts of the ship are still visible below the bridge on which a simple monument stands. I went there one evening towards twilight; there were no tourists, no ships were moving and only a tiny breeze ruffled the waves. All was silent and it was almost impossible to believe that such horror had happened in so peaceful a place. I was deeply moved.

Every morning that week I had a quiet little swim on the edge of Waikiki, and then usually made my way to Waialea where the tournament was being played. The course, close to the ocean, a joy of blue and silver as the great breakers toss their heads, is flat and exposed to the impatient bustle of the trade winds. All the golf I had seen previously in the United States had been played in comparative calm, never in winds as strong as the trades, and I was eager to see their effect on the 1.68 ball.

In Britain the seemingly interminable arguments as to the respective merits of the two sizes of ball were approaching their tedious peak. To my delight the wind seemed to have precious little effect. The way in which the ball held its line was proof that if struck truly it could be controlled as accurately as the small one. The trade winds were warm and this helped the distance the ball flew but I was convinced then, as almost before, that the large ball should be adopted for universal use.

Tony Jacklin was playing in the tournament and showed that he had developed a swing which would control the large ball in testing conditions. That spring he had given a fine account of himself in his first Masters and was glowing with enthusiasm for the competition and the atmosphere of American golf. After the event, in which he finished eleventh, I wrote that he clearly had a future in the United States provided he maintained his admirable attitude and the slower rhythm which had served him so well of late. Some six months later he won his first victory in the United States and his golden years were unfolding.

The 1969 British season ended at Wentworth with the Piccadilly championship in which Bob Charles beat Gene Littler at the 37th in the final, a classic example of the old adage that golf is not a game of how but of how many. It has always seemed unjust that a golfer can produce, as Littler did, a prolonged series of perfect strokes through the green and lose to a man whose golf in this respect was vastly inferior.

The orthodox, effortless simplicity of Littler's swing has always enchanted me. The quiet, relaxed approach to every shot, the gentle half swings and the stance taken so naturally suggest that he might have been born playing golf. The smoothness of the take-away, the unhurried start to the downswing and the purity of arc could be those of a man practising before a mirror. Watching him could be almost hypnotic. Beauty can be an ephemeral quality; rarely in any golfer has it been as enduringly expressed as in Littler.

At that time Charles had no superior as a putter and the fortune involved in holing numerous long ones during the afternoon round was less than it would have been for other golfers. In effect he won the match with one club while Littler's superb striking with the remainder was of no avail. It seemed a miscarriage of justice but such is often the way with the golf. Whenever Littler was playing I would hasten to watch him not only for the beauty of his style but because one knew it was fashioned by one of the gentlest and most modest of men. As of De Vicenzo I never heard anyone speak ill of Littler nor him speak ill of anyone else.

The year was alive with the unusual. I doubt that I shall ever again see a golfer of Trevino's class suffer a disaster comparable with that which befell him in an Alcan tournament in Portland, Oregon. With three holes to play Trevino was six strokes ahead of Casper who was playing immediately in front of him. Casper, who was concerned only with making sure of second place, finished with three birdies and was quite unaware of what was happening behind him. Trevino dropped a stroke at the 16th, hit a careless shot to the short little 17th, was bunkered, failed to get out at the first attempt and took six. His lead had gone in two holes and with it $40,000. His par on the long 18th was not good enough to tie. Casper's astonishment at having won was profound.

Calamity, but nothing like as costly, befell Kel Nagle on the third day of the same event. When signing his card he did not notice that his marker had inserted Nagle's total of 35 for the outward half in the space for the 9th hole. Under the Rule the 35 had to stand and Nagle's score was over 100, but he accepted the mishap as graciously as Vicenzo had done the previous year at Augusta.

As autumn slipped away I went back to the United States for the fifth time that year, and once more to the western shores. This time Jean was with me and the journey was intended as an escape from the golf which had crowded so many months but, within a day or so of arriving in a San Francisco shining in the crystal light of autumn, Bing Crosby was saying 'Have you got your sticks with you?' and a game had been arranged.

Five of us gathered at the San Francisco Club, a lovely golfing oasis seemingly, but not actually, remote from the purlieus of the city. It is a graceful place, with folding sweeps and falls amid gentle woodland, always appealing and never forbidding, although demanding high skill if it is to be conquered.

Going to the tee Sandy Tatum, my host, declared that he and I would play the others — Bing, Robert Cameron, a skilled photographer who publishes the superb aerial studies of cities (most recently London), and Bill Docherty who rejoiced in the unusual calling of growing rice.

It was one of the rare times that I have played in a five-ball and probably the only one that I have really enjoyed. That I contributed little to our cause was hardly surprising because Sandy played beautifully and was round in 68. I did however improve our score on the 17th and Sandy's birdie on the 18th enabled us to win. After the wagers beloved of American golfers had been settled, a process that always leaves me totally confused, Bing handed me 35 dollars.

Tatum, who was a Rhodes scholar at Oxford where he played for the university, has remained an impressive golfer ever since. In 1961 he won the pro.am. section of the Crosby tournament, improving on his professional partner by no fewer than 37 strokes. His swing became famous for its pronounced pause at the top which helped him to preserve a constant rhythm, but Hogan once remarked that if he did not 'stop and visit' he would hit the ball further. Nonetheless Tatum has been long enough for all normal purposes, and I much admired his control and variation of flight with the driver, a certain mark of class.

That day was so beautiful and the golf so enjoyable that we played again the next day. Legal affairs demanded Tatum's presence and this time I played with Docherty who bore the burden nobly. Thereafter we pursued our journey south by the coast route. Sandy most kindly had arranged for us to stay a couple of nights in the clubhouse at Cypress Point, and any American golfer would realise what a rare privilege that was.

As always in America, and particularly in California, our journey was one of extremes: the wonder of Disneyland, and wonder is the word even for jaundiced middle age; the extraordinary clutter of antiquity at San Simeon; the fascinating horror of the Los Angeles freeways and the relief of knowing that the desert, in all its austere loneliness, was only an hour away; the long hours of still sunshine in the valleys where, almost without exception, the towns were a hideous sprawl and then the overwhelming awesome beauty of Yosemite. Its vast granite peaks reached to ice-blue skies and although any thought of golf seemed trivial a charming little course lay in the threshold of the valley. I would love to have played it but Napa, a very different kind of valley, was calling.

This gentle country, an hour's drive from the Golden Gate, was a promised land of quiet green hills, meadows, scattered woodland and long reaches of vineyards, their leaves turning gold, that can produce finer wines than many Europeans imagine. American golfers rarely visit a more agreeable setting than the club by the old Silverado Trail that bore seekers after gold a century ago and inspired Robert Louis Stevenson to write 'The Silverado Squatters'. We stayed there for the finish of the Kaiser tournament, and Nicklaus won as he almost always did when I was in the western states. Soon a memorable year was done.

I greatly enjoyed these visits to the United States. The travelling had been a joy; the driving more comfortable and disciplined than in any other country I knew and the service generally far more agreeable than it was becoming in Britain. At the same time it was a pleasure to return home. There was escape from the syndrome of steaks the length of a missable putt, baked potato and the three sauces seemingly common throughout the nation, overpoweringly huge sandwiches, burnt wisps of bacon and weak coffee, apparently inevitable in the restaurants of motels where perforce one often had to stay, but the fruit was fine and I loved the cornbeef hash for breakfast.

CHAPTER 11
THE CONQUERING OF BONALLACK

For some years the old Penfold tournament was played in Llandudno, usually in the early summer before the place became crowded with visitors. I used to stay in one of those hotels which still echoed days of Edwardian splendour and look out across the handsome curve of the bay and dwell on happy memories of a distant youth. I had been at a preparatory school not far away and had spent many holidays on that coast.

In 1957 I wrote my first commentary for *Country Life* about one of those Penfold events which a year later heralded a particularly absorbing season.

In the winter the PGA in their wisdom had decreed that all their official tournaments were to be played with the 1.68 ball, a practice which happily became permanent. It helped to further an important cause and added interest to the professional events. During that summer Michael Bonallack dominated the amateur scene in Britain to an extent that had not been approached for at least forty years. At the Spring Meeting of the Royal and Ancient Club it was announced that Gerald Micklem was to be their next captain. It was fitting that this should coincide with Bonallack's greatest year as a player. In their various ways they were two of the most influential figures in the golf of my time.

Generations may pass before British golf produces an amateur golfer of Bonallack's stature. For ten years he had no peer as a competitor and his tally of achievement may never be surpassed, especially if professional tournament golf continues to prosper and attract some of the finest young players. I had no intention of dwelling on records in this book; numerous sources of reference exist for the purpose, but in recent years amateur golf has not received its due attention. If the unfortunate trend persists the next generation of golfers may not appreciate the extent of Bonallack's supremacy. Between 1961 and 1970 he won the Amateur and English championships five times each and won or tied for the English strokeplay on four occasions. Twice he won both matchplay events in the same summer. The second time was in 1968 when he also won the English strokeplay championship, and the *Golf Illustrated* Gold Vase. To one who watched all his championship victories, as I did, and lesser triumphs besides, his success was saved from becoming monotonous by the differing ways in which it was achieved, and the unfailing grace and modesty with which it was borne. Year after year writing of his golf became an exercise in restraint of superlatives and seeking varied phrases with which to analyse and praise him.

Bonallack was a classic example of the truth that there is far more to the winning of championships than elegance of style or accurate striking of the ball through the green. There were times when his game embraced both these virtues, as for the most part they did in 1968, but there were others when neither his swing nor his striking were impressive and it was then that his abundant gifts as a competitor more than compensated. Winston Churchill once said that balance was a great characteristic of the British temperament. This may not be true of an increasing proportion of the race nowadays but it certainly has been true of Bonallack. His reaction to competition was never extreme or intense; he faced the desperate situations with phlegmatic calm and the prosperous in exactly the same way.

His remarkable temperament, allied to an exceptional short game, enabled him to survive many an apparently hopeless cause in a match, and in strokeplay hold together a good score when his golf through the green would have left another man struggling in the high seventies. No opponent could assume that Bonallack was beaten until defeat became a fact. Time and again in matchplay events he would scramble through early rounds, sometimes because opponents grew anxious at the prospect of beating him or because he could make devastating thrusts when least expected. And, no matter what the other man did, Bonallack was always the same friendly companion for all that his manner concealed a ruthless determination. Like all great champions he would dismiss lesser fry, even close friends, in merciless fashion. Then, having reached the later stages, he had the capacity to raise his game often to a masterful level which brooked no opposition.

There were numerous instances of this, notably in an English championship at Ganton. He had several untidy passages on his way to the final and needed all his skill around the greens to beat, among others, Gordon Clark and, in the semifinal, Michael Attenborough. That evening a group of us, including Bonallack and David Kelley who was to be his opponent in the final, dined together. Bonallack spoke of continuing anxiety about his swing. It had improved somewhat that day but on the Thursday he had been picking up the club too quickly, taking it back on the outside and chopping rather than swinging at the ball. He had suffered spells of this in previous years, not that they cost him too dearly. His short game invariably came to the rescue. In one final of the English championship at Burnham he was quite outclassed by Alan Thirlwell's majestic striking. But twenty times in 33 holes Bonallack was down in two from off the putting surface and poor Thirlwell was cruelly beaten.

David Kelley was an experienced golfer and an English international. He knew well enough how unpredictable Bonallack's golf could be and said that he would try to ignore him and concentrate on playing to par. He did so for thirteen holes the next morning and was seven down for his pains. As Michael Reece dryly remarked later 'Play to par and leave the door wide open.' He had lost to Kelley in the semifinal and was grateful not to be receiving Bonallack's treatment. Allowing Bonallack two tiny putts which Kelley had conceded, he was round in 61, probably the deadliest golf ever played by an amateur in a British championship. Admittedly it was a heavenly, still summer day and the greens were perfect but Ganton measured 6900 yards and the way it was playing the strictest par was 69.

There was nothing amiss now with Bonallack's swing. He was striking the ball with power and authority and his putting was lethal, of the order of Bob Charles and Bobby Locke, two of the greatest putters of modern times. The shortest one he missed was about twelve feet. It all looked marvellously simple. Crouched low over the ball he gave it a sharp rap with his crisp little stroke and time and again, from all the middle distances, it vanished. His putting stroke was individual in the sense that when it worked it was admirable but sometimes in later years it did not look convincing.

In no form of golf had Bonallack ever broken thirty for nine holes but he was home in 29 that morning and the hapless Kelley was eleven down. He was able to win one hole in the match which ended on the 7th green after lunch. At this point Bonallack had played 25 holes without a five in 89 strokes. It was one of those occasions which even the finest golfers rarely enjoy when everything comes together in one round; if memory serves Bonallack missed only four greens in the entire contest and those by only small margins. When I saw him at lunch his first remark was to ask how his swing had looked. This was indicative of a true champion's outlook, and especially so then because a month later he was due to play in the United States championship.

As if the quality and manner of his golf were not enough Bonallack served the game in numerous ways, as captain and selector of teams, and on various committees of the Royal and Ancient and the PGA. Rare is the golfer of whom it can be said that he never failed the high esteem of everyone, not least those who knew him well.

Throughout all that time the Bonallack influence was not confined to

Michael's feats. In that same summer of 1968 his sister, Sally Barber, was English champion. Even before his mark was made his wife Angela, then only 18, played a considerable part in winning the Curtis Cup at Prince's in 1956, and in defending it successfully two years later. She was twice English champion, once when Michael won the men's title, and for twenty years and more was one of the foremost women golfers in the land. In the sixties she and Marley Harris (then Mrs Spearman) shared a delightful and amiable rivalry. When they met in championships the outcome was a tremendous contest between two women, whose uncommon determination was cloaked by their charm of manner and attractive appearance. These qualities, allied to comparable skills, have not been conspicuous in British women's golf since.

The golfing world was delighted, but not at all surprised, to learn that Micklem would be captain of the R. and A. I doubt that anyone in the game's history gave more of personal gifts, time and means to the cause of golf in all the obvious aspects and a host of anonymous ways besides. I am certain, although there can be no way of proving the fact, that no one has ever watched as much golf as he has, or watched it with more intense concentration and interest. His devotion to the game, which amounted to a passion, and dedication to its organisation and the encouragement of innumerable players, have had no peer in my experience.

Micklem's influence has been profound on championship, rules and selection committees and, at the time of which I write, much of the progress in the organisation of championships at every level of competition was due to his alert mind, imagination and not inconsiderable powers of persuasion. The improved process of selecting international teams from the middle fifties onwards was due almost entirely to Micklem and Raymond Oppenheimer. Unfortunately Micklem was taken ill during the Open championship at Carnoustie and was unable to drive himself into office at the Autumn Meeting. The following year he became the first captain to undergo that strange ordeal at a Spring Meeting.

In all the time of following golf few occasions have been as rewarding as the Walker Cup match. Inevitably the United States has held the balance of power and the outcome of the contest has often been disappointing, but in the long view this has not seemed to matter greatly. At a time when, to an increasing extent, sport is influenced, if not dominated, by commercial interests the Walker Cup has no need of sponsorship in any form. It is a purely amateur contest which expresses, like no other event, the mutual good will existing between the foremost governing bodies, as well as being a symbol of the spirit in which the game should be played. The same is largely true of the Ryder Cup match but this has become dependent on sponsorship, and its form has been altered so often in the past twenty years, in an attempt to make the contest more even, that in my view it has lost something of its stature.

Time and again I have looked forward to the Walker Cup match in the hope that Britain and Ireland would triumph. Occasionally victory did seem possible, but save once the prospect proved too great a burden and never more so than at Baltimore in 1965. Even when the Americans were conquered six years later at St Andrews there was no lively hope of victory when play began on the last afternoon, whereas at lunch in Baltimore the Americans were in a desperate plight. The British needed only two points from the eight singles to become the first team, either professional or amateur, to win in the United States. I cannot recall spending an afternoon of greater suspense, mounting to growing fear that Britain might even lose. For once I took a camera on to the course in readiness to photograph various people such as Joe Carr, the captain, and Gerald Micklem at the moment of triumph. Not once in the long afternoon did the camera emerge from its case. Gordon Cosh won the first point but Peter Townsend and Sandy Saddler lost their matches on the last green. Four others had gone to the Americans and Clive Clark was two down and three to play. He won the 16th with a birdie; his opponent was the luckiest man on earth to halve the short 17th, after shanking his tee shot into deep woods, but Clark saved his side untold remorse by holing from eleven yards on the last green and halving the whole contest. His finish was as brave as any the match had known by a British golfer.

The crowning point of Bonallack's career came a year later on the Old Course when he led Britain and Ireland to victory in the Walker Cup match for which amateur golfers had been praying with no very lively hopes for a generation. Hopes were the reverse of lively soon after lunch on the last afternoon. Britain and Ireland needed five and a half points from the eight singles for victory and Bonallack was soon down to formidable golf from Lanny Wadkins, and Geoffrey Marks was in a like state against Tom Kite. If anyone had then said that the home team would win the remaining matches he would have been regarded as an idiot.

I walked out on the course expecting to watch an academic American exercise. Even when the scoreboards shows that all the matches were even or slightly favouring Britain I was not optimistic. Often in other years such situations had held false promise because the Americans had much more experience of hard competition, especially from college golf. We awaited the inevitable American recoil but to our astonishment it never happened in the face of splendidly attacking golf.

The progress towards victory began with Warren Humphreys holing two long putts against Steve Melnyk, while Hugh Stuart was beating Vinnie Giles in the match ahead. Then, to British eyes, came the joyous spectacle of American golfers making the very mistakes on the closing holes that we had grown painfully accustomed to expecting from the British. In succession Charles Green, Roddy Carr, whose father, Joe, had spent a torturing afternoon, and George MacGregor won on the last green, and there back on the 17th fairway David Marsh was about to play the stroke of his lifetime. When his three-iron, a magnificent stroke at such a moment, found the heart of the menacing green, where disaster ever lurks, and he became dormy the deed was done.

One after another the conquerors came into the timeless setting of Old Tom Morris's green, with thousands gathered against the fences, on roofs, balconies, at windows and on the fairways. Cheers and tears of joy, relief and pride were mingled as they had not been for many a long year. The triumph belonged first and foremost to Bonallack who, in his calm, unshakeable fashion, had instilled in his team confidence and faith in their ability to win. He said later that he had never doubted their capacity to do so. That they succeeded was his fitting reward. No golfer could have served the British cause in international competition more selflessly than he did.

The early part of that evening was about the most exacting I endured as a golf correspondent. Until the last hour or so of the match I had been prepared to write of an American victory. The sudden transition to triumph and all the excitement paradoxically made the writing harder. After all it had been an historic moment. I had to write and phone upwards of a thousand words to the *Guardian* and do a short radio interview. This left one hour to write what was supposed to read as a leisured commentary on the whole occasion for *Country Life*. A telephonist was waiting in London at a specific time and if I failed to meet it the article would not appear in the next issue. I finished with a moment or so to spare.

Soon afterwards I ran into Gerald Micklem who invited me to lunch at Gleneagles the following day, a kindly thought typical of him. He understood far better than most that even a golf correspondent's job can be exhausting, and exhausted I was. The next morning I relaxed in the back of his car and gradually regained my senses.

International matches on the highest level of men's and women's golf have left many stirring memories. Some have been recalled elsewhere but the most recent in my experience did not receive the attention it deserved. The media (will anyone ever think of a pleasanter word?) generally have become so obsessed with professional golf that, apart from a very few newspapers and journals, the main amateur events are largely ignored. When the 1976 World Team championship for the Eisenhower Trophy was played at Penina in Portugal *The Times*, the *Telegraph* and the *Guardian* were the only British newspapers represented there. Lewine

Mair, John Campbell and I had the privilege of watching Ian Hutcheon play one of the finest rounds ever by a British amateur in an event of such importance. Lewine, an attractive, gifted person and her husband, Norman, who writes with rare fervour and skill on many sports, play no small part on the golfing scene.

The last afternoon at Penina was enthralling. With eight holes to play on a long demanding course where the damp greens became increasingly difficult Britain's destiny lay entirely with Hutcheon. John Davies, Michael Kelley and Steve Martin had done their damnedest, leaving Hutcheon to overcome the challenge of Mori of Japan and Tony Gresham of Australia, who were playing with him, and any threat from the last Chinese and American ahead. Hutcheon, a shy, impassive man, responded with deathless calm and courage, playing those holes in four under par and missing two other birdies by the tiniest fraction. He won a famous victory by two strokes from Japan. I have rarely seen a performance of comparable character by anyone playing for a team when the responsibility is more intense than in an individual contest.

I left Penina at dawn the next day and arrived in Lisbon with ample time for the flight to London which was due to arrive at noon. This left hours to spare before telephoning an account of the British triumph to the *Guardian*. As irony had it the flight, due to call at Oporto, could not land there because of fog so back we went to Lisbon. A few hours later the same dreary process was repeated. I tried every way I knew to telephone the copy to England, a totally futile endeavour from a Portuguese airport on a Sunday. Everyone from whom I sought help was charming and useless. At last we were flown to London but it was too late and I missed the first edition with one of the most worthwhile stories in a long time.

Telephoning from the southern Continental countries has improved somewhat but for years it was a nightmare of frustration for those whose calls were fairly urgent. Editions could not wait. Even from Paris there were delays, bad lines and interruptions. One of the best ways of getting a call through was to take a bath; often when one was thoroughly immersed the phone would ring.

Throughout these years I had less time for playing golf than I would have liked but one particularly pleasant occasion comes to mind. At the height of summer in 1973 Royal Montreal, the oldest club in North America, held its centenary and, together with Gordon Youngs, the late Frank Brett, long a pillar of Norfolk golf, and Donald McCullough, famed for the Brains Trust, I represented Royal West Norfolk. We did not excel but were far from last and I had the pleasure of a practise round with Sandy Somerville, one of the greatest of Canadian golfers. He won the United States Amateur championship in 1932, having also given Bobby Jones

121

food for thought at Merion in 1930. The centenary week immediately preceded the Walker Cup match at The Country Club near Boston, and the journey there from Montreal was a welcome opportunity to stay with Gene Sarazen who then had a summer home in New Hampshire.

Sarazen and I had been friends since, in the early fifties, he resumed pilgrimages, begun in 1923, to the Open championship. At this writing he is 79 and the most enduring of all the great champions. Sarazen is the oldest link with the generation of golfers who thrived half a century and more ago but is the last person to dwell on the past. He is always forward-looking, forthright, pragmatic and sometimes provocative. From his Italian parentage he inherited the flair and inspiration that made him a superb competitor, and a hard American upbringing gave him the toughness of spirit and the ambition to succeed. Gene and Sam Snead had the finest natural swing, simplicity itself of any golfer I have seen.

For over fifty years he has been blessed in Mary, his wife, whose gentle manner and intellectual tastes complement him perfectly. Always they were kind, attentive hosts. Jean and I had stayed with them when Gene had a farm in the foothills of the Catskill mountains. I also spent a few days at their winter home on Marco Island in Florida where we would swim together after his, not my, early morning walk on the beach. He would splash about lively as a boy. We then played a few holes. Every year at Augusta I would look forward to seeing the sturdy little figure with nut brown face and engaging grin, welcoming and eager for talk and far from drowsy with old age.

In New Hampshire Sarazen had a long meadow, falling away from the house, which he used as a practise ground, mostly for his young grandson who showed promise. I remember hitting my first shots with a graphite-shafted club there; they spread far and wide but this did not matter. Gene would speed away on a little tractor and collect the balls. When I produced my own driver and told him that Palmer had given it to me he said that the face was set slightly open to help counter the hook that Palmer always had to guard against. He seized the club from me and set to work with a file in his garage.

That was a soothing interlude in 1973 before we moved south through the folding green and wooded hills of New Hampshire and Vermont, some of the loveliest country in America, towards an enthralling Walker Cup match. The contest remained vividly alive until the last moments, as had the two previous matches in the United States. With all to play for in the last few singles to finish the Americans had a very slight edge and won by two points.

CHAPTER 12
TWO GREAT BEARS

Unreliable though memory may be, often discarding the notable and retaining the trivial, there are golfing events which make so strong an impression that they never fade. I can think of perhaps a dozen such occasions and two of them concerned Roberto De Vicenzo, the imperial golfer from the Argentine.

Adversity in golf can take many forms. One of the most acute is the repeated failure of a distinguished golfer to win the Open championship when his ability clearly is greater than that of many who have succeeded. The irony besetting such men is that they can become as famous for their narrow failures as for the skill which made these possible. When the golfers assembled at Hoylake for the Open in 1967 not many believed that Vicenzo could win. In some ten previous attempts over a period of almost twenty years he had been third five times, second once and fourth once. No golfer had ever been so close so often without winning, and Vicenzo was 44.

Argentinian golfers had often challenged for the Open since Jose Jurado erred sadly on the last two holes at Carnoustie in 1931 and allowed Tommy Armour to win. After that it seemed that the gods had turned their backs on golfers from the Latin countries, but Vicenzo still kept faith with his superb talent. It was an enduring technique founded on immense strength, simplicity of movement and a wonderful rhythm. For years he was one of the great long drivers; no one except Snead hit so far with such ease, but his strength was also revealed in his pitching. He hit the ball so hard and so late that the whole process seemed effortless, but often his putting was uncertain. This cost him dearly but Vicenzo bore his disappointments with grace and dignity. Like many strong men Vicenzo is a gentle soul, kindly and charming to everyone. The Latin in him never exploded; rather were there sad little shrugs of resignation when things went amiss.

Hoylake was in benevolent mood that year, the fairways firm and fast and the perfect greens holding. After 36 holes Vicenzo was among the leaders as he had been so often before and then a third round of 67 thrust him right into the melting pot. Hard on his heels were the formidable figures of Player and Nicklaus, two and three strokes behind respectively. Whether he could withstand the pressure of yet another chance at the title at first seemed doubtful. Much would depend on his putting but he had found a good stroke and had not been under strain on the greens. Also he appeared more relaxed than usual and was helped by the feeling 'that many peoples are with me.'

The situation at the outset of the last day of an Open could hardly have been more compelling, or as sentimental in its undertones. By their voice alone one knew, as did Vicenzo, that the people wanted him to win. They would have loved a British victory but this was not the time. Admiration for Nicklaus, Player, Clive Clark and others was warmly given but their hearts were with Vicenzo.

That afternoon's watching was among the most enthralling and enjoyable I have known. The background of the old links was at its most beautiful in the warm sunshine, the dunes, the silver spread of the Dee and the Welsh hills softly outlined in the distance. After a few holes it seemed that Player was more tense than usual and this was comforting for Vicenzo, his companion, but the mighty Nicklaus was immediately ahead and Vicenzo could see what he was about. When Nicklaus holed for a two at the 7th and then hit a four-iron which pitched on the back of the 8th green, an enormous shot which brought him another birdie, it seemed that Vicenzo would be sorely pressed.

After Player had taken three putts on the 10th and hooked far wide of the 11th green, where Vicenzo saved his three with a masterly chip from a treacherous sandy lie, it was clear that the issue lay squarely between him and Nicklaus. The next few holes were crucial as Nicklaus, three behind, was not hitting his approaches close enough to have reasonable hopes for birdies.

When Vicenzo boomed a huge drive far down the 14th fairway he had to wait for Nicklaus who was striving to make a birdie after driving into the rough. Vicenzo walked across to where a few of us were standing and said, as Nicklaus missed his putt, 'He make his par like a good boy — I feel better now.' A few moments later Vicenzo almost holed a little chip and was four ahead. I thought then that he was safe even though there was no telling what Nicklaus might produce, and Vicenzo did drop a stroke at the 15th, but the decisive moment was at hand, never to be forgotten by those who were there.

Everyone familiar with Hoylake knows how a corner of the Field, the practise ground which is out of bounds, cuts sharply into the 16th fairway. It is embraced by a shallow bank over which a ball can easily hop. I stood inside the Field as Vicenzo drove. For a ghastly second or so it seemed that he had taken too straight a line and that the shot was too long. Happily it came to rest just five yards short of the bank.

Very few golfers have hit as many shots as Vicenzo in their lifetime; to strike a solid spoon from a good lie was second nature to him in the ordinary course of things, but think of what depended on that particular shot! Nicklaus had holed for his birdie and might easily make two more as the closing holes were playing very short. As it happened he did make one. A mistake at that point could cost Vicenzo what, at his age, had to be the last chance of achieving his greatest ambition. I doubt that any such frightening thoughts plagued his mind. He struck the shot as promptly and decisively as he always did; he was never a fidget. The ball thundered away over the Field and not for an instant was it going to finish anywhere but in the heart of the green. The rest was academic. The magnificent driving that had served his so well as the pressure gathered left him pitches with only a nine iron to the 17th and 18th.

Vicenzo, the look of an emperor about him, strode into the amphitheatre by the last green towards a reception the like of which I had never heard before. Its sustained warmth and affection were tribute to a fine human being as well as to a great golfer and a victory nobly won. As Vicenzo left the last green Nicklaus, smiling as always in defeat, congratulated him and made some jest about a great big bear whereupon Roberto said, 'I don't want to see you any more, Jack,' and two strong men laughed together. It was a vintage golfing day, but such can be the perversity of fate that Vicenzo's triumph was shadowed the following spring by as harsh a quirk of fortune as ever beset a champion golfer.

On Easter Day in 1968 Vicenzo was 45. It was to be a birthday that neither he nor anyone who watched the Masters at Augusta that year is likely to forget. It was the last round, and for once I was in the right place at the right time, standing behind the first green as Vicenzo's second shot with a nine iron floated down the enamelled sky, pitched a foot from the hole and vanished within. The crowd erupted into a pandemonium of noise and the singing of 'Happy Birthday' which lasted for minutes. I wondered whether Vicenzo's concentration might be disturbed but need not have worried. As he walked to the next tee he said to me, 'I need seventeen more of those.'

His drive was so easy and smooth that nothing might have happened. It flew away down the plunging fairway, a four-wood rifled just through the green and a little chip almost fell for another eagle. When he pitched dead at the 3rd he was four under par and I was so excited that my cigarette burned my neighbour's shirt. There followed hours of suspense as Vicenzo, playing with effortless authority and accuracy, moved towards his destiny. When he came to the 18th he needed a four for a 64 and probable victory although Bob Goalby was maintaining a marvellous pursuit behind him. Vicenzo's drive was good but his medium iron was pulled slightly, slipped off the green and he took three more.

Angry with himself because he thought that he had thrown away the tournament, and mentally exhausted after his tremendous effort, Vicenzo failed to check his card carefully. He did not notice that Tommy Aaron, who was playing with him, had marked a four instead of a three for the 17th and signed the card as correct. Later Vicenzo told me that he had looked at the card three or four times but saw nothing amiss. Under the Rule the four for the 17th had to stand and his total became 66 instead of 65.

Had Vicenzo known before he signed the card that Goalby had dropped a stroke at the 17th and needed a four to tie he would probably have been more careful. Although the fault was Vicenzo's it pointed to a flaw in the organisation. There was no procedure for making certain that a player checked his card properly before signing and that he could do this in private before being set upon by a mob of autograph hunters. Thereafter a system was introduced, similar to that used by the Royal and Ancient for the Open championship, which greatly lessened the risk of a player signing an incorrect card.

As it happened Goalby made the bravest of fours at the 18th. Trees had impeded the progress of his drive, leaving him a two-iron to reach the green. Finally he holed from four feet to tie, as he thought. He did not know that Vicenzo's mistake had given him a stroke to spare and this made his finish all the more courageous. A putt to tie is harder than one to win.

In their anxiety to try to remedy the situation members of the committee rushed to consult Bobby Jones to see if he could find a solution. His wife, Mary, told us the next day that when she saw all the men in green jackets running across the lawn towards the cabin she thought there had been a fire. Doubtless the committee would have preferred a modest fire to the embarrassment of the incident. Of course there was no solution except to observe the Rule which was absolutely clear, and as Jones said, 'Golf is a game where only the player can tell exactly what goes on; his word must be the final one.'

Obviously Jones was right and no exception could be made for Vicenzo but it did seem absurd that a simple, pardonable error should cause so much turmoil. Much was made of the fact that thousands following the golf and millions watching on television must have seen Vicenzo hole for a three at the 17th, but it sometimes happens that a player's ball moves when he is addressing it on the green and he alone is aware of it.

He tells his marker that he has incurred an extra stroke but the spectators know nothing of this, and so the argument that Vicenzo's three was seen by millions would have no substance in law.

Some time elapsed before the press and public knew what had happened. I was about to phone my story of a tie and the magnificent golf that Vicenzo and Goalby had played when the announcement was made, and a joyous tale became a sad one. It was one of those occasions when the golf writer's task is far from enviable, especially when within moments the main edition in England is about to go to press.

Vicenzo was brought into the press centre for the mass interview. He sat on the dais, for all the world like a great wounded bear, and faced a barrage of questions, many of them uninformed and inconsiderate and designed to snare him into criticising others, but he steadfastly insisted that the fault was his alone. So persistent were the questions that I became increasingly irritated and asked that delightful man, Dudley (Waxo) Green who I think was President of the Golf Writers' Association at the time if he would stop the interview. He agreed and Vicenzo was escorted away by police so that he would be pestered no more.

Hours later I was in an almost deserted clubhouse when Frances Jones, Bobby's daughter-in-law, appeared with two teenage daughters.

A few moments later Vicenzo came in, having endured an official dinner. When I introduced him to them he said to Frances that these young ladies cannot be your daughters you must be their sister. The man's innate courtesy and charm never failed him.

If the fates had wrought a cruel prank on Vicenzo they did not allow Goalby to escape. In the end he suffered possibly more than Vicenzo and he was not involved in the affair. All he had done was to play one of the finest last rounds in Masters history and beat a sentimental favourite. Rarely can the victor of a great occasion have been so modestly rewarded compared with the vanquished. On the eve of the Masters a year later Goalby told me that he had earned little from the victory apart from the automatic bonuses from equipment contracts. Vicenzo on the other hand made a great deal of money, partly from what might be termed sympathy, in spite of the fact that had he tied it was by no means certain that he would have won the play-off.

Furthermore, for a while afterwards Goalby was insulted and abused by an idiotic minority who considered that he was responsible for Vicenzo's failure. That a fine, handsome golfer could be treated thus was wretched, but I understood that he accepted it with dignity and restraint and rightly refused lucrative television offers to meet Vicenzo in a kind of phony play-off.

All in all it was a strange Masters, the one above all the others that I shall not forget. Aside from the splendour of the golf and the extraordinary climax there was an undercurrent of sadness. In the beginning there was a day of mourning for Martin Luther King but within the policies of the club all was peace and beauty, remote beyond belief from the anguish and strife fomenting in many parts of the nation. There was, as always, so much evidence of leisured wealth about the people strolling over the smooth green lawns in the soft sunshine that the scene stirred images of the last days of Versailles. And the days were to be the last that Bobby Jones would spend at the Masters.

By then Jones was grievously stricken and weighed little more than eighty pounds but he still welcomed chatting — or 'shooting the breeze', as he called it — in his bedroom. The morning after the tournament he spoke of his distress at not being able to attend the presentation, even though it was only a hundred yards or so from his cabin. If ever the occasion needed the authority of his presence and his clarity of mind and speech it was that evening. Soon after Jean and I had taken our farewells he was carried to his car. I never saw him again but the memory of his courage and gentleness will never fade.

After an emotional Masters it was a relief to escape to Florida for a while before returning to the rigours, if that is the word, of the British season. It had been arranged that we stay for a day or so with Truman Connell who would take us to Great Harbour Cay, an island in the Berry Group, where a major golf development was in embryo. Unlike many of the Bahama islands it undulated pleasantly and I have often wondered whether the course became as beautiful and challenging as it promised to be with its glorious setting of ocean, ever-changing in its hues, and gleaming white beaches. Never have I enjoyed swimming more; for once there was no sense of disappointment as on many a famous beach, not least some of the miserable little strips that masquerade as such on the Mediterranean coast. I could have lingered there for days but as always on the brief American trips there was much to be seen and done, especially the playing of Pine Tree, a fine example of the late Dick Wilson's work. It was said to be the pride of one of the finest contemporary architects and a few miles north lay Seminole, conceivably the masterpiece of all the famous courses designed by Donald Ross. I asked Hogan once which was his favourite course and he said that Seminole offered him most of what he looked for in a golf course. After playing it I soon understood why. It is a wonderful blend of varied challenge with over 200 bunkers but menacing though they may be fear is leavened by the artistic way in which they are arranged and the awareness that every hole is fair. One could play Seminole for ever and never be weary of it; there can be few, if any others, of its particular quality. A day or so after I had been there Nicklaus was saying that it was probably the finest course he knew.

For the last part of our stay we were in a hotel on the coast north of Palm

Beach. Every morning I took a gentle swim in the soothing ocean until one afternoon we heard that a little boy had been attacked by a shark while lying on a raft only a few yards from the shore. Happily someone frightened the shark away but the boy was badly injured and thereafter my daily immersions were taken in a foot or so of water with an anxious eye ever scanning the horizon.

Meanwhile we had been in touch with the Nicklaus's who lived at Lost Tree not far away. Jack had been on a fishing trip and one day after his return he said that he needed some practice before going to the next tournament and would I like to play nine holes. It did not take me long to answer that one, and it was arranged that Jean would visit a zoo with Barbara Nicklaus and the three children they had then. On my first meeting with Barbara many years before it was obvious that Jack was, and is, greatly blessed in his marriage. In spite of the wealth and enormous success that has come his way she remains a natural, unaffected person, friendly and charming to everyone and, as I have seen on several occasions, content to remain aside from the glare of adulation and publicity.

When I arrived at Lost Tree Nicklaus was on the practice tee thundering balls into the sunlit distance. He looked massively strong in tennis shorts and socks; this was before the famous weight dissolving began. Members drifted by watching and chatting as he worked on problems with his driver which was producing a rich variety of strokes, unlike the searing straightness of his irons.

There is no more stirring sight in golf than to see long-irons hit by men like Nicklaus, Palmer or Snead. Nicklaus was about to pass from the two iron to the spoon when I asked him to punch a few low with a one iron. To my mind this is one of the ultimate revelations of power. The ball tore away not rising more than eight feet until it had gone a hundred yards or more and then finishing in the remote distance.

Some 30 yards ahead of the tee were two seats of the pattern familiar on any golf course, with backs of wooden beams about an inch thick and a few inches apart. Jestingly Nicklaus asked which gap we would like him to hit through and unleashed another fearsome missile. The ball struck one of the slats, leaving a perfect semi-circular hole, just as a bullet would have done, at the point of impact and splintering it vividly on the other side. The ball whistled on quite a long way and we shuddered at the thought of what it would have done to a human body.

Later I asked what he thought was the source of his power; he patted a hefty haunch and said he guessed it was there. The movement of weight at speed is the foundation not, as some believe, the strength of the hands. Nicklaus's hands are on the small side and his grip is not one to make you wince, whereas to ask Palmer to grip hard would be to invite a bone-

129

mincing. Once I tried to snatch a club suddenly from his hands; it never moved and he said 'There is no way you can get that club'.

However well one may know great golfers the opportunity to play with them in private is rare indeed. That day at Lost Tree the two of us were alone except for one caddy who carried both bags, and later Jack's son Stevie, then five, who hit balls along with his little club and the absorption of the very young.

To watch Nicklaus in a tournament or at practice is one thing; to play alone with him is quite another. Then one can really appreciate the enormous difference that exists between the kind of golfer who hopes to break 80, and is very pleased when he does, and one such as Nicklaus. In all the game's history there have been few men whose golf approached the dimensions of his and this thought is somewhat awesome as for the first time you stand on a tee with him, but I was not that anxious. After all to press would be asinine. There was no call to strive beyond trying to make a good swing. My best that day was far from wonderful, neither was it too bad. We hit two or three balls from every tee and although concerned with his own play he took time to watch mine, and without being asked to do so.

Knowing that Nicklaus never paid idle compliments about anyone's golf I asked him about mine. He said 'I would expect you to hit the ball further with your swing, your right hand is not working hard enough' and showed me how a change in weight distribution might help. I realised yet again how observant he was, without appearing to be so, and never once during the nine holes had I asked him to watch me or tell me what I was doing wrong. Looking back now over the twenty years I have known and watched him I think that his powers of observation have been one of his greatest strengths. Hogan and Cotton come first to mind as being of his company in this respect.

That evening we sped over Lake Worth and out into the ocean in Nicklaus's boat. We saw the plot of land where his present house was to be built and he talked of how Florida was to become a permanent base, and of how he hoped to be playing tournament golf for another five years or so because he loved the competition, and that was in 1968. Earlier I had asked him what he liked most in golf and he said that it was to have to make a birdie and three pars on the last four holes to win.

As we bounded over the darkening ocean and the warm twilight fell I remarked that the four-foot putts did not seem to matter out there and he agreed. He seemed absolutely identified with the ocean and boat, standing easily as it bucked over the waves. Golf was in another world; it could never be an obsession with him; he has always had the priceless gift of detachment. Never has the ancient phrase about a healthy mind in a healthy body been more true of a golfer than it is of Jack Nicklaus.

130

CHAPTER 13
BING

As far as golf was concerned the centrepiece of 1969 was Tony Jacklin's victory in the Open championship, a triumph which brought renewed heart and pride to British golfers as no other individual achievement had done since the War. That was in high summer whereas one of my most memorable years began in January when Bing Crosby invited me to California for his tournament at Pebble Beach.

This came about because Bing, as I appreciated later, was a regular reader of *Country Life*. To my surprise one day in 1964 a letter arrived from him. We had not met or corresponded before but he had read an article I had written about Hogan playing with Billy Joe Patton at Augusta and wanted to reproduce it in the souvenir programme for his tournament. The editor of *Country Life* agreed and I thought no more of it. Then, a few years later he took amiable issue with me because I thought Billy Casper had been mistaken in his tactics at a crucial point in a match with Nicklaus at Wentworth. This led to an intermittent correspondence.

Months might pass and then Bing would write about something that had interested him. His letters often were quite long and revealed the depth of his knowledge of the game, down to its very roots. He had a good feeling for words and would have made a splendid golf writer. After Nicklaus had taken a horrific 45 on the last nine at Pebble Beach in 1976 when in sight of winning the tournament I very soon had a graphic account from Bing. It ended with three sentences, admirable for their simplicity. 'He [Nicklaus] never lost his smile. He was just in disbelief. But he continued to play.' The television commentaries he did on his own tournament were excellent; he was never one to talk unnecessarily in private or into a microphone, unlike the majority of commentators.

Towards the end of 1968 Tom Harvey, who had met him in London, told me that Bing would invite me to his tournament. My suspense was short-lived, an air ticket arrived and everything was arranged, but at the last moment the flight was changed to one due to call at Los Angeles before

San Francisco, where I wanted to be. To my relief an hour or so from the end of the journey the captain announced that owing to bad weather in L.A. we were going direct to San Francisco. Imagine being diverted to your intended destination! This seemed a good omen, but I was still late and the connecting flight to Monterey had been cancelled.

I was prepared for a long wait when I was called to a telephone and Bing said he would be along to buy me a drink while I waited. He had met the flight on which I was expected but had taken the trouble to come again. As he and his wife, Kathryn, walked towards me across the airport lobby I had the strange feeling that I had known him for a long while. I suppose it was because his appearance and his voice had been so familiar throughout my adult life. Yet at first it was hard to believe that he was the man, and a shorter one than I had imagined, who had become a universal legend. His manner was totally relaxed and unaffected and he sat quietly puffing his pipe as the talk turned from golf to Kathryn telling of her day's teaching. Among the many accomplishments, aside from acting, of an exceptionally bright, attractive person were qualifications for nursing and teaching.

Bing had arranged for me to stay with friends of his, Dick and Helen Snideman, whose house was a short walk from the course at Pebble Beach. On arriving in Monterey I was taken to a dinner party at about six in the morning British time. It was my first experience of as long a time change as eight hours, but it had little effect because I went to bed at a normal American time. I have always found this to be the best course however tired one might be on arriving in the United States.

During the tournament I had several chats with Bing. He said that golf had been a profound influence on his career. It afforded relaxing interludes in a frenetic life and he would escape on to a course whenever there was a chance. He soon became a good golfer with a handicap of two and competed in championships, including the Amateur at St Andrews in 1950. An enormous heterogeneous horde pursued him in streaming rain that day but he began with two perfect birdies and we knew his golfing reputation had not been exaggerated. He lost his match to J. K. Wilson but clearly had enjoyed himself and soon afterwards was elected a member of the Royal and Ancient.

Bing started his own tournament before the War as a means of gathering his golfing friends, amateur and professional, about him, rather as Bobby Jones did when launching the Masters at Augusta. In fact Bing was probably the founder of the pro.am. movement on the highest level, which was to become so popular.

The tournament was most enjoyable in spite of rain which caused the first day to be abandoned, and the difficulty of trying to cover an event taking place on three courses some distance apart, and cope with the time

132

difference. The noble settings of Pebble, Cypress Point and Spyglass; the lighter side of watching such as Jack Lemmon, a slight intent figure with cigar in mouth as he played, Andy Williams, Sean Connery and others, all determined to give of their golfing best, and the more significant part of the event more than compensated. Michael Bonallack, in splendid form, and Casper failed by a stroke to tie for first place in the pro.am. section. Bonallack received only four strokes a round but they finished 30 under par and he did his share at the very least.

Towards the end of the week Kathryn Crosby invited me to spend a night with them in San Francisco. Their main home was there, rather I imagine, as a retreat from the Hollywood-Beverley Hills environment although Bing still had an office there. The house was large and handsome but not ostentatious. The swimming pool had been filled in and the lawn where I played football with Harry and Nathaniel, Bing's two sons from his marriage to Kathryn, was no manicured surface.

The boys had been introduced to soccer by the English butler the Crosbys had then. At one point I was showing Nathaniel how to head the ball and kicked it too high. It was wet and quite heavy and landed squarely on the top of his head. I was horrified to think that I might have hurt him, and he must have been shaken but bravely showed no sign. We then tried basketball of which I had little knowledge but such was their courtesy to a guest that they often insisted I had suffered a technical foul so that I might have a free throw at the net. Both boys became good golfers, Nathaniel exceptionally so, much to his father's pride.

The house within was a warm and gracious place with beautiful furniture and china. Bing had assembled many fine pictures, among them a huge Munnings which hung in the hall, and some splendid western scenes by an artist whose name unfortunately I cannot recall. And Kathryn showed me her considerable collection of works by Fabergé.

Rarely in American households does one hear the welcome tinkle of teacups around four o'clock but both afternoons I was there tea duly arrived. It was their custom, not simply a gesture to an Englishman. Two other guests, George Coleman and his wife, came to dinner, when the talk turned on many things from pictures to writing books, from slow play to education, and from religion to Hogan hunting deer and what fun he could be when away from golf and with close friends. After dinner Harry played his guitar for a while and when he came to 'Little Green Apples' Bing sang the lyric. It was so effortless that I could readily believe the stories of what a pleasure it was to work with him on recording sessions, so swift was his sense of how a song should be treated. He told me once that singing had never seemed like work to him because he got such a kick out of it.

Admittedly Bing was over sixty when I first knew him but I cannot recall having met anyone who seemed to move through life on such an even keel. I never saw him impatient or intolerant, or raise his voice in anger. Occasionally his casualness may have been disconcerting to those whose ideas of timing differed from his unhurried tempo. He appealed to me as a constant person, perhaps most of all because he was kindly and unfailingly genial towards everyone, no matter their importance or lack of it.

One summer, a year or so later, Bing came to see us in Norfolk. He had telephoned to ask if I would join him for golf at St George's, one of the famous courses in Britain that he had not played. I had just returned from a tournament, had little time to spare and could not make the long journey down to Sandwich so I suggested that he come to Brancaster instead. Rather to my surprise he needed no persuading.

A day or so later he caught an early train from Liverpool Street and arrived at Downham Market bearing his driver and spoon. We paused a while at home before going to the club, where we were to play with Tom Harvey and Bobby Selway. Much to our relief it was a heavenly day, isolated in a spell of indifferent August weather, and he was able to see the links at their most beautiful. As we mounted the last hill before the coast and the club came into view I remarked that he was about to see the absolute antithesis of an American club. By most standards the clubhouse at Brancaster is a spartan place, existing solely for the purposes of playing golf and providing essential sustenance. That is the way we intend it to remain. I had no thought of apology in mind, knowing that Bing, a devoted Anglophile, appreciated the simple values of British golf. He loved the game for its intrinsic merits and not for the rewards it might bring or for the publicity sought by lesser members of his calling.

Whenever or wherever one played with him, and hundreds would agree, one was soon aware of the quiet pleasure he took in amiable talk, gentle ribbing with his friends and chatting afterwards over a few 'potables' as he called them. There was nothing of the legendary star of show business about Crosby the golfer, either on the course or, for that matter, off it. His manner towards anyone, however humble or exalted their status, was always constant.

Bing's golf was an expression of the remarkably unhurried person he was. In those years he would break 80 more often than not. His woods had soft shafts which to me felt like fishing rods but his swing was slow and measured almost to the point of laziness. He rarely mishit, always played within himself, and drove particularly well that day at Brancaster. All was sunshine and enjoyment and Bing neither did nor said anything beyond the call of a sociable day. Naturally we had kept quiet about his coming, not wishing him to be pestered. Later, when it became known that he had played, a newspaper rang the club secretary and asked why they had not been told. They received a fairly sharp response.

After the golf we called to collect Jean on the way to the Harveys for supper. Tom was to drive Bing back to London that evening. A man from the village who used to help in our garden happened to be there; Arthur has many qualities, is a forthright citizen and no great respecter of persons whoever they are, but he had always admired Bing's singing. When my wife told him that Bing was sitting in the car his face melted with joy. After being introduced his opening remark was, 'My wife would be happy to wash your shirts, Mr Crosby.' He then said that he remembered all the old songs and when he mentioned 'Home on the Range' Bing responded with the next line 'Where the deer and the antelope play'. Arthur was almost ecstatic but I gather it was some while before his friends believed him, and all kinds of crazy rumours spread through the village.

Watching the unchanging rhythm of Crosby's golf reminded me of a day a few years earlier when I had played with Rita Hayworth. Alistair Cooke was in London to celebrate with the BBC his thousandth *Letter from America*. We had arranged to play when I noticed that Rita Hayworth also was in town. Knowing that Alistair knew her well and that she was a golfer I suggested that he bring her along. We played at Swinley Forest. Rita was a delightful companion, natural and joyous and yet, appealingly, rather shy. When I had suggested to Alistair that I find a fourth for our game he said, 'Heavens no, I have already had to persuade her to play with one stranger as it is.'

During some cheerfully apprehensive moments on the first tee it was obvious from her grip, stance and approach to the ball that she had been well taught. Our golf was not remarkable but enough good shots were hit to sustain a happy day, and when Rita's putt for a two at the 8th rolled into the hole her joy and ours for her were complete. I was impressed by her rhythm. Even a longish absence from the game did not betray her into hurrying the swing; the take-away was smooth and easy.

She was graceful in all her movements and, when very young, had begun a career as a dancer. Rhythm and balance had been an integral part of training from childhood, and have, I am sure, helped her golf. I thought of Marley Spearman, as she then was, who always had a fine rhythm, and was not surprised to learn that Fred Astaire, Gene Kelly and Roy Bolger, among famous dancers, have played golf well.

Opinions vary as to the most important qualities in the golf swing, but I have always thought rhythm was foremost. No matter how correct in outline a swing may be, it will not achieve its maximum potential without rhythm, on which timing depends. Whether a man swings like Palmer or

135

Snead, Boros or Trevino, Nicklaus or Hogan — they all have perfect rhythm, but how elusive it can be for the ordinary golfer. Those, like Rita Hayworth, practised young in a rhythmic art, have a precious gift.

CHAPTER 14
JACKLIN & CO

During the practice for the 1969 Open at Lytham it was clear that Jacklin had found a true, measured rhythm for his backswing which in earlier years had been too fast. Furthermore, the confidence gained from experience in America was revealed in his short game. Frequently, towards the end of the third round, beautifully played bunker shots saved his pars and enabled him to overtake Bob Charles who had led for the first two days. I always felt that this was a key phase in his triumph. Had he let slip a challenging position his confidence might have been undermined. As it was he played such unyielding, solid golf from the outset on the last afternoon that the prospect of his victory grew ever stronger. Gradually, threat of close pursuit waned as Nicklaus, Thomson, De Vicenzo and others failed to make telling thrusts. Only Charles, Jacklin's inscrutable companion, was an immediate danger.

Although the long dark night, during which no British golfer had won since Max Faulkner in 1951, was ending I felt less of the tension and suspense than one might have expected. So smoothly was Jacklin swinging, so true was his striking and so confident the stride of his jaunty figure that it seemed almost impossible for him to fail. Although he made a couple of errors towards the end there was never a point of real crisis.

No one who watched could forget the moment as Jacklin stood on the 18th tee two ahead of Charles. This was the last anxiety. Many a golfer, not least Nicklaus in 1963, had failed to hit the last fairway when victory beckoned. If ever Jacklin needed a good drive, evading the diagonals of grasping bunkers, it was then. He knew it, everyone knew it, but when I saw the smoothness of his swing I felt that all was well. One of the finest drives that can ever have been hit by a man on the threshold of achieving his greatest ambition soared far beyond all the dangers to the heart of the fairway. It was a magnificent stroke but there was always the possibility that Charles, the supreme putter, might make a three. Jacklin still had work to do but made nothing of it with a perfect seven-iron shot which stifled any hope Charles might have had of a tie. Jacklin was the first golfer to beat a powerful overseas field in the Open since Henry Cotton in 1937.

Jacklin now was the ultimate hero in British golf as he showed later that year at Birkdale when the Ryder Cup match was halved. That was an extraordinary affair, without parallel in the evenness of the contest. For once the British and Irish played as if sure of their ability; gone were the tremulous starts and finishes that had haunted them in the past. The whole team, finely led by Eric Brown, responded splendidly to the occasion and no one more so than Jacklin. He was the great inspiration, unbeaten throughout and finally the saviour.

The teams joined battle in 32 separate matches of which no fewer than 18 went to the last green. For three days the whole match was delicately poised and it seemed only fitting that the greatest players of their respective sides should be involved in the climax. When Jacklin and Nicklaus stood on the 18th tee of the final match they were all square and so were the countries. Everything was to play for, win, lose or tie.

Jacklin, who had played with a champion's assurance, had beaten Nicklaus handsomely in the morning but was one down going to the 17th. As he waited to play his second shot he asked the state of affairs and on being told said, 'I knew it would come to this.' Nicklaus hit a perfect second shot a few yards past the hole but Jacklin was a little fortunate to finish on the green some fifty feet from the hole. When his huge putt vanished the summer's mightiest cheer exploded. Jacklin looked to the heavens in relief and wonder as Nicklaus, crouching behind his putt, gave him a coolly old-fashioned look. We knew then that a gallant little Huggett had halved with Casper in the match ahead. Nicklaus missed his putt for the half and after 31 matches, as dark evening winds came down from the sea, the destiny of the Ryder Cup depended on the play of one hole.

As they left the tee after two solid shots Nicklaus asked Jacklin whether he was feeling nervous and if it was any consolation to him he was too. Both hit fine second shots, then Nicklaus overhit his putt by a good yard, perhaps more. I doubt that a soul in the vast crowd hoped he would miss, even though it would mean a British victory. The contest had been too great to end in sad anticlimax. Nicklaus obviously thought so too. After holing his putt he instantly conceded Jacklin's which was short but not dead. This was true to the spirit of the man and of an unforgettable occasion.

When the players and multitudes gathered at St Andrews for the 1970 Open the thoughts and dreams of golfers throughout the land were concentrated perhaps more intensely than ever before on the eve of a championship. For the first time in history the Open was to be defended by a British golfer who was also champion of the United States. A month earlier at Chaska in Minnesota, Tony Jacklin had massacred the establishment of American golf, and massacred is the word. He won by seven strokes, the largest margin for half a century, and only Casper and Trevino of the world's foremost golfers were within thirteen of his total. Nicklaus, Player and Palmer, still deemed by some to be the mighty trio of golf, were left floundering in the ruck more than twenty behind.

It mattered not that many did not like the course which had, I understand, for sadly I was not there, numerous dog-legs, blind holes and vast greens, or that the weather varied unpredictably. The conditions were the same for everyone. A true champion accepts them as he finds them and in the words of an ancient golfer makes the best of bad luck and the most of good. Jacklin led throughout and with Trevino is still the only golfer in the 80 years of the championship to have been under par for every round. Whatever reasons or excuses the vanquished may have entertained for their failure there was no denying the wonder of Jacklin's achievement.

When, late in the afternoon of the first day at St Andrews, Jacklin was eight under par for ten holes and threatening to make a nonsense of the Old Course, a great defence of his title was in the making. The course was playing easily as Neil Coles had proved that morning with a record 65 but Jacklin was in sight of beating that splendid score. The deluge that halted play for the day undoubtedly arrested his impetus and he dropped three strokes in finishing the round the next morning.

It would be absurd to claim that the storm cost Jacklin the championship any more than it did Trevino, who had seven holes to play on the second morning and yet was leading the field at the day's end. Although they and Harold Henning, one of the most delightful of men, remained hard in the hunt until almost at the end it fell to Nicklaus and Sanders to be involved in as dramatic a climax as the Open had known.

From early days on narrow, wooded courses in Georgia the skill with which Sanders could manipulate the ball had become famous. The unusual flatness and brevity of his backswing made the whole process seem like an elongated flick but its extension through the ball was marked. When he played one of the finest sand shots I have seen, from the Road bunker at the 17th in the fourth round, his victory seemed inevitable, except to some who knew the cruel subtleties of the Old Course. They took dreadful toll of poor Sanders.

His pitch over the Valley of Sin was too firm, a pardonable error, and the putt down the hill was slower than Sanders realised. The final one of a yard broke fractionally from left to right, but knowledge rather than eyesight was the only key that it did. Later Gerald Micklem took me to look and although I lay down behind the line I would have sworn the putt was straight. The long slope of the green down the mound, which was an ancient burial ground, has not quite expired when it reaches the championship pin position.

As far as my researches show no one in seventy years or more had missed as short a putt to win the Open. Everyone's heart went out to Sanders, an amusing, agreeable person, who had played superbly after having to qualify for the championship, and the Fates had not finished with him. The final act had a powerful undercurrent of sadness, even tragedy, bearing in mind the failure of Sanders that had reprieved Nicklaus and the courage with which he fought back from what seemed a hopeless situation in the play-off.

At the last he had to watch as Nicklaus, in an unconsciously theatrical gesture on the 18th tee, peeled off a sweater for greater freedom and unleashed an enormous drive which raced through the green into thick rough beyond and, finally, holed from six feet, the ball just catching the right lip before falling. Sanders then had to dodge Nicklaus's putter hurled high in triumph which revealed the tension and relief that he was feeling. Clearly overcome Nicklaus turned away for a moment and Barbara Nicklaus said to me that she had never seen Jack cry on a six-foot putt before. William Whitelaw, who was to become Home Secretary, was captain of the R. and A. that year and presented the prizes. Nicklaus, in accepting, had no little difficulty in controlling his voice just as Sanders seemed to have no difficulty in accepting his cruel disappointment in the most sporting manner.

I shall not forget that week. On the first morning I woke to a sudden combined attack of housemaid's knee, tennis elbow and writer's cramp. There had been slight, but not troublesome, indications of rheumatism earlier that summer but now walking was a burden and writing by hand difficult. The doctor told me to take it easy — as if I could during an Open. When it was over I was exhausted. Jean drove me home and soon thereafter to the hospital in King's Lynn where rheumatoid arthritis was diagnosed. Visualising myself in a bathchair I thought it could be the end of golf writing but the specialist was not as pessimistic. Gold injections were prescribed and gradually began to work. Whenever I went abroad I took the injections with me and one year in the medical centre at Augusta when a nurse asked me where I took them, I pointed to my backside whereupon she said, 'You mean your fanny.' Jean's command of English did not extend to all the crucial differences in meaning between some of the English and American slang terms. When she repeated the phrase to an English friend she was enlightened. Mercifully the arthritis burned itself out after a year or so. I was mightily thankful as I have been thus far not to be ill in America where hospital and medical costs are horrific. Anyone visiting the United States at their own responsibility should take hefty insurance against accident or illness or they could find themselves in dire financial trouble.

Whenever possible I have avoided describing run of play but those days at St Andrews were exceptional. There were the Vicenzo years and several occasions later when the quality of the contest and the golf reached a higher pitch but few championships made a more lasting claim on the memory.

Once at a tournament in Melbourne I had a long talk with Jacklin about his attitude to competition. He had played indifferently that day and spoke of how he needed to be almost frightened into playing well; of how he needed a spur. Presumably the indifferent round he had played that morning acted as such; the next day he played the Yarra Yarra course in 63 and went on to win the tournament in commanding style. Later in talking of his great respect for Nicklaus he said, 'Money is not the all-important thing with Jack, neither is it with me.' I am sure he was speaking honestly then but I believe that the sudden wealth that had come his way had a decisive influence on his golf. The temptation to make the most of the abundant rich pickings that were there for the taking after his Open victory at Lytham must have been extremely hard to resist for one who a few years before had very little. I think that the victories which made him into an instant and isolated hero in British golf and the constant adulation betrayed him into forgetting that his basic purpose in life was to play good golf, and that even the finest talents must be cherished by concentrated work and practice.

Success was so swift that he was not conditioned to overcome the effects of a Muirfield. I think also that he became preoccupied with the trappings of fame. I remember him saying that he wanted to have the finest house of any professional golfer in the world. I wonder if anyone told him not to waste his thoughts and money in such pointless fashion. In endeavouring to do so Jacklin landed himself with an unnecessary and costly burden, which cannot have helped his concentration on golf.

It seemed that he needed someone to insist that his first priority was golf even if this meant sacrificing easy money. He had three outstanding examples, all of whom he knew very well, in Nicklaus, Palmer and Player who would never jeopardise their talent for trivial, if lucrative, causes. They appreciated that the very best way to become rich was to win championships and important events and thereby enhance commercial value. Above all their ambitions to remain the world's foremost golfers transcended the making of money.

Whenever a young golfer has soared to the heights, as Sandy Lyle has in recent years, there is always the fear that money may breed contentment and sabotage the resolution that is the foundation of greatness. Thus far in the chronicling of the game a golfer is remembered longest for the

141

championships he won and the way he played, rather than the money he made.

Two such who spring immediately to mind are Christy O'Connor and Neil Coles. The consistently high quality of their golf was a constant factor on the British scene long before and after the brief incandescence of Jacklin and Peter Oosterhuis's dominant spell. O'Connor won the first thousand-pound prize ever offered in a British professional tournament at Southport and Ainsdale in 1955. Although he was then 30 he had competed in few important tournaments. Fred Daly, a rare competitor on the great occasions, and the round, lovable Harry Bradshaw, one of the great short-game players of the age, were the foremost Irish professionals of the time.

In the far west of Ireland O'Connor had not had the advantages his British contemporaries had enjoyed but had developed a splendidly uninhibited natural style and a beautiful rhythm. I still have a clear impression of the way he attacked the closing holes that day at Southport when so much was at stake for him. Over twenty years later in a tearing gale-force wind he played Lindrick in 69 and finished fifth in the Dunlop Masters.

Although playing in strong winds had been second nature to O'Connor since his boyhood in Galway it was a masterly performance but, as he modestly said afterwards, all you need to do is take one or two clubs more than usual for the distance, swing slower and never try to hit too hard. In my view O'Connor, an amiable soul who enjoyed the convivial things of life, was the most accomplished stroke-maker of the post-Cotton gener-ation in these islands. He was worthy of an Open championship and frequently finished high, seven times in the first six, but the indefinable quality or fortune was missing.

One of my happiest memories of O'Connor was when Westward Ho! celebrated their centenary in 1964. As an epilogue a contest was arranged between ancient dress and equipment, worn by O'Connor and Faulkner, and the modern represented by Peter Alliss and Brian Huggett. It was wonderfully entertaining.

The 'ancients' wore Norfolk jackets and breeches with deerstalker hats. Faulkner cut a dashing, somewhat Sir Jasperish figure while O'Connor resembled an amiable poacher in his Sunday best. Each had five clubs — driver, iron, mashie niblick, niblick and a wooden-headed putter — carried by assistants from Westward Ho! and Saunton clad in corduroys and bowler hats.

Soon the old sharp click of the gutty ball was heard when Faulkner opened the proceedings but O'Connor was soon to be the hero. His fine free swing and natural genius for the game were well suited to hickory clubs. He gave a marvellous exhibition of strokes — faded, drawn, flighted

142

high or low — with a real museum piece of a driver. Its aluminium head, weighing eight ounces, had a leather-faced inset. The club felt astonishingly light but O'Connor rarely mishit. He was round in 83 in a fresh wind on a difficult course he had never seen before. He and Faulkner, who received strokes on twelve holes, greatly enjoyed themselves especially when O'Connor holed a pitch of some 35 yards over the stream at the 18th to win the match.

In an age when the personality of games-players often attracts more attention than their ability Coles has rarely received more than basic tribute for his achievements. He is a modest, retiring man not interested in projecting himself. When asked about his golf he will always reply pleasantly but unless hard pressed will never elaborate, to the despair of those seeking a lively quote. Like other golfers, uncommonly gifted from youth, such as Gene Littler and Thomson, Coles sees nothing remarkable in playing well and seems to wonder what all the fuss is about when he excels in a tournament. Once, when someone asked how he was playing he replied 'Almost quite well.' It sounded like a masterly understatement but, by his standards, was probably a fair estimate.

There is a cool, contained intelligence about the way Coles approaches the game; far less than most does he play automatically. His strong, sensitive hands enable him to vary the flight and strength of his strokes without losing control. Although his attitude on the course as he strolls along, head down, hands in pockets, impassive and silent, might suggest despondency and indifference there are forces at work within, as rare flurries of anger with himself reveal. There is nothing insipid about Coles, a fine example of how it is possible to be shy, gentle, even withdrawn in manner yet stern of purpose.

Coles is a golfer to be envied because he always seems to have known his priorities and been faithful to them. He dislikes flying and while others pursue the frenetic chase around the world each winter Coles is usually in his Surrey home. His philosophy has been that a man can have a good and fruitful life in professional golf without devoting his whole existence to it. This is one reason why in 1980, his 26th season as a professional, only five British players won more money than he did and all played more often.

No doubt Coles has been fortunate in having the talent to make a handsome living from tournament golf without becoming a teacher or club professional in the full meaning of the term. Tournaments are his business. Often they are profitable, sometimes they are not but he seems not to mind overmuch, aware with reason that the balance will be in good order at the season's end. No British golfer of the past fifteen years has been more accomplished in the varied arts of stroke-making. At his best he has been masterful and has been rewarded with more victories and considerably more prize money than any British golfer of his time.

Of the young golfers who developed during the Jacklin era the most admirable was Peter Oosterhuis, not so much for the style of his play, which was effective rather than elegant, but for his character. When he finished third in the 1973 Masters, by far the best performance ever by a British golfer at Augusta, it seemed that he was on the threshold of an exceptional career. Since he won the Berkshire Trophy while still at Dulwich School it had been clear that he had great talent. For several years thereafter the graph of his progress was a smooth upward line with scarcely a curve in it, and certainly no jagged breaks. He made the transition from amateur to professional golf with remarkable swiftness and success.

Early in 1972 I wrote that progress would probably continue, with the reservation that he had yet to acquire an enduring consistency of method. My hopes were based largely on his temperament. His attitude to tournament golf was that of a mature, clear-minded, ambitious man, aware of his destiny and determined to pursue it in his own fashion unaffected by those around him. To this end he became something of a loner, never hanging aimlessly about the clubhouse as many young professionals do, but his manner towards everyone remained as courteous and pleasant as it had always been. He had acquired a quality of detachment which implied a single-mindedness of purpose rare in a young golfer. Had the same been true of Jacklin how much more strongly armed he would have been.

Throughout the four years when Oosterhuis led the British order of merit his greatest strength was a calm, phlegmatic and mightily determined temperament. This was reflected in a remarkable short game. No golfer in Europe was more skilled in recovery; none had a stronger nerve when faced with treacherous holing-out putts, but always there was the lingering doubt about his long game.

Unlike other uncommonly tall golfers, such as Weiskopf, Hyndman and Bill Campbell, all of whom have superb styles, Oosterhuis was relatively longer in the leg than the back. His stance never gave the impression of lasting stability and his swing was so short in relation to his height that in moments of stress he had difficulty in staying behind the ball. An inevitable tendency to block shots became famous. Frequently his short game would compensate but with every passing year the strain upon it must have intensified.

Oosterhuis's first full season in America was encouraging. In 1975 he finished respectably in the money list and was only two strokes behind Lou Graham and John Mahaffey when they tied in the United States Open at Medinah. This was a severe course, tightly wooded in parts, but Oosterhuis controlled his game extremely well. By the end of that season hopes were high that he might make a considerable impact on the

144

American tour but sadly his playing fortunes have declined these past two years. Possibly his swing has been the basic cause but I shall be delighted if future events prove me wrong, not least because he is one of the most agreeable of golfers.

CHAPTER 15
WITH TREVINO INTO THE SEVENTIES

Of all the golfers I have watched Lee Trevino has been one of the most compelling. Alone of his famous contemporaries he is a throwback to the age when great players like Hagen, Sarazen, Hogan, Snead and many others began their careers in golf at the humblest level. So did Trevino; he had none of the advantages of years of college golf which produces the great majority of the American tournament players. At a time when swings and appearances were becoming standardised to a degree that threatened monotony Trevino emerged with a unique style, a skill in the execution of varied golf shots that has rarely been approached, a distinctive personality and a vivid sense of humour.

At first many scorned his style but soon came to realise that the pronounced open stance ensured that his downswing moved under rather than, as they say, over the top. He keeps the clubface square to the line and down through the ball longer than anyone of his build. His swing is one for a powerful, sturdy man, which he is, and has enabled him to become one of the straightest golfers of his time. His consistency year after year, and the winning of the United States and British opens twice each, are evidence enough of remarkable control.

In 1971 he joined Jones, Sarazen and Hogan as the only golfers to have won both championships in the same summer. The Open at Merion, where he beat Nicklaus in a play-off with something to spare, was one of the finest I have seen. Merion measured only about 6500 yards, very short by modern reckoning, but it examined all the delicate arts of golf. Above all accuracy was the theme. Considering that of eleven par fours the longest was 430 yards, and that the two finest golfers in the field alone could equal par for 72 holes, some idea of the difficulty and subtlety of Merion can be appreciated.

In some respects Trevino reminds me of Sarazen. Both are of pure Latin parentage; both acquired through hard, unprivileged upbringings the tough, aggressive realistic approach to life wellnigh essential for survival in a fiercely competitive society when a man starts with little or nothing. Both were endowed with quick, native wit and perception but Sarazen, for all that he communicated so readily with those about him, was never as extrovert on the course as Trevino.

Neither Sarazen nor, for that matter, Palmer in spite of his uncanny mass appeal, entertained the crowds as Trevino has often done. It would seem impossible to play fine golf and joke and chatter at the same time even though they are a means of releasing tension. On first acquaintance I thought that the spate of wisecracks was rehearsed and the work of others, as those of many comedians are, but it was soon clear that Trevino can be a spontaneously funny man. He has too a generosity of spirit, not altogether common in a selfish game, which on occasion has taken substantial practical shape.

Not everyone has been amused by his ebullience and playing with him could be a strain for some. There was a famous match in the Piccadilly tournament at Wentworth when Jacklin, round in 63 after lunch, lost on the last green. I recall him hanging back on occasion so as not to have to listen. At times it seemed that the chatter verged on gamesmanship but I doubt that it was intentional. Trevino has said that if a companion seemed disturbed by his talk he would stop. In a person whose moods can vacillate so swiftly the jester can vanish and a less agreeable side of his nature appear, but few famous players have not had their dark moments and his have been rare as far as I know.

Few golfers I have known can analyse a course's problems as quickly as Trevino, sometimes after only one round. His speed of reaction to people, circumstances and ability to summon instant concentration at times are extraordinary. There never was a more revealing instance of his mercurial character than his play of the last two holes at Muirfield in 1972 when he stole the Open from Nicklaus and Jacklin. When his fourth shot ran through the 17th green his whole attitude was that of a beaten man. It seemed certain that Jacklin, playing with him, would become one ahead but as most of the golf world knows Trevino, playing almost heedlessly as if resigned to defeat, holed the chip, Jacklin took three putts and was one behind.

Transformed in the instant from despair to elation Trevino then showed his greatness. It is one thing to have a monumental turn of fortune, quite another to make the most of it. Trevino, who normally bustles along between shots, restrained the impulse to hurry, which might have overtaken a lesser competitor, and lingered so that he would not have to

147

wait on the last tee for the crowds to settle. He then struck two of the finest and most decisive strokes any champion could have played at such a moment and slammed the door on Jacklin and Nicklaus.

The disaster at Muirfield doubtless left a scar on Jacklin which does not seem to have healed. Apart from having to endure Trevino's good fortune at the finish and in the third round the knowledge that failure was partly of his own making must have sorely undermined his confidence. For the next eight years he was never in contention for the Open and his capacity for winning day to day events waned. There was nothing wrong with his technique, and when his rhythm was right he remained as fine a striker as anyone in Europe. The lack of success stemmed from indifferent putting, and when this persists in a first-class golfer the cause is loss of confidence and, eventually, nerve.

Countless fine golfers have suffered in this way. Hogan and Palmer were cases in point but when stricken they were much older than Jacklin and had competed far longer on the highest levels. Jacklin was just 28 that fateful day at Muirfield and had only been established as a world-class golfer for three years. The decline from that estate, which led to a defensive attitude, was too swift for one endowed with a talent such as his, and sadly so for British professional golf which had long needed a golfer who could hold his own with the finest as well as having an appealing presence which Jacklin has.

By the seventies my golfing horizons had expanded greatly and journeys abroad were a constant part of the yearly scene. The Continental championships were embraced into the official PGA calendar, much to the benefit of the leading professionals, whereas in earlier years the French Open alone attracted a strong field from Britain and elsewhere. Invariably the championship came after the Open in Britain and made a soothing contrast for the writers.

The French Federation, of which the late Jacques Leglise was president, would invite a few of us to stay in a pleasant hotel in the heart of Paris. This was delightful but for players like Peter Thomson, who had either won the Open or been in close contention the previous week, the golf was something of an anticlimax, though it had memorable moments.

In 1955 the great Byron Nelson played superbly at La Boulie in winning the last important event of his career. I can still see his iron shots, struck with immense authority from any range, squirming to a stop within a few feet of the hole on the heavily watered greens. It was my first sight of American type target-golf. In later times I had many an interesting talk with Byron, one of the nicest of men and in his conquering years a peerless striker.

Flory Van Donck, with his courtly manner and perfect style, and

148

Vicenzo often played supremely well in France, and watching was a pleasure because there were only a hundred or so spectators. Quite often they included the Duke of Windsor who made a most agreeable and keen watching companion. He was always interested in the Argentinian players, Vicenzo, Tony Cerda and others and would hasten in pursuit of them.

Occasionally I went to Spain in the blessed years before the mass tourist invasion but the greater part of travelling was within the shores of Britain and Ireland. I have always been grateful that I was able to see the most beautiful parts of those countries as I never would have had I been in most other professions.

With the growth of jet flights excursions abroad became more frequent. For the most part they were a great experience and a pleasure but so crowded was the season's calendar that there was little time for lingering. Once the job was done one usually had to scurry home again but there were interludes, refreshing because they were remote from golf.

On the way back from Australia one year I stayed with Sandy Tatum in San Francisco. One evening he asked if I would like to see a football game the following day. As became a good host his face was impassive and he even murmured of alternatives, revealing nothing of what I soon discovered was a passionate desire to see the game, but he did say it was at Stanford. That was an inducement. I would see a great university and perhaps learn something of an esoteric cult.

We drove along the pleasant valley to Palo Alto, past the Stanford golf course where the mighty Lawson Little, my host and, long afterwards, Tom Watson had excelled. An agreeable prelude to these occasions is the tailgate party when the rear of a station wagon is lowered, bottles, ice and food produced and friends come a-calling.

While fortification was under way high school bands from all over the district poured into the huge stadium which seats a hundred thousand. Its massed terraces made brilliant patchworks of colour the like of which I had never seen. Neither had I heard such a torrent of sound, music, cheers and commentary that persisted throughout the game. Both sides had their cheerleaders and ever-dancing pretty girls on either side of the pitch. Their exhortations rarely ceased. It was a great occasion. If Stanford, the Indians, could beat Washington University, the Huskies, they would qualify for the Rose Bowl match in Pasadena for the first time since 1951.

The game is highly specialised. The coach at Stanford had seven assistants; every team has two separate elevens, one for offence, the other for defence, and these are switched constantly according to which side has possession. This is determined by downs, that is when a man with the ball is brought down in a tackle. A team is allowed four downs and if it can progress ten yards before the downs are exhausted it has four more. Thus it makes progress towards openings for a touchdown.

The game resembles a sort of chess in which openings are made by clearing paths through the defence by blocking, that is, the calculated obstruction of an opponent. For this purpose footballers have developed into a race of near supermen. Only a third of the 56 players on Stanford's roster that year were less than 200 pounds and six feet. I tried to imagine, and shuddered as I did so, the sight of one of Stanford's strong side tacklers thundering at me with only one purpose in mind, to flatten me. It was no wonder that the players were so heavily armoured that they looked like enormous astronauts. And yet the violence seemed impersonal; I saw no sign of malicious retaliation, no sickly pretence of sportsmanship as in professional soccer. My expert companions agreed that it was a remarkably clean game.

The focal point of attack is the quarterback who bears a heavy responsibility. If his passing is off the most elaborate moves are useless, and how elaborate they are. The quarterback, possibly by instruction from a coach on the touchline, decides which of a multitude of plays will be used before each down. The ball is then snapped back to him; he makes space for himself as the other players race to their appointed tasks, and then releases his pass. The ball, flatter and more pointed at the ends than a rugby ball, hurtles through the air like a projectile, sometimes 40 yards or more, to where the predetermined receiver can take it, often while moving flat out. The skill involved in propelling a ball with such speed and accuracy is remarkable especially when massive opponents are bearing down on the thrower.

In this art I was fortunate to see one of the great masters in Jim Plunkett who fired three wonderful passes which brought touchdowns (tries) in the first quarter. One was so beautifully timed, so lethal in its splitting of the defence that I found myself standing and cheering as if Stanford had been my alma mater, as well as that of Tatum and his friend.

In this game Plunkett broke the college football record for passing by bringing the total for his career to over 7000 yards. Facts and figures are sacred in American sport. When I visited the press box, almost the size of Wembley's, with hundreds of writers and broadcasters in it, sheets giving precise details of every move in the game thereto were being distributed. It seemed that the writers need scarcely have troubled to watch unless the spirit moved them.

To one accustomed to British football the American game lacks the sudden inspiration leading to unrehearsed moves when attack develops in unlikely quarters. The forward passing was admirable but one never saw what are known as lateral passes mainly, I understand, because they are vulnerable to interception. There were no handling moves flowing across the field which can be a joy in rugby. On the other hand the game never degenerated into the disorganised mess and endless touch kicking which can make rugby a bore.

The one tiresome feature to British eyes was the stop and start nature of the game with considerable intervals between the action. In the end someone stole victory for Stanford when he received a Plunkett projectile in the last quarter. As we drove back towards the twilit city I realised that a great deal of previous prejudice against American football had vanished, simply because I had learned something about it.

Barcelona may not be the fairest city in Spain but it does have one of the finest courses in the Real Club de Golf, 'El Prat'. Many years ago I was fortunate in playing there with Javier Arana, its creator. He never worked outside Spain but his designs of courses such as Campo in Madrid, La Galea, El Saler and many others revealed rare artistry and imagination.

A great course should examine the mighty with a variety of testing strokes; should not frighten the humble; should be fair, pleasing to play and agreeable to look upon. Arana achieved all these things within a context of remarkable moderation, so that no aspect of the course is overwhelming. Some of the holes are graceful curves through sombrilla pines but these are not dense. Balls are not lost and a measure of recovery is always possible. A third of the holes are in open country where judgement of length and strategic driving are essential and contrast is splendidly furthered with holes along the coast with more than a hint of links to their character. Throughout the course the bunkering is admirable in its economy and beautifully varied shaping. The attacking shot is always rewarded, the frail and the erring punished, but never cruelly so. I always enjoyed 'El Prat' and the championships there and one year was particularly memorable.

The day after watching Dale Hayes win the Open I saw Jackie Stewart win the Spanish Grand Prix. Not having watched motor racing in any shape or form I was fascinated beyond imagining. The track is in the heart of the city, an ordinary road winding and climbing its way past the old buildings. We were able to watch two severe curves at either end of a brief straight, and appreciate the skill with which the drivers rocketed their cars around the corners, time and again with inches to spare on first one side and then the other.

Stewart was always leading and I found it strangely moving to think of a wisp of a man controlling so much beautiful, but brutal power with such delicacy of timing and judgement. Above all I wondered at the continuing concentration that for some two hours could never falter even for a second or so, with the constant knowledge that if it did so death could easily be the price.

Later that day we talked with Stewart and were taken with his modesty and charm. He said then, and confirmed after the season was over, that it had been one of his hardest races, rather like having to play the last round of a championship in 64. Never in some 60 laps was he more than a few seconds ahead.

Stewart's golfing analogy was interesting, particularly from the aspect of concentration which obviously is a crucial quality in all great golfers, but how different their command of it can be. Hogan and Cotton played with an intensity of single-mindedness which they would not readily permit anyone or anything to break. At the other extreme Trevino, like Sarazen before him, will chatter happily between shots. Concentration in golf is an entirely individual matter, as it is in other games or sports, but invariably there are moments when a man can relax, if but briefly. Not so the racing driver.

Another fascinating aspect of motor racing was how the drivers resisted the dangers of monotony, of doing the same things over and over again even though they had to be done so swiftly. No golfer could become bored with hitting perfect shots; most of us are lucky to hit two or three in succession, but who at some moment in a round has not thought 'I will try to fade this one' or some such notion, not that the stroke is essential but simply as an improvisation, a relaxation.

The racing driver, coming to the same old corner for the 56th or whatever time, can hardly permit himself any margins of relief from a pitch of concentration and technical execution close to perfection every single time. His swing, so to speak, must always be in the groove. The race was a stirring experience; it emphasised in dramatic fashion the qualities which enable men such as Stewart to reach the highest peaks.

CHAPTER 16
THE LAND OF PLAYER

For many years I had wanted to visit South Africa but it was never likely that the *Guardian* would send me there to cover golf. The cost of trips to America and elsewhere was burden enough for the sports budget and so we decided to go on our own account. When I suggested to Alistair Hetherington, then editor of the *Guardian*, that I should cover the South African Open he was doubtful because of the paper's policy regarding apartheid. However I learned that for the first time in a long while the championship was to be open to golfers of all races and it was agreed that I should write some articles. Thus work intruded upon the holiday but it did help towards the expenses.

Our stay began in Durban where George Blumberg had lent us an apartment overlooking the Indian Ocean. George and his wife, Brenda, have long been familiar figures at great golfing occasions in many parts of the world. George had been a generous patron of professional golf in South Africa and numerous British players had cause to be thankful for his kindness, as indeed did we. He arranged for us to have a car throughout our month in South Africa, and thus we saw a great deal more of the country than we might have done.

While in Durban I had the pleasure of playing at the Country Club, a lovely course, undulating through trees and shrubs close to the ocean, where two years earlier Tommy Horton had become the first British golfer to win the Open. The club itself was as impressive as any I had seen for the way in which comfort and convenience had been blended. The food and service were incomparable in my experience of golf clubs. There was, of course, no shortage of staff, mostly of Indian origin, and the club then was superbly run by Peter Van Diggelen.

Days in Natal were enriched by a visit to Derek and Biddy Heaton-Nichols in Zululand. When I phoned from Durban he told us to meet him at a hotel in Mtubatuba, the small town where he lived, from where he would direct us to his estate. We arrived a few minutes before he did and within seconds of his appearing it was as if time had no meaning. We were talking as if continuing a conversation begun 28 years before in a German prison camp. His manner was as appealingly casual and unaffected as ever; nothing, save the mild evidence of passing years, seemed to have changed in all the while since the War.

Neither Jean nor I are enamoured of reptiles but we were fascinated when Derek said that his foreman specialised in collecting them. When we enquired if he had any it happened that he had already sent some deadly specimens to the zoo. It would have been interesting to see how he handled them. I was glad to be in a Jeep as we drove through a sugar plantation where snakes were found. We came to a river where crocodile were pleased to attack anyone lingering too close to the edge, and yet the brown, gliding water looked innocent enough. We loved our stay in Mtubatuba but time was pressing and we had to make haste for Johannesburg.

No more idyllic escape from winter could be imagined for a golfer than to compete in South Africa, and countless British players should be grateful that they have had the opportunity to do so. Every day while I watched the Open at Royal Johannesburg the light was diamond sharp, the sunshine hot but never oppressive. Not since Mexico had we enjoyed such a flawless climate and the course was beautiful, its woodland holes curving between abundant willow, acacia, jacaranda and heavy-scented pine.

At 6000 feet the ball flies abnormal distances through the pure air and even the longest holes were within range of a medium-iron second shot. My immediate impression was that golf was easier in South Africa than Britain, but I never felt the force of the winds that can attack courses at the Cape and Port Elizabeth.

I was not surprised to learn that the majority of good South African golfers, from Locke and Player downwards, developed in the wonderfully sympathetic conditions of the Transvaal. The foundation of successful golf is a constant swing, rhythm, and confidence, all of which are not easy to acquire in Britain where, within a short period, the golfer may be battered by winds, chilled to the bone, drenched or occasionally find himself playing in perfect calm. An unstable climate is no help at all.

That Open was memorable for the presence of the non-Europeans, as they were called. Six qualified for the first two rounds and Vincent Tshabalala and Moergerane played through to the end. Four years later Tshabalala won the French Open at Le Touquet and became the first black golfer to win an important event in Europe. Another who failed to qualify fascinated me nonetheless. Chowglay played left-handed with the right hand below the left and competently at that.

As the championship approached its climax I was hoping that Harold Henning would win. Few golfers of my time have been more quietly appealing or as respected and I recall a happy evening with him and his wife, Pat, in their home. For three rounds he led the field but suddenly his short putting withered and Player beat Bobby Cole by one stroke.

I first saw Cole when, soon after his 18th birthday, he won the Amateur championship at Carnoustie. Although he was so slightly built and slender his beautifully wide arc of swing and perfect timing enabled him to drive enormous distances and he pitched with a lovely rhythm, but his exceptional promise has rarely been fulfilled. At times he did play superbly as one year in Venezuela when he and Dale Hayes won the World Cup for South Africa. I have rarely seen such driving as Cole's and he easily outscored everyone including Hale Irwin and Trevino. Watching was most frustrating when one thought of what might have been, and what nearly came to pass the following summer in the Open at Carnoustie. If he could have played the last five holes in par, and four were downwind and very short for him, he would almost certainly have been champion. As it was he failed by one stroke to tie with Watson and Newton.

Player's victory that week was his eighth in the championship but he pursued it with his usual tenacity, determined that nothing and no one should threaten his eminence in South Africa, even though it was then, and probably will remain, beyond dispute for generations. No golfer that I have known, not even Hogan, Nicklaus or Palmer, has been more lastingly consumed with desire to conquer and to prove himself the greatest of all golfers.

Years ago after he had won the United States Open and had joined Hogan and Sarazen as the only players to have won all four major championships open to a professional I asked what further ambitions he had. He said, in as many words, that he wanted to become a great man. This, I believe, has been the motive force which has driven him beyond all normal barriers of ambition since the day, shortly before he was fifteen, his father suggested that he try his hand at golf.

Thenceforth Player drove himself with unquenchable dedication. His zeal for fitness was wellnigh fanatical and involved years of exercise and discipline. At times his sermonising on their virtues could be tedious but few men of his size could have made themselves as powerful while retaining perfect athletic proportions. His capacity for exercise involving abnormal strength was far beyond the compass of ordinary men. A year or so ago during a clinic at West Runton in Norfolk, Gary produced a practice club weighing ten pounds. Gripping it about six inches from the end of the shaft between the first and second fingers of one hand with no assistance from the thumb, he held it horizontal for several seconds. The strength of his fingers is astonishing; the majority of people would be pressed to hold an ordinary club as he did. Later, he swung the same club effortlessly with one hand and no trace of weakness at the top while I managed some rather wobbly laborious swings using both hands.

Player's quest for fitness and appetite for practice have long been famous but it is his character that has interested me. As a golfer he has always been a symbol of the little man relishing challenge and fighting adversity. When these are obvious, such as being many strokes behind or holes down or in contention with Nicklaus, they will inspire most great golfers as they frequently have Player, but when they were not obvious he would create, consciously or otherwise, crises to overcome. This was to emphasise that he was facing fearsome burdens and that overmuch should not be expected from his golf, but I think he believed in what he was saying. He would talk of an onerous life, of a dislike for flying, of longing to be at home and not playing golf; of the strain of winning, of a course's difficulties, of a disastrous tendency to hook and so on with such wide brown-eyed earnestness that those unaccustomed to him in such a vein would be moved to sympathy. Those who knew him well learned to beware such outpourings; as like as not the very next day he would conquer all the odds, real or imagined, and often win the tournament.

I recall the eve of an Australian Open. Player had been troubled with hooking, possibly the one most troublesome recurring problem of his career, and agonised about it to the point where it seemed that only celestial guidance or Hogan's advice could save him. After an opening 71 Gary said it would be a miracle if he won. The Australian writers listened faithfully but I was not in the least surprised when he was round the next day in 65 and eventually was champion.

At times Player would dwell on the power of positive thought, on religion or self-hypnosis and being able to induce a trancelike state on the golf course. It was easy to be cynical about such attitudes but they have worked for him. It is hard to imagine that any golfer will ever be as successful outside his own country as Player has been. Certainly no one has approached his tally thus far.

Over the years one saw many sides to Gary. He could be most appealing and occasionally tiresome, provocative and stimulating and at times his intensity could be disturbing but a lively sense of humour makes him an entertaining companion. His playing achievements have quickened admiration, at times even wonder throughout the golfing world. I admired him for the way in which he dealt with questions about political issues in South Africa and incidents arising from them. These must have imposed considerable strain. There was a period in the United States when he competed knowing that detectives were in the gallery in the event of possible demonstrations or even assault. This could hardly aid concentration but his survived. It was another challenge to be met.

No other golfer can have been pestered or threatened by letters and phone calls to anything like the extent that Player was during those unfortunate years, but he never used them as an excuse for failure. On one occasion when he had played moderately he told me that he had been troubled with threats but not until he had extracted my promise not to write anything of them. I was at Dayton for the United States PGA championship in 1969 when demonstrators threw things at him and ran on to a green where he and Nicklaus were putting. The common sense and tact with which Player spoke of the incidents afterwards at a press conference commanded everyone's respect. Eleven people were arrested and extra police drafted in for the last day. There was no further trouble, but who, and most of all Player, knew that there might not have been, and yet he finished second, only a stroke behind Raymond Floyd. Courage and resolve were never lacking in a remarkable little person.

After the Open in Johannesburg Player departed for the United States. We did not envy him because we were on our way to a tournament at the Royal Swaziland Club. Driving in the cloudless heat across the long rolling green veldt with its wonderful limitless skies we were hardly prepared for the tumbling mountainous land as we descended into the charming little country, then, as now the kingdom of King Sobhuza. The cloistered valley, on one side of which lay the course and its handsome attendant hotels, could have been in the Welsh borders, green wooded hills, occasional outcrops of rocks and cloud prowling the peaks. There the resemblance ceased for colour was everywhere in flowering shrubs and plants, hibiscus, Australian flame and moonflower. Never before had I seen caddies so gaily clad; all had to wear brilliantly coloured toga-like garments. It was a delightfully relaxing place and a ready escape for South Africans from some of the restrictions of their country.

Although I had to produce an article every day my watching of the golf was not as earnest as it might have been, and I had two expert informants in Gerald Micklem and George Blumberg who made a diverting study of how compulsive watching can become. Each day they would lay their plans as to whom they would follow. Some flexibility was permitted according to the run of play, but slacking around the clubhouse certainly was not. Away they would go their separate way while as often as not I would write beneath an umbrella of beautifully wrought thatch beside the swimming pool looking towards sun-shadowed hills beyond. On a table by one's side was a little red flag which when raised indicated urgent need for sustenance. Towards gin time Gerald and 'Uncle George', as hosts of young players called him, would return and as often as not George would say 'I want to tell you, Gerald' and two of the most passionate followers of golf I have known would be launched for the evening.

In a land of sunshine we were unfortunate in a visit to the Kruger Park. Long in advance Micklem had been in touch with Basil Keartland, then president of the South African Golf Union, who kindly invited us to spend three days with him and his wife at their house in the park. The owners of such houses are, if I remember rightly, allowed to use them for only thirty days a year. We were therefore privileged, but it rained and rained. The animals had no need of the watering holes visible from the roads but we had some fascinating drives. To leave the car is forbidden but we saw a pride of lions and hosts of other animals. We enjoyed our stay and were happy to have been in a remarkable place. The Keartlands continued their hospitality for our last days in Johannesburg where I did manage to watch some cricket with Eddie Barlow pounding away at the *Wanderers'* ground.

Some examples of apartheid that we saw seemed unnecessarily hurtful, even childish, but often I have wondered whether the British and other nations would be so self-righteous if faced with a situation similar to that in South Africa.

CHAPTER 17
AUSTRALIA —
AND WIDENING HORIZONS

For some years after a boyish obsession with cricket had taken hold I was probably more conscious of Australia than of any other foreign country. Every four years the awesome figures in the dark green caps would tour the land, and every fourth winter came the dark mornings when one longed for tidings of how England were faring. Nowadays, when Test matches are two a penny and the finest overseas cricketers are familiar in the county game the romance of those long-ago tours has faded.

Nonetheless Australia has always had a special place in my mind, though even when men like Norman Von Nida, Peter Thomson and Kel Nagle were making their impact on the golf world I never expected to see their country. Then, during the Open at St Andrews in 1970, I was invited to cover the Australian Open which was sponsored by Qantas. John Spooner, then an executive of the airline, offered to fly three writers there. This was a wonderful opportunity not only to see the country and some of its golf but to travel round the world.

Our introduction to Australian golf was fortunate in that the Open was at Kingston Heath, one of that rare concentration of splendid courses near Melbourne. They lie, about a dozen, on gently undulating land, with sandy subsoil ideal for golf. Thomson showed us several of them, including that of the Victoria Club which in 1954 had the distinction of producing the Open and Amateur champions of Britain. Both Thomson and Doug Bachli were members of the club.

The masterpiece of this great gathering of golf is Royal Melbourne where the two beautiful courses provide probably the finest examination of the game in the southern hemisphere. The greater part of the design was the work of Alister Mackenzie who was also responsible for Augusta National and Cypress Point, a remarkable legacy from one architect. The holes roll and curve through groves of trees and shrubs without being

159

overly confining and have much of seaside character in the playing, notably in the firmness and pace of the greens. It is small wonder that Thomson, who learned his golf on courses of this nature, should be so successful on British links.

Essentially Royal Melbourne demands thought and control, placing rather than power, and care with the approach shots so as not to be putting downhill. When I watched the World Cup there in 1972 the greens were among the fastest I had seen and contributed to the deadly slowness of the play. Some rounds took over six hours, an appalling test of endurance and concentration for the golfers and a massive bore for a writer, but I loved the course which, in Thomson's words, could humble the giants or confirm their greatness.

Of all distinguished golfers Thomson is one of the most able writers. For years he has been a correspondent with the *Melbourne Age*, where through Ranald Macdonald I was often welcome. Thomson produces his copy with clarity, speed and firmness of view. The majority of books and articles purporting to be written by games-players are either the result of edited tape recordings or the work of 'ghosts'. When I was involved in *The World Atlas of Golf* for Mitchell Beazley a few years ago we needed a writer to describe the Asian and Australasian courses. Immediately I thought of Thomson and the outcome was admirable.

As I have said before Thomson was not one for dwelling overmuch on his own golf. In his home one would be pressed to find any evidence that he had played the game seriously. I saw no cases of trophies, no array of medals and, as I recall, few golf books in his library. Thomson is a man of varied tastes as could be judged by the people one met in his house. Although playing golf, designing courses and writing have been his profession he and his appealing wife, Mary, do not seem to allow them to obtrude into their private life. Thomson and Nicklaus are outstanding for their sense of proportion.

That first trip to Australia gave a welcome glimpse of Canberra. The beauty of Burley Griffin's plan, based on circles rather than squares, was compelling for the spaciousness of setting, for the clinical shining buildings and width of avenues where the trees had taken on their spring raiment. The encircling hills, distant snowy mountains and water made a lovely background to a fine course designed by John Harris, where the greens were said to be the largest in the country.

On the way from Canberra to Sydney we drove through a country town rather too swiftly for the liking of a local policeman. He roared after us on his motorcycle and was sounding pretty formidable until we explained that we were British golf writers on our way to Fiji. Whereupon he said 'In that case there isn't much I can do about you,' and within seconds we were talking rugby and cricket. Sport is never far from Australian conscious-ness, but had we been natives we would have been in trouble.

While watching the Open, and the Dunlop tournament at Canberra, both of which were won by Player, we heard criticism which, I believe, still exists of the custom of paying fares, expenses and often substantial appear-ance money to overseas players, mostly of course Americans. Resentment by Australian players is understandable because such payments give a few players a distinct advantage over the domestic golfers who are competing under greater financial pressure. At the same time the presence of famous overseas golfers gives the public a rare chance to see them, attracts larger crowds and television which otherwise might not cover the event, and possibly ensures the future of a tournament. This must benefit the home professional in the long run.

Some may wonder why wealthy men, as most of the world's leading golfers are, should need inducements to compete. Could they not afford an occasional trip somewhere for the good of others rather than for them-selves? Obviously they could but golf is their profession and simply because it is a game is no reason to expect golfers to be more altruistic than many a similarly prosperous businessman.

The prospect of a few days in Fiji was appealing but our hotel was some 70 miles from the airport. Before setting forth the Indian taxi driver insisted that we call at his house for a beer or two. We took off in the dead small hours of the night then the driver suddenly declared that he must sleep. He passed out in the back and I found myself wrestling an ancient taxi over terrible roads through what looked like semi-jungle. Ben Wright and Raymond Jacobs, my amiable companions for the trip, were to take their turns at the wheel but the driver revived and they were spared. The native Fijians were delightful, friendly people and we relaxed on the beach before the long trail home.

When Donald Steel and I went to Australia the following year we broke the journey in Singapore. Unfortunately we were advised to stay in a modern hotel which, for its lack of Oriental atmosphere, could have been in Kansas City. When we paused for a drink at Raffles the next day I was sorry that we had not stayed there. It may not have been as fashionable as in the days of Somerset Maugham's stories but it stirred echoes of that other age.

Since the independence of Singapore its two great clubs merged into the Island Club which when we were there had some 7000 members, half of whom played golf, and four 18-hole courses. We walked the latest of these, one of Frank Pennink's attractive creations, and were impressed by the quality of the golf and the superb condition of the courses, which was not surprising with a greenkeeping staff of almost 200. The courses are so busy that there is a strict awareness of slow play to the extent that everyone's time of starting is checked and laggards reported. Handicaps are assessed by computer and cards have to be handed in for every round although there was no insistence on all putts being holed. I can imagine the reaction at my club if such a system were imposed.

I regretted having only a day in Singapore, but such has often been the way of my journeys. One has to learn to resist temptations to linger and Tasmania was on our horizon that year. I have always blessed Qantas for taking the Australian Open there because I had never dreamed that I would see that remote, beautiful place. As we emerged from a turbulent overcast above the Bass Strait it was hard to believe that we were not approaching the west coast of Scotland. Here were great inlets of gunmetal seas, tumbled masses of mountains and below, rich green pastureland that might have been in the Borders.

Hobart is one of the most attractive harbours in the world. Boats dance and gleam on the water, white and red houses rise on the green flanking hills towards Mount Wellington, its peaks then lightly dusted with snow. It was springtime and the chill air reminded us that Antarctica was not far away. One morning the peripatetic Peter Dobereiner, one of the most fluent of writers, and I were flown in a light aircraft to the western part of the island, glorious desolation beyond imagining for one who had always thought of Tasmania as an orchard. We saw vast estuaries with mile upon mile of deserted sand and lagoons that looked tropical in the brilliant light. It seemed an enchanted land, Van Diemen's Land, as compellingly beautiful as any I had seen.

We were fascinated by the abundance of Georgian-style houses, mostly built by convict labour, even though their classic outlines sometimes contrasted vividly with corrugated iron roofs. This, I gathered, was because of the shortage of slate.

The Royal Hobart course lies in a quiet valley, flat and serene, amid groves of gum trees, titrees and wattle bush, but it was no match for Nicklaus that year. He mastered it and a powerful field in effortless fashion and won by eight strokes. One evening we discussed with him the possibility of anyone achieving the professional Grand Slam and he made a logical case for his own prospects in 1972, saying that the four courses involved, Augusta, Pebble Beach, Muirfield and Oakland Hills were among his favourites. As it proved he won the Masters, the US Open and was but one stroke behind Trevino in the British.

I had always known that *Country Life* was an enduring magazine in that it tended to lie about houses for ages but I was pleasantly surprised at a party one day in Hobart. My hostess said she had just read an article of mine about an event in Wales. I could not recall having been there for some

162

time and then saw that the article was in an issue from 1964, eight years previously.

Rarely have I been as loath to leave a place. Two or three days more would have sufficed to explore more of the island and to play the Tasmanian course which rises and falls about a rockbound peninsula in glorious fashion. I had not seen a more beautifully sited clubhouse anywhere in the world, with its magnificent views of sea and mountain and green pastures but to stay in Tasmania would have curtailed a rewarding spell in Sydney. There for the first and last time I watched cricket in Australia.

Although Lawry, somewhat surprisingly, and Stackpole, naturally, put bat to ball in impressive fashion it was a sombre occasion. Only a few hundred watched, sprinkled in the great stands, stately symbols of Victoriana. The famous Hill was at peace, no holocaust of noise; a voice occasionally roared therefrom but otherwise the match might have been played in a museum of memories. For this was the place of Bradman, McCabe, O'Reilly, Hammond and all the noble host before them.

Donald Steel is as absorbed in cricket as I am. One morning before going to Tasmania we stood in the vast emptiness of the great Melbourne ground with Ian Johnson, who had captained Australia in the fifties. We relished his memories and I thought of a boyhood when Hobbs, Sutcliffe, Tate and all the worshipped host of the time dominated many a winter's waking on the other side of the world. Later that day Lyndsay Hassett helped to gladden an hour's watching of a golf tournament, and before leaving Sydney there was a pleasant evening with Richie and Daphne Benaud in their apartment high above the incomparable harbour.

I loved these associations with cricket but we remained mindful of golf. A peaceful round at Royal Sydney was only slightly saddened by the way in which suburbia has enclosed the course. But the great turreted clubhouse, of a much older fashion than most in Australia, stood proud above the gathering roofs around it. Another day John Spooner took us to Pymble, a delightful course, almost Augustan in the lovely rise and fall of its fairways amid great stands of eucalyptus. It was there that Nagle's long career began.

Once again California and the coast of Monterey were calling. The US Open the following year was to be at Pebble Beach and Sandy Tatum had much to do with its preparation. While there we met Jack Neville who, with Douglas Grant, had designed the course during the First War. Few architects can ever have been blessed with so marvellous a setting. For a while then I had been afflicted with rheumatoid arthritis, happily not in a virulent form, but tiresome enough to hamper my golf. I played so poorly that day at Pebble that I decided not to play the next morning at Cypress Point but when the moment came I could not resist it and was glad that I played. On the 5th, a majestic hole rolling upwards through the woods, Steel hit two perfect shots with a spoon, the second of which went into the hole for an 'albatross', or double eagle in American parlance.

Kathryn Crosby was on hand with a camera to record Steel's enviable moment and then, remarkably, Richard Snideman holed his tee shot to the short 7th. Bing Crosby and I were denied any such exalted feats, but Bing was one of the only two or three to have holed in one at the famous 16th, the hole that would be any golfer's first choice for such a turn of fortune.

On the way to New York I remember envying Steel who was returning directly to England. Wonderful though many of these trips could be there were times when suddenly one had travelled enough, but I was committed to a week in Florida and the World Cup. The flight from New York was, I think, my first in a 747 and not improved by a garrulous captain who delivered endless homespun homilies to hosts of purple-hair-rinsed women on their way to Florida, which in some respects is like a waiting room for the mortuary.

Within three weeks I had been in Singapore, Melbourne, Tasmania, Sydney, Honolulu, San Francisco, Monterey and writing on most of the days. I would not have missed it for anything but it had all been too swift. However the climate of Florida had its soothing effect and Nicklaus had brought his transcending form from Australia. On a long, demanding course he was 17 under par and helped by Trevino won a commanding victory for the United States. I remember Nicklaus saying one evening that he enjoyed playing with Trevino and that he admired his generosity of spirit. Their rivalry was to continue for years to come. One of the most warming aspects of professional tournament golf since Palmer first exploded on the scene has been the grace and good humour with which powerful rivalries between the great men have been pursued.

When Qantas repeated their invitation to Australia in 1972 and I knew that the Open was to be played in Adelaide the possibility of meeting Sir Donald Bradman immediately sprang to mind. Thanks to the kindness of Jim (E.W.) Swanton, who wrote to Bradman on my behalf, hope became reality. Soon after I arrived in Adelaide he telephoned saying he was going to watch the championship at Kooyonga and would collect me at the hotel. As we drove to the course I could hardly realise that the quiet, slight figure beside me was the same person I had watched with awe on the cricket grounds of England.

Bradman was most agreeable to meet, pleasant and courteous, but one was soon aware of an extremely positive manner, clarity of mind and economy of speech. Nothing about him was vague, casual or uncertain. We followed the play together for an hour or so, talking of cricket and golf. I asked if it was true that as a boy he would throw a golf ball against a wall so that the rebound would quicken his reactions. He said that he did so but not with any specific intent because at that age, 'I knew nothing of the technique of cricket.' It was simply that he often had to play alone but he supposed that it might have helped.

When I remarked on the wonderfully fast footwork which was such a feature of his batting he said that it was purely a natural gift. He spoke so modestly that it was difficult to believe that he was the man whose astoundingly swift reaction and movement had enabled him to destroy bowling as no one else has ever done.

The following day Sylvester Phelan, an Australian writer, asked if I would like to make up a four with Bradman, Bill Ackland-Horman, a former Australian amateur champion, and Phelan himself. I needed no second bidding; the Open could be spared my presence for a while. I had heard that Bradman was an accomplished golfer and was curious to see how good he was. Many eminent cricketers have played golf well. The names of Dexter, Graveney, Cowdrey and Simpson come readily to mind and, of an earlier vintage, Hammond was no mean golfer, and McCabe, I was told, had a very low handicap.

The techniques involved in the two games do not seem to conflict at all. The difference between striking a moving ball or a stationary one might appear to be great, but the art of doing so successfully requires the same basic skills of balance, rhythm, co-ordination and timing. It would have been remarkable if a man as abundantly endowed with these qualities as Bradman could not master any game if he were so minded. And, from what one heard, when Bradman was minded to do anything he excelled at it. I was told that at one time he was the best billiards player in Australia after Walter Lindrum; he became an able stockbroker and a successful business-man. In some respects Bradman reminded me of Hogan. Beneath the quiet, inconspicuous manner there was a ruthless determination, far beyond the ken of most men.

We played on a perfect sun-filled morning at Royal Adelaide, a course of considerable charm and quality. Bradman's first act, after driving straight down the fairway, was to retrieve my ball from the nearby railway line where a hook had deposited it, the almost inevitable consequence of borrowed clubs and arriving in a somewhat anxious rush not having played for weeks, but that had become a common experience. It mattered not for we played what they called a Canadian foursome or, in English terms: a greensome, and my partner, the huge, amiable Ackland-Horman, drove so far that my best drives were academic.

Straightaway I was impressed with Bradman's method. His address and grip were perfect and might have been modelled on Peter Thomson's, but when I asked who had taught him he replied crisply, 'Self-taught'. His backswing was contained, designed for straightness rather than length, and this seemed in character. Less often than any other great batsman did he hit the ball in the air; in his merciless fashion he gave the fielders the least possible chance. His golf was played as if he regarded hazards in the same light; they never interfered with his progress that day. In the whole round I can recall only one bad shot from Bradman and two or three indifferent ones. It was easy to see how he had been scratch. His handicap of seven seemed an understatement, but I did hear whispers that the twitch occasionally beset him, as it does legions of golfers much younger than 64, as he was then.

The golf was taken carefully as we were playing in a competition. What with this, watching Bradman play, struggling with my own game and thinking mostly about cricket it was a conflicting kind of morning. Many questions remained unanswered but I did ask Bradman which bowler had caused him most problems before the war. He paused and said with a smile, 'I don't think any of them troubled me too much.' He then went on to say, to our great amusement, that he should have retired in 1938 and that he was not too good afterwards, (he only averaged about 85 in ten Tests against England) but he did concede that Alec Bedser bowled pretty well.

In an earlier chapter I referred to my frustration at Lords in 1934 when he was out after a brilliant innings of 36. I asked if he remembered. He did so with great clarity, saying that Woodfull, his captain, suggested that he slow down and play for the close. The thought betrayed Bradman into a checked stroke and it was then he returned the simple catch to Verity; otherwise he thought he might have made a hundred that evening. I had heard that he did once score a century in three overs in a country match. Without thinking I asked if they were eight-ball overs. 'Yes,' he said, 'but don't denigrate it; I lost the strike for two balls.' When I enquired for details of the innings he said that I would find them in his book in the London School of Economics. The retort was not out of character.

Meanwhile Thomson was moving steadily towards victory at Kooyonga although he had to beat David Graham in a play-off. His golf was not as infallibly straight as of old but the effortless simplicity of his finest strokes was a joy to see. The conditions suited him because the greens were rather of the traditional seaside character he loves, demanding thought and a variety of strokes for the approaches. I wrote then that Graham would become one of the most significant golfers on the international stage because there was an intensity of purpose and fire within him and he had a swing which would withstand the pressures of his ambition. For once prophecy has been fulfilled.

I found Adelaide an engaging city, admirably planned with much space and green. No wonder cricket writers are captured by the setting of the handsome ground with the cathedral soaring nearby and the hills of the Lofty Range in the background. When I saw it, deserted and at peace one morning, I thought how strange it was that such a tranquil place should have been the scene of so much bitterness during the body-line tour forty years earlier. Through the kindly offices of Tom Porter, a former mayor of Adelaide and a friend of Swanton's, Dobereiner and I were made members of the Adelaide Club for our stay. We spent some rewarding hours in the wine country and I left the city with nothing but pleasant memories.

No sooner had I arrived at a tournament in Melbourne than one of the golf writers insisted that I meet a remarkable man, Legh Winser, who lived at Barwon Heads on the coast some 60 miles from the city. In a recent competition, shortly before his 88th birthday, he had returned a 76 at Barwon Heads, a considerable course that was said to be the nearest approach to a links in Australia.

The crispness of Legh Winser's voice on the phone warned me that I was about to meet an exceptional person. I drove down from Melbourne and he was awaiting my arrival, an erect, slender figure bearing no traces of the frailty common to the greatly aged. No sooner were greetings over than he suggested a few holes before lunch and a round afterwards. His attractive daughter suggested I might like some coffee but I was hastened away to the club nearby. When I gently implied that one round would suffice for me, after all I was rising 60, he proposed a walk instead. The talk turned to cricket and when he mentioned that, as a boy at Oundle, he had kept wicket while the great bulk of W. G. Grace was at the crease, and that for three years he had played for Staffordshire and kept wicket to Sydney Barnes, all thoughts of golf fled from my mind.

Winser, who was born in Cheshire, went to South Australia in 1909 because his health was delicate, and took up fruit farming. He played for the state and was recognised as one of Australia's finest wicketkeepers to the point where Clem Hill invited him to go to South Africa but the tour was cancelled because of the War. As we walked he spoke of Trumper, Hill, Armstrong, Bardsley, Cotter and a host of legendary figures, and I wondered at the glory the clear old eyes had seen.

In 1921, the year after he last played cricket for the state, he won the Australian amateur golf championship. He was champion of his state eight times and for some twenty-five years was secretary to successive governors of South Australia. He held this office during the MCC tour in 1932–3 and as the governor was in England at the time was intimately involved with the famous messages concerning the body-line bowling.

When we played golf that afternoon it was immediately clear to me that he was capable of beating his age almost at will. To have done so by eleven strokes surely is a record. I cannot believe that anyone, even James Braid, long famed at Walton Heath for doing so regularly, ever achieved the feat by such a margin. With a beautifully firm, orthodox grip and short simple swing Winser struck the ball true and straight time after time. His drives, which approached 200 yards, would be followed on the longer holes with another quiet, steady wood, probably a five. Then an ancient Ben Sayers hickory mashie-niblick would appear, and as often as not the ball would finish within likely holing distance. The whole process seemed enviably simple, a marvellous example for anyone, not only those full of years.

We played 14 holes in the lovely sunshine, Winser pulling his clubs on a cart and walking quite fast enough for me. Much of history was quickened that afternoon, not only by my companion but by Bud Russell, the club's admirable professional for over 40 years. His career had started at Gullane with Jack White who, in 1904, was the first man to break 300 in the Open.

On and on the talk flowed until what had been an invitation to lunch extended into the evening. As I took a reluctant leave of gentle, hospitable people and drove back to Melbourne I could not recall having spent a more absorbing day. Aside from the joys of sharing so much precious recollection I had come to know a most remarkable man.

Before leaving Australia, sadly for the last time, I dithered for days as to which route home I would take. Many people said that I must see Perth and I was tempted, but the thought of glimpsing another country made me decide to break the journey at Kuala Lumpur. Also I would be able to see the Royal Selangor Club which was to be the setting for the World Team championship for the Eisenhower Trophy in 1974. As it happened politics intruded, as to a tiresome extent they so often do, and the event was taken to another country.

One afternoon I played nine holes with the captain of the club, a high court judge, and two other members. Elsewhere on the course the king, a keen golfer, was playing and so, to my surprise, was a Russian diplomat, a useful performer, so it was said, and the first member of his race whom I had seen with a club in his hands. Huge black thunderheads weaved down from the misty hills, savage lightning darted between them and my golf was not as resolute as it might have been. Suddenly the storm exploded, its fearsome flashes ever nearer. My hosts seemed undisturbed but my last backswing, as the rain came crashing down, hardly rose above ankle height and I hope the speed with which I returned the club to the caddie did not appear too cowardly.

The Malaysians had been as courteous and gentle as I expected them to be and I now regret that some of my journeys did not embrace the Far East. I left Kuala Lumpur with pleasant memories, lastly of the beautiful girl who escorted me from the departure lounge for my flight which left at midnight. She was a blend (rarely encountered in the western world) of striking appeal, gentleness and a total lack of affectation. A weary traveller was refreshed as we talked awhile before I had to board. For once, of course, the flight had to leave on time.

CHAPTER 18

LEARNING NOT TO WAFFLE IN HOLLYWOOD

For the most part a golf correspondent's life is clearly ordained. Usually he knows months in advance where he will be at a given time, but occasionally the unpredictable arises. It did so for me one December evening in 1972 when Jay Michaels called from Los Angeles. It appeared that Trans World International, of which he was president, were producing a television film of a year in the life of Arnold Palmer. Jay suggested that I do the script and added that I would probably write better if Jean were with me. It was one of those rare occasions when there was no question of having to make a decision, one of the great curses of middle age. I had no sooner put down the phone than my thoughts were in Southern California.

The following January we arrived at the Century Plaza Hotel, hard by the ghostly remnants of the 20th Century-Fox lot, and I was launched into the unfamiliar world of films. For one who had always been accustomed to writing at length, producing a script was a fascinating exercise in economy of words. Not for years had I found writing as stimulating.

Throughout 1972 Jay and a camera crew had pursued Palmer all over the United States and far beyond, to Britain, New Zealand and Sweden, in hope that he would win a tournament but always he failed, although sometimes by narrow margins. An enormous footage had been shot and I did not envy Jay, Ted Parrish, his principal assistant and Don Shoemaker, the editor, the awesome task of cutting to some fifty minutes of film. Towards the end of this process we all went down the coast to Dana Point where Shoemaker, a delightful young man, had a small studio. There we would work in peace. Any thought that Jean and I might have of stealing an hour or so on the beach was killed dead by incessant rain during the wettest winter California had suffered in 40 years.

That same weekend Palmer was competing in the Bob Hope tournament in Palm Springs just over the mountains from where we were. Splendid irony had it that after Jay and his men had chased Palmer all over the place for a year he was about to win, and we had no television or radio in the studio. This was the height of frustration but Jay was equal to the challenge. He knew that Mark McCormack would be watching the tournament on television at his home in Cleveland, some 2000 miles away, and called him. For the better part of an hour while Palmer, and Nicklaus his closest challenger, played the closing holes Mark gave a running commentary on an event that was only a hundred miles from us. A few feet of Palmer's triumph were included at the end of the film and I wrote 'Ecstasy that victory alone can bring came once more to Arnold Palmer.' It was his last important victory in the United States.

The final writing was an absorbing exercise involving a stop watch and an editing machine. I worked with Parrish, an attractive and highly-skilled film man from whom I learned a great deal. His experience and advice were invaluable and after many hours of the most intensely concentrated work I had done in years the script was finished. I had enjoyed every moment of it.

The question of who would do the voice-over had already been resolved. From a long list of actors Jay had found Jason Robards who, by remarkable coincidence, was the only one of them I knew. Once, in New York, Alistair and Jane Cooke had taken me to supper with Betty (Lauren) Bacall and Jason, then her husband, after her theatre performance. I was fascinated to meet Betty and immediately took to Jason. He was particularly famous for his performances in Eugene O'Neill plays. When I asked if it was hard to escape the effects each day of playing such powerful roles, he agreed that it was, and this may have contributed to his problems in private life. Another time in London Jean and I dined with Cooke and Robards, whose appearance and manner might have been those of a quiet successful businessman, and not one of America's finest actors.

At the time of the film Jason was divorced from Betty Bacall, had married again and was living on the coast north of Malibu. We drove to his house so that he could read the script and spent a pleasant afternoon with him and his attractive new wife. Not long previously Jason had suffered a serious car accident, from which he was lucky to escape alive, but his teeth had been damaged. This caused some delay in recording his voice but he made it the day before we had to leave for home.

Much to my delight towards the end of the year we were back in California. This time Palmer had been filmed playing 18 of his favourite holes in the United States, each one with a famous player — Trevino at Baltusrol, Player at Oakland Hills, Floyd at Merion — a pretty feminine touch with Laura Baugh at Seminole, an evocative moment at Olympic, where Palmer and Hogan had suffered crushing disappointments, and so on.

171

The film was split into three separate shows for television, and Jay said I must write opening and closing speeches for Palmer who was due to arrive soon to record them on film. Early one morning we gathered at the Lakeside course where many of the film people played. A site was chosen, camera set up, and Palmer was to read my words from a prompt board. Simple enough, I thought, but five hours later we had not finished. Although Palmer well knew what he had to say he is not an incisive speaker. His remarks, timed to seconds, had to be prepared in advance. Time and again there was a slight flaw, a false inflexion in Arnold's voice, a hesitation, a wrong expression, and Jay would say, 'Could we try it just once more?' Never once did Palmer complain, and when I suggested that I change some of the words or phrases he said, 'Hell no, it's my fault, not yours.' He remained wonderfully good-humoured throughout what became a wearisome chore. The patience of film-makers is boundless. Never did I hear grumbling from Jay or any of the crew. They shot 43 takes that morning before we retired for lunch. Fortunately I knew most of the courses used in the film and the writing was easier, but I still welcomed the shrewd, steadying influence of Ted Parrish during our dark hours in the studio.

There was little time to spare during those weeks but Hollywood and Beverley Hills became familiar places. Hollywood's era as the film capital has now faded. One afternoon Jean went to see a Barbra Streisand movie at the famous Grauman's Chinese Theatre, scene of the great world premieres of the past where the stars' footprints are impressed on the pavement outside. Gradually she realised that she was the only person in the whole theatre and came out feeling like a ghost.

One evening too she forgot that taxis do not cruise for fares in Los Angeles, and must be sought at hotels or other key points. On my way to the studio I left her in Wilshire Boulevard near museums she wanted to visit. Hours later I returned to the hotel but she was not there. Darkness had fallen and instantly I was worried. Los Angeles must have the most inadequate public transport of any city in the world! Buses do appear occasionally on some of the main streets, and not finding a taxi Jean walked to a stop. No bus, so she walked on to the next. Suddenly it dawned on her that she was alone. No one else was walking. As in most American cities buildings ablaze with lights give a false impression of companionship. A solitary feminine figure is easy meat for the vicious who abound in Los Angeles and, in the event of an attack, it is highly unlikely that anyone would come to the rescue; the cars would stream past, their drivers unseeing and uncaring if they did. As it proved my anxiety was needless. When Jean eventually returned she found me heartily relieved and furious!

The Michaels, the Parrishes and Arthur Rosenbaum and his wife were kind to us during both our visits. Everyone who worked on the films was helpful and welcoming and I was grateful for the novel writing experience. We became attached to the Century Plaza. Each morning we would breakfast on a wonderful array of fresh fruit, read in the *Los Angeles Times* of the plight of Britain and feel momentarily depressed. Our balcony looked out over the lights of Santa Monica with the gleaming spire of the Mormon Temple towering above. It was pleasant to sip our evening drinks while the sun went down over the Pacific, but early one morning our room felt far from pacific. We were awakened by the trembling of our beds and the sight of the pictures shaking on the walls. We hastened to the doorway, the safest place relatively speaking, and some seconds later it was over. The epicentre was a few miles up the coast, causing damage but no loss of life.

Although both films were shown on a national network in the United States, they did not appear in Britain, for some reason known only to the BBC. Palmer was not the dominating figure of old but he was still immensely popular and I am sure the British golfing public would have enjoyed the shows, particularly the best 18 holes. They were superbly photographed and most had been the scene of an historic occasion.

CHAPTER 19
A WOMAN'S WORLD

One blessing of the golf correspondent's life is the opportunity to play some of the finest courses in countries other than his own. After numerous visits to the United States I had known the joy of Pine Valley, Pebble Beach, Cypress Point, Merion, Seminole, Shinnecock Hills, The Country Club and others, but had never been to Pinehurst in North Carolina. The chance to visit one of the great golfing places in America came about in unexpected fashion.

In the early seventies the Diamondhead Corporation bought the Pinehurst estate and its several beautiful courses from the Tufts family who had owned them for generations, and decided to build a World Golf Hall of Fame. This sort of thing is common in America but has never commended itself to followers of sport in Britain. The Hall at Pinehurst was opened in 1974 by President Ford and all the obvious people, Jones, Hogan, Hagen, Nicklaus, Palmer, Vardon and others were, as they say, inducted. Each year thereafter further names were added and I was asked to suggest a few from the past in Britain. The first that came to mind was Lady Heathcoat-Amory who, as Joyce Wethered, was supreme in her time and the greatest woman amateur of all golfing ages.

It happened that the induction of this next group was to coincide with a tournament on the Pinehurst No. 2 course to be played the week previous to the Ryder Cup match at Laurel Valley. This was admirably convenient and the Hall of Fame people asked if I would accept the various awards on behalf of Lady Amory who was unable to attend the ceremony, and ceremony it was in elaborate American fashion.

The Hall of Fame itself, costing about a million pounds, is a massive structure, white and columned, set alone within a pine forest and embraced by pools and fountains. It could well be a government building in, for instance, Canberra. Aside from being a kind of shrine for the great players, living and dead, it also contains a museum. Each player has a separate wall with a portrait and a bronze plaque with a likeness in heavy relief. The whole affair is admirably arranged save that some of the likenesses are not as true as they should be.

Among those to be anointed that year were Sarazen, Charles Evans, the first man to win the United States Open and Amateur championships in the same year, Glenna Collett Vare, America's greatest player between the wars, and Joe Dey for his remarkable services to golf. That same month he drove himself in as captain of the Royal and Ancient. Francis Ouimet is the only other American to have held that office.

Sarazen, Evans and Dey were there in person and they and the stand-ins for the others were assembled behind the 5th green on the No. 2 course. Army parachutists then made precise landings in front of us. Each bore a small plaque and in alphabetical order we had to walk forward and receive them. As a 'W' I was last and the smart airborne officer in charge of the affair announced to the company that Miss Ward-Thomas would accept for Joyce Wethered. As I rose amid the laughter he swiftly made amends but I wished afterwards that I had thought to curtsy.

We were then stationed in front of the hall to receive a large replica of the principal plaque, and to make a speech of exactly one minute. The plaque was far too bulky for me to take home but eventually it reached Lady Amory by other means. The next step was a press conference to enlighten the writers about ourselves or those we were representing, and that evening a dinner at which we each had to speak for, I think, six minutes. On such occasions it is easier to speak about someone else than about oneself but Joe Dey was as accomplished and modest as ever. Sarazen had no trouble at all but Patty Berg, with every justification, lauded Mrs Vare, who could not attend, in tremendous style. I was next to speak and had to tone down the fact that on the three famous occasions when Joyce Wethered had played Mrs Vare she had won.

I have never been enamoured of pro.am. tournaments and the only ones in which I have taken part were in the United States. The one at Pinehurst was my only chance of playing the great No. 2 course and as they had invited me, I girded myself at the appointed hour. It was pleasant to potter about the putting green with every right to do so as one awaited the starting time. After I had holed one or two putts Sam Snead's high-pitched voice behind me said, 'I always knew you (expletive deleted) Scotsmen were good putters.' Having swiftly adjusted the question of nationality I was called to the tee. Snead was playing behind us and a largish crowd had gathered but apprehension served as it can at such moments, intensifying determination to complete the backswing and look at the ball. The drive was solid. Much of the rest was not but I had played the lovely course and enjoyed the round with Jerry McGee, an engaging young man, and Dean Cassell, an attractive person whose solid golf befitted an executive with the

Acushnett Company, and more recently Dunlop's.

Among few regrets in the watching of golf is that I never saw Bobby Jones or Joyce Wethered play during their great years. Every contemporary account has it that Miss Wethered's golf was as near flawless as it was possible to be. Jones himself wrote 'I have found many people to agree with me that Miss Wethered's swing was the most perfect in the world.' Raymond Oppenheimer, one of the seven who had the privilege of winning the Worplesdon Foursomes with her, and as exacting a critic of the golf swing as anyone I know, said that if the Almighty were asked to make a women with a perfect swing he could not imagine any improvement upon hers.

The swing was absolutely simple and, like its owner, free from affectation of any kind. The wonder of her golf was that it was not the product of years of striving and experiment but of an innate talent. In all her life she had only two lessons but played a great deal with her brother, Roger, when he was developing into a first-class golfer, and his friends. This helped greatly but she has said that playing with Jones had the most profound influence, especially in the way he took the club back, and in his rhythm.

Of the eleven national championships in which Joyce Wethered competed in Britain she won nine, lost one final and one semifinal. In so doing she revealed, as did Jones, all the qualities of greatness: absolute sternness of purpose, the capacity to destroy without mercy, courage and resilience in adversity, grace and modesty in triumph. Her retirement from championship golf in 1929 was not because, as with Jones, all worlds had been conquered and the strain was becoming intolerable, but because she never regarded golf as other than a game. Her love for it never became obsessive.

Soon after her marriage to Sir John Heathcoat-Amory they created one of the most beautiful gardens in England. This became a consuming interest and, together with music, pictures and no small skill at casting for trout, meant that golf became only a casual pastime. Many years ago she gave away her clubs and the putting course, of which Bernard Darwin wrote lovingly, is no more.

A few summers ago I spent a day with Lady Amory at Knightshayes Court in the heart of Devon. It is a tranquil place, so far removed from golf that it was almost impossible to believe that my hostess had once been an incomparable player. The only indication I saw that she had played the game was the golf umbrella which sheltered her from occasional showers that swept over the green hills as we wandered about the garden. It covers some 25 acres, an enchanting variety of flowers, azaleas, rhododendrons and many less common shrubs glowing beneath the trees. These are never

176

overwhelming but lend ever-changing light and shade and, fittingly, a sense of peace.

Lady Amory is a serene, gentle person, a firm believer in Christian Science for forty years and more during which she suffered no illness. As we talked I realised how the planning and tending of the place had easily supplanted golf in her affections and those of her husband. On his death in 1973 Knightshayes was acquired by the National Trust, greatly to her relief. She knows that the beauty they created will be preserved and that to her, I think, is a greater reward than the winning of championships long ago could ever be.

From the earliest years of writing I had always been interested in women's golf and tried to cover one or more of their championships every season. They made a soothing contrast to masculine affairs and although the striking of the ball was in different context to that of the men the same qualities of character were involved. Throughout the fifties there was a nucleus of fine players: Jessie Valentine, a marvel of enduring skill, Jean Donald (now Mrs Anderson) a true and powerful striker, Jeanne Bisgood, who had a rare capacity for winning, even when not at her finest, Elizabeth Price Fisher, the personification of steadiness, Philomena Garvey, the most accomplished of all Irish players, Jeanette Wright, an appealing little golfer, and Frances Smith.

Frances was the least naturally gifted player of them all, but one whose character made her into an indomitable competitor, and enabled her to endure awareness of cancer, from which she died in 1978, without trace of complaint. Her courage and stoicism were reflected in her golf. Under the tuition of her father, Fred Stephens, she worked as few women ever have done to develop a swing technically perfect in all its parts. No excuse for failure was ever permitted. A gentle, retiring manner belied an inflexible will which thrived on adversity in golf and in private life.

Outward appearance often is no indication of the force of character which makes a great competitor but there was no mistaking the resolve of Catherine Lacoste de Prado. I have not known a golfer, except Nicklaus as a young man, whose manner and golf were more revealing of enormous self-confidence. She was always cheerful, assured and extremely positive in her approach to the game and might well have echoed Walter Hagen's famous remark before a tournament, 'Who is going to be second?' At its finest her golf was immensely strong for a woman. She was the only one I can recall who used a one iron, and with great effect.

In 1969 Catherine stirred the pride of women golfers, and many a man besides, by winning the United States Amateur championship, having already acquired the British and French titles that year. The British championship was at Portrush and that, sadly, was the last time I saw those links I have always admired. On an exacting driving course Catherine often was able to keep the ball in play with her one iron and without appreciable loss of length. In the 18-hole final against a fine golfer in Ann Irvin she lost the first three holes and seemed likely to lose the 4th but, as she passed me on the fairway, she made some bright, smiling remark as if to say 'There is nothing to worry about, I'll win in the end.' This was typical of an attitude which gave her a psychological advantage over many opponents. She beat Ann Irvin by one hole and decided to compete in the United States championship. I then realised that I would be in Dayton, Ohio watching the PGA championship the same week.

It was agreed that Peter Ryde and I would phone her each evening to see how she had fared. Day after day her voice bubbled with triumph as eventually she beat Anne Quast Sander and reached the final. The next evening we called several times but she was not there. Ryde grew pessimistic, thinking that she had lost and had begun her journey home, but I felt in my bones that she had won. Whether or not Catherine believed in her destiny I did.

When, eventually, I spoke to her that evening from Ohio I learned that she had beaten Shelley Hamlin in the final. This was a rare achievement in Texas temperatures sometimes over one hundred. Having won the United States Open championship two years earlier, the only amateur to do so, which cannot have amused the world's leading professionals, her conquest of women's golf was complete. She never had the slightest inclination or need to turn professional, but she was a golfer of the very highest class with a formidable attitude to competition. She was, of course, blessed in her heritage; Rene Lacoste had been one of the great lawn tennis players of his generation and her mother, as Simone Thion de la Chaume, had been the finest French woman golfer and had won the British championship.

Catherine was one of a gifted trio of French women golfers. Brigitte Varangot, a most accomplished stroke-maker, won the British championship three times, and Claudine Cros Rubin, with her lovely style, was unlucky not to do so at least twice. That France should produce three women golfers of their quality, following the Vicomtesse de Saint-Sauveur, as she was then, was an extraordinary coincidence and a happy one for those who followed women's golf as I did. They were a joy to watch and greatly enhanced the stature of the British championship and other events.

In 1951 a small group of American women professionals headed by 'Babe' Zaharias, that formidable athlete, and Patty Berg, a highly-accomplished golfer, made a brief visit to Britain. Both women were lively extrovert personalities and Mrs Zaharias was my first sight of exceptional power in a woman golfer. Her death some years later was sadly premature for she was a remarkable person, but Miss Berg remains, a kind of mother figure to the professional tour which she, perhaps more than anyone else, helped to found. I was fascinated by these women and looked forward to watching one of their tournaments in the United States. Unfortunately the dates never fitted until David Foster, chairman of the Colgate Company, who was born and educated in England, decided to lavish millions on golf, particularly the women's game. He believed that the women professionals would be a fine advertising medium for his company's products.

The centrepiece of Foster's endeavours was the Colgate-Dinah Shore championship at Mission Hills, near Palm Springs. It became the richest women's event and Foster personally ensured that nothing was spared in its presentation. This included inviting guests from Britain and for four successive years Jean and I spent a happy springtime week in the desert sunshine, either before or after the Masters at Augusta.

The women professionals have abundant cause to be grateful to David Foster. Through his tournaments and television, and with the aid of Dinah Shore's lasting appeal, he exposed the players to a huge public, the like of which they had never known before. This made them acutely conscious of their appearance, which had variety, taste and colour, and of their manner on and off the course. In this I found them to be invariably pleasant, not least in the pro.am. competitions. Always they were helpful and kindly towards their amateur partners, unlike some men professionals who, in their stupidity, make it obvious that to them such occasions are a chore.

Mission Hills is one of those vivid, emerald oases that abound on the desert floor. All around savage mountains rise to snow-clad peaks and even when the temperature is in the nineties the air is so pure and dry that playing and watching are never trying. One charm of Southern California is the enormity of its contrasts. No greater could be imagined than that between the coastal courses and those in the desert and they are but a hundred miles or so apart.

The climax to the championship the first year I was there gave Peter Ryde and me a demanding hour. While four women were in a sudden-death play-off for a huge first prize, which Jo Ann Prentice eventually won, Peter Oosterhuis and Lee Elder were similarly involved at precisely the same time in Pensacola 2000 miles away. If Oosterhuis won it would be his first victory in the United States, and if Elder succeeded, which he did, he would be the first black golfer to qualify for the Masters. Ryde and I were determined to have both results in our final editions. In between watching the women on television in the press tent we took turns every few minutes to call Pensacola. From there that kindly man, Tom Place, who does such an admirable job as Director of Information for the men's tour, kept us posted. Both play-offs lasted for several holes but we had the results in time.

For years I had been hoping to see Mickey Wright play but injury had prevented her from emerging from semi-retirement until my third visit. I was beginning to feel like a golf correspondent who, after twenty years, had never seen Nicklaus but Miss Wright had never played in Britain, more is the pity. I only needed to watch her strike a few shots to wonder whether anyone, since perhaps Joyce Wethered, had matched her perfection and grace of style. She is taller than average with, in her words, strong under-pinning. From the moment she stood to the ball there was an impression of authority seen only in the finest men players. No woman can have achieved greater power with a swing of such effortless smoothness. In one spell of five years from 1960 she won 50 of the 130 tournaments in which she played.

Talking with her one would not suspect that she had been a supreme golfer. Her manner was gentle, her handsome appearance, emphasised by glasses, quietly studious and her conversation revealed a mind attuned to things other than golf. And yet, as Joyce Wethered did in her generation, she had set standards of achievement that have not been surpassed, the most lasting contribution any player can give to their game, especially when, as with Mickey Wright, it is gracefully borne.

One year at Mission Hills I had the pleasure of playing in a pro.am. tournament with Amy Alcott, then clearly on her way to the heights, and Jack Kramer, one of the great lawn tennis champions. I was much impressed with Amy's crisp, controlled swing, intensely determined approach and application to every shot. Four years later she won the US Open by a record margin in dreadful heat and is now one of the foremost players in the world. Kramer, an amiable companion, hit many powerful strokes and a middle-aged lady with a high handicap often contributed to our cause which was prospering when we came to the 15th. I was the only one with a chance of making a net birdie. The drive left me a medium iron to the green but, of course, the lie had to be downhill and a little grassy, and a lake had to be carried. I remember Amy saying, 'If ever I needed you I need you now.' I would have given a good deal to hit that green but naturally my shot was heavy and just failed to carry the water. Nevertheless we finished third and a handsome cut-glass bowl sometimes reminds me that but for my lapse we would have been second.

It was customary for winners to donate some of their prize money to the local hospital. As we were guests I told Dinah Shore, who was running the prizegiving, that I would give my share, some $400, on behalf of the British golf writers, some of whom were also there as guests. Misunderstanding what I had said Dinah announced to a large assembly that I was donating my prize to the British golf writers. Naturally nothing was further from my thoughts and I hastily asked her to make amends.

On another occasion the great Willie Mays, one of baseball's immortal figures whom I had watched in New York and San Francisco all those years before, was in our four. He is an impressive, superbly-built, attractive man and I was anxious to see what he made of golf. He made no bones about it at all. With a short, simple swing his massively powerful hands delivered the ball enormous distances. His drives were not always straight but he was no mere slugger. His handicap was eight and his game pretty solid throughout. As with Bradman, Kramer and others, I had seen how the great players of various games could readily adapt to golf.

Apart from the affairs at Palm Springs David Foster had cast Colgate's blessings on a tournament in the Far East, and at Sunningdale where for six years British followers could watch the finest players in the world. In Judy Rankin, who won twice there, they saw that a tiny figure need be no handicap to the playing of splendid golf; they saw the beautiful measured rhythm of Donna Caponi prevail one year and Chako Higuchi, with her quaint style, leave everyone far behind on another occasion.

The last two years, before economy sadly halted a splendid event, belonged to Nancy Lopez, now Mrs Melton, as indeed they had in the United States where she had dominated the women's world in her first full seasons as a professional. At the time I wrote that it is one thing to be gifted with great natural talent, it is another to compete with the freshness, charm and obvious enjoyment that Miss Lopez brings to it. Whatever the fate of her shots the finely determined lines of an appealing face invariably softened into smiles, and what a joy that is when so many are grimly earnest. Her manner has nothing of the professional gloss which many players strive to acquire for their public relations. There is about her an innate gentleness, courtesy and warmth.

It was a strange coincidence that Trevino and Nancy Lopez, the most striking personalities to achieve great distinction in their respective spheres these many years, should both be of Mexican parentage. Trevino rose from hardship and Nancy's parents made great sacrifices for her to play golf. When she was twelve her father sought Trevino's advice, which was not to change her swing as long as it worked. It is not classic but it is powerful, beautifully rhythmic and has worked wonderfully well thus far. May it long do so and may she continue to delight everyone who watches her play. Would that one such as Nancy Lopez Melton could arise in British women's professional golf, which in a short time has made a promising start.

CHAPTER 20
JACK NICKLAUS SEES ME THROUGH

From the beginnings of tournament golf more than a century ago there have always been golfers who, by their achievements and uncommon personality have stood far above their fellows. Jack Nicklaus, of course, is the supreme example. Since 1960 when, as an amateur, he finished second to Palmer in the US Open, he had after 1980 played in 80 of what are regarded as the four major championships open to a professional. Aside from his 17 victories he had finished in the first four on 32 other occasions.

Within a year or so of turning professional in 1962 Nicklaus was the standard-bearer of greatness, always the man who could never be discounted. His record, which is nothing less than astounding, may never be approached, at least not in the foreseeable future. For eight years Bobby Jones enjoyed even greater supremacy, as did Hogan for a similar period, but no one in the game's history has had such a commanding impact on competitive golf for anything like as long as Nicklaus. Nor has any overseas golfer had as beneficial an influence on the Open in Britain. He has competed every year since 1962 and only four times has finished lower than fourth. More than anyone else he has ensured that the old championship would remain the foremost golfing occasion in the world.

Occasionally his eminence has been threatened. Palmer, Player, Casper, Miller and notably Trevino and Watson have had their great, even tremendous years but always Nicklaus was thereabouts. When he won the US Open and PGA championships in 1980 even Watson's triumphant season paled by comparison. Every year ambitious determined young men with strong nerves and sound technique pour from the college golf factories, but twenty years after his own college days Nicklaus has shown himself capable of beating them all when it mattered most.

I first became fully aware of Nicklaus in 1959. It was obvious that he was uncommonly blessed. When I saw him win his second US Amateur championship at Pebble Beach I was so convinced of his talent that I wrote 'Of all the golfers in the world I cannot believe that anyone will make a

greater impact upon the championships than this very tough, very determined, likeable young man.' I have not felt the same about any golfer since.
Apart from a remarkable aptitude for the game, great power and sensitive
touch, abundant good health and a comfortable happy family background,
it was clear that he had exceptional mental qualities. The development of
his character doubtless owed much to his father. Charlie Nicklaus, a warmly
sensible man, would stand no nonsense from the boy; there were to be no
tantrums. Between father and son there existed a strong affection and
understanding and I think that the first, and possibly the only, real
adversity Jack has experienced was when his father died, in 1970.

If I had to express the foundation of Nicklaus's success in a single word it
would be balance. This was one of the fundamentals of the swing that Jack
Grout, his only teacher and an exceptionally wise one, has always stressed,
but balance of mind has been Nicklaus's greatest strength. The impact of
failure, even when the fault was his, never lingered long. There seemed to
be no quirks in his temperament and yet he is far from being unfeeling. His
attitude to disappointment or success is constant. From early in his career
he has invariably been gracious and generous in defeat.

Balance has enabled him to control his nerve and judgement in situations
of acute pressure and thereby command absolute concentration to a greater
extent than any contemporary golfer. Rarely has he lost patience with a
course or the tide of affairs, and any impatience with himself which he
must feel at times is subdued. As a golfer his mind has always been in
control of his emotions.

From the beginning too Nicklaus has maintained balance in the pattern
of his life, not permitting golf, no matter how rich the inducements to play
may be, to interfere with his plans. Family life, business and other sporting
interests have always had their share of his time and thus he has not been
vulnerable to the dangers of staleness. Nicklaus too is an observant person,
extremely attentive to details. If some may have found this tiresome it is a
contributory factor to his success. He misses little of what is going on
around him. In conversation he listens and concentrates and if the talker be
vague or muddled Nicklaus will demand explanation, sometimes with
disconcerting directness. In youth he could be disturbingly outspoken, tact
was not his forte, but this stemmed from honest reaction and not rudeness.

In the autumn of 1966 Nicklaus was involved in an unfortunate affair
during the final of the Piccadilly matchplay championship at Wentworth.
On the 9th hole of the morning round Nicklaus disputed the decision of the
referee, Tony Duncan. It was a matter of opinion whether part of a
billboard was on the line of Nicklaus's third shot to the green and whether
he should have a free drop. Duncan said that it was not, a reasonable
decision, and after some discussion withdrew in favour of another referee

so that the harmony of the match, which Gary Player won with plenty to spare, would not be further threatened. I am sure that Nicklaus came to regret the only incident, in all my knowledge of him, when his behaviour on the course was less than impeccable.

Golf has been singularly fortunate in having men of the calibre of Nicklaus at its head. It has always seemed to me that he played professional golf of the highest order with the spirit of an amateur. His conduct has been a splendid example in an age when some eminent games-players behave like spoiled children.

I once spent an evening with him at La Costa where he was staying. We were talking in his condominium when he suddenly asked if I had a cigarette. By the time I left we had finished a pack. Nicklaus was a spasmodic smoker, a session like that would be followed by none perhaps for days, and he never smoked on the golf course. He said once that long ago he had seen himself on a film walk across a green with a cigarette in his mouth and tap in a short putt. The sight disgusted him and he vowed never to smoke on the course again and, as far as I know, never has.

Such has been the increasing strength in depth of professional golf, particularly in the United States, that it may soon be impossible for one or two individuals to remain outstanding for any length of time. Tournament golf could well become an exhibition of technical efficiency by a host of somewhat faceless young men and the age of enduring heroes will have vanished. There would be a fresh one every week. As the time for my retirement from the *Guardian* approached I was anxious that this should not happen while I was having to cover many tournaments each year and write about them daily. After dinner one night during the Open at Birkdale in 1976 I was taking the air with Nicklaus before retiring and said to him in as many words, for heaven's sake keep going for another couple of years and see me out, I don't want to have to adjust to a new generation of college boys. Nicklaus smiled and said that he hoped to do so. This was a natural reaction on my part. Nicklaus had been prominent in so many events I had watched that I had no desire to be writing of his decline or disappearance from the scene.

There was no sign then that he was on the threshold of, for him, a comparatively lean period in championships. In the Masters the year before he had survived what I am sure must be the finest three-way contest ever fought between golfers of the stature of himself, Johnny Miller and Tom Weiskopf. It was wonderful stuff. After two rounds Nicklaus led the field by five strokes; the next day Weiskopf had gained six on him and was one ahead, and Miller no less than eight and he was still three behind. Nicklaus was not always at ease with a large lead; he preferred close combat. Leaving the club that evening I ran into him coming from the practice ground. He was relaxed and cheerful as if saying 'Now we really have a game of golf coming up tomorrow.' What a game it was. I shall never forget Nicklaus's one-iron shot over the lake at the 15th, the huge putt on the next green which gave him the lead, or the suspense as first Miller and then Weiskopf just missed putts to tie on the last green. Miller had played the final 36 holes in 131, a marvellous performance. As Nicklaus said later, 'Tom had every right to win, so did Johnny. I was just damned lucky that I did.'

Later that summer Nicklaus won the PGA championship, but no major title came his way in 1976 and then at Turnberry the following year there was the most absorbing two-way contest I have seen on a great occasion, unforgettable for the sustained splendour of its skill and character. The two finest golfers in the world fought to the death with scores the like of which had never been approached in the Open. Watson was 130, Nicklaus 131 for the last two rounds and the previous Open record was made to seem futile. That spring Watson had narrowly beaten Nicklaus in the Masters and after Turnberry people were saying that he had established right of succession to the throne. Nicklaus was not of the same mind. ·

Not since James Braid in 1910 had any golfer been Open champion twice on the Old Course, and when Nicklaus's masterful golf prevailed there the following summer he had won all four major championships three times or more. It was fitting that he should reach this lonely peak at St Andrews. When he walked into the incomparable setting of the last green the warmth of the acclaim that greeted him was as much for the man himself as for the greatest golfer of the age.

A few weeks earlier I had retired from the *Guardian* and Nicklaus, with help from Watson, had seen me out in style. Others also contributed to making the closing years memorable. A day or so after my plea to Nicklaus in 1976 the whole golfing world became aware of Severiano Ballesteros. For three days he led the field and, far from being unnerved, continued to attack until the end. This was joyous youth, at 19 abounding in confidence, but on the burnished links that torrid summer, attack was his undoing. Control from the tees was the essence and Miller played beautifully for a final round of 66. Ballesteros tied with Nicklaus six strokes behind, but he had given wonderful entertainment to a crowd that had taken him to their hearts. No young golfer since Nicklaus was a like age had shown such power, flair in recovery and command of all the little shots. But Nicklaus never evoked the same sense of adventure; his was the Germanic approach as opposed to the Latin.

It seemed but a matter of time before Ballesteros was champion and three years later he triumphed at Lytham. Again the theme of his golf was uninhibited attack. Unleashing his driver with furious abandon he found

185

only one fairway with it in the last round. Such driving would have been sorely punished elsewhere, but the trample of tens of thousands of feet had rendered most of the rough harmless and Ballesteros knew what he was about. He played the links as he found it more effectively than anyone else and his closest pursuers had no just cause for complaint; all, including Crenshaw, whose love for the Open and the old traditions and history of the game have rarely been approached by an American golfer, and Nicklaus, made errors that had little to do with the condition of the course.

By then Ballesteros had won tournaments in numerous countries, including the United States, and when he dominated the Masters the following spring the world lay at his feet. The youngest Open champion of the century was the youngest Master and one of the most handsome and appealing. Never before at Augusta had the might of American golf been routed in such fashion; around the turn on the last afternoon he led the field by ten strokes. He had anxious moments thereafter, as did some British correspondents who, working against the clock, had already prepared their tributes but Ballesteros won at his ease. His score of 275, the fourth lowest in the history of the event, showed that he had the control and intelligence to master a course as different to Lytham as could be imagined.

Whatever reasons or excuses were offered Ballesteros's failure to arrive on the tee at the right time on the second morning of the US Open two months later was unforgivable. Nonetheless he had a successful season in Europe and at the outset of another year I wonder what lies ahead for him. For all his gifts I would hesitate to predict a future of lasting greatness, but every watcher of golf will hope that he has the character and health to remain in the forefront for many years to come. Professional tournament golf, especially in Europe, has sore need of men such as he for the excitement and beauty their golf can give. At the same time I trust that he does not allow undue cupidity, such as haggling over appearance money, which should be banned in Europe as it is in the United States, to mar his image and talent.

Technical efficiency is not enough in itself and the spectacle of non-descript young men plodding gracelessly about the business of earning a living is not inspiring. Their contribution to society is slender and they are fortunate that sponsors find golf a good medium for advertising. Vast sums are not poured into golf as a tribute to the players. Unless they appreciate that tournaments are promoted solely to attract publicity and good will, and set a good example by the standard and manner of play, it is hard to see a lasting future for tournament golf in its present form. Fortunately, on this side of the Atlantic about half the events are held in Continental countries, or there would be a real danger of saturation.

This is not a sour view, rather one of concern. I have had great pleasure from professional tournaments and have enjoyed many of the people involved, but a return to matchplay for some events may become essential. Three and three quarter days or thereabouts for a strokeplay tournament to approach a climax is a long time when cricket, for instance, has shown how successful one-day matches can be, both financially and as a means of entertainment.

Apart from a few major occasions, such as Opens or the Masters, I prefer watching amateur golf. The main championships are decided by matchplay and there is no odour of the commercialism which is inevitable in the professional world. From a competitive viewpoint amateur events can be most rewarding. Although no monetary prizes are at stake the pressures on the players are relatively the same; their technique, control and nerve are tested to their limits at every level from boys' golf to the Amateur championship and Walker Cup. A finely fought match in the first round of a championship between two comparatively unknown amateurs can be as compelling to watch as a low score by a known professional on the first day of a 72-hole event.

The best scoring in amateur golf may be several strokes a round higher than that in a professional event but scoring is far from everything. Watching the President's Putter at Rye in January, when the most vicious elements of winter may have to be overcome, is often greatly entertaining. The Putter, like the Halford Hewitt tournament at Deal with its numerous desperate finishes as the schools fight to the death, is a perfect expression of the true competitive spirit and challenge of golf when honour is the only reward.

The crowds at amateur golf are not as large as once they were, but the watching is more comfortable; so too are the catering arrangements and a car can usually be parked in a convenient spot. Parking, as my writing friends would confirm, has been something of an obsession with me, partly because I frequently use the car as a refuge for writing. Concentration in a press tent can be difficult with a few high-pitched voices around. In the clamour at a big championship it is easy.

When the Open was last at Lytham I was the butt of some amusement. Arriving late one evening I could not get the parking pass necessary for those staying in the dormy house. At breakfast the next morning Michael Williams, who writes most ably for the *Daily Telegraph*, said that the police had towed a car away from the dormy park. Thinking nothing of it I returned to my room and saw the space where my car had been. The police were understanding and when I produced the pass they brought the car back. Williams, who rarely fails to see the funny side of such situations, even when they happen to him, was highly amused, as I was when he told me of discovering halfway across the Atlantic that his visa had expired. Fortunately, the US immigration were sympathetic and passed him through.

Occasionally friends say that my golf should be better than it is because I have seen so much good play, but this works two ways. I have learned a great deal from watching the finest players but doing so does tend to diminish tolerance of my own imperfections. Although I may not have played for two or three weeks this seems no reason to hit dreadful shots. I am neither so vain nor so stupid as to expect to hit good shots all the time. It is the difference between the moderately adequate and the ghastly that is hard to tolerate. Unlike some people I do not find the latter amusing. For instance, to smother a four wood shot from a good lie in calm air when little or nothing is at stake is unforgivable; or to leave a straight, level putt of five feet to win a hole short on line smacks of cowardice.

I have often failed to come to terms with the fact that to err is human. Many years ago I heard Cotton say to Nicklaus that he sometimes wondered why he did not win more often than he did. Jack smiled and said 'Don't forget, Henry, I am human.'

From the foregoing the reader, unaware of the mercurial nature of my golf, will gather that my temperament for the game is far from classic. After a tournament in Spain one year groups of players and golf writers were striving to leave Malaga airport amid the total bureaucratic confusion for which the Latin races have such a remarkable flair. After much anguished argument I reached the sanctuary of the departure lounge. A moment later Gary Player appeared laughing and saying that he would not forget the sight of me at the desk crying, 'Why cannot these people ever do one thing at once?' He added that it was a good thing I did not play golf for a living. I would certainly not dispute that, but my agonies as a player have greatly helped me to understand and sympathise with failures in others, even the great ones.

CHAPTER 21
ESCAPE TO NORFOLK

After leaving Manchester in 1954 we lived for several years in Weybridge, an appealing little town until it became crowded by dormitory development. It was a good base for my purposes but we could not visualise an apartment, comfortable though it was, in an old house as a permanent home. Our thoughts turned to more distant pastures. Having been to Hunstanton for various golf events I had seen enough of Norfolk to be attracted by its remoteness from cities and by its varied beauty. The unspoiled north coast and wild sea marshes made a rare contrast to the lovely folding arable and wooded country so close at hand. Most of all I was fascinated by the links of the Royal West Norfolk Club at Brancaster which offered the wonderfully natural golf by the sea that I have always preferred to any other setting for the game.

Unaware at first that the *Guardian* would relieve me from covering hockey, and that I would be needed in the London office less often than before, we searched north and west Norfolk for something we could convert, while keeping a small place near London. Fortunately we had friends in Norfolk. I knew Tom and Lady Mary Harvey, Bobby and Bunny Selway, and Laddie and Jill Lucas, who then had a house at Titchwell. All were kind in having us to stay at various times while we explored. Tom Harvey, gifted, graceful man, who was to be captain of the Royal and Ancient in 1976, had been chairman of the Championship Committee during the early years of Palmer in Britain, and had survived two weather crises which caused postponement of play. Had the rain persisted at Birkdale in 1961 the Open might have been abandoned for that year. Palmer would not have won, might not have come again and that could have had a serious effect on the future success of the Open.

Bobby Selway had been chairman of the same committee. He also had a crisis at St Andrews. On the last hole of the 1957 Open, Bobby Locke marked his ball on the green but failed to return it to the proper place. This was not noticed until later when seen on a film but Selway's committee rightly decided that as Locke had three putts from inside a yard to win they would waive disqualification under Rule 36 (5). Since university days Selway, like Harvey, has been an accomplished golfer and is a world authority on the paintings of James Pollard.

Golf with Lucas has always been a joy. Although he has not played serious competitive golf for a long while his striking has lost little of its purity and skill. He has been one of the very few who have made left-handed golf look entirely natural. My pleasure at holing in one for the first time was the greater because I was playing with Laddie and his son David, who was a strength in the Cambridge University side for three years.

A year must have passed, and hopes of a home in Norfolk were declining when we were told of some land for sale on the Sandringham estate. It lay on the edge of a village with a lovely southern aspect. We decided to build a small house and were pleasantly surprised when Queen Elizabeth herself signed the contract for the purchase of the land. The document has attracted envious glances, especially from American friends.

While I was delighted at the prospect of living in Norfolk and playing most of my golf at Brancaster, Jean was uncertain. She would miss the convenience of London and all it offered, mainly in the artistic respects which interested her. Early one miserable November evening after buying the land we paused in the road nearby. Darkness had fallen, the pub had not opened, the one shop was shut and the only sign of night life was a telephone kiosk. I asked Jean if she could bear the deep silence of winter in the country. To my relief she agreed to try.

Fortunately Jean is a most adaptable person and was swiftly accustomed to the new life especially after we had acquired a bull terrier from Raymond Oppenheimer's Ormandy Kennels. Priscilla has been a great joy and protection these many years.

Some of our friends, Alistair Cooke among them, thought we were crazy to live in Norfolk which they visualised as the bleak flatlands of the Broads and the eastern part of the country. On one of his visits Cooke was accompanied by a banker friend from New York, Paul Manheim, and I was determined that they should see Brancaster in all its glory. Cooke, of course, was well aware of English climatic extremes but Manheim's exper-ience of golf was riding in a cart round beautiful sunlit parks. Brancaster was another world to him and he was soon wondering whether we were totally out of our minds.

It was raining as we set forth with Tom Harvey, and by the distant turn we were soaked but still had to fight our way home into a lashing gale. I can still see Manheim, glasses streaming and solid figure drenched, plodding bravely on with unfailing humour. Later Cooke wrote of the ordeal, saying that the course had been designed by Lady Macbeth, but did not mar his

190

story with any reference to the heavenly day that followed.

At times Norfolk may be fiercely cold and windy but we have never regretted the move, and soon decided that with an extension to the house we could live there all the year round. The pursuit of golf did involve more travelling but I did not mind. Even when returning from faraway beautiful places there has always been a feeling of pleasure and none of regret as the last homeward country miles pass by.

As I write on a chill December morning every prospect is peaceful. From my windows the land spreads away to the south and east towards distant woods. Not a building is in sight and the only movement is that of cattle in a far meadow, and the friendly plover who, day after day, seeks sustenance in the garden. Gradually it has become a kind of sanctuary for pheasants who wander about at will or shelter in our hedgerows as if sensing safety, especially when there is shooting in the season over the neighbouring land.

Quite often families of partridge, English and French, trot happily over the lawns and every year martins come and go in abundance. Soon after the house was built they decided that its walls were suitable for summer homes. In spite of the mess they leave beneath their nests we look forward to their coming and are sad to see them go. On good summer days we still have a feeling of being on holiday. Whatever daily tasks await it is no hardship to have meals in the garden, unseen by anyone, and to take long country walks without having to drive anywhere.

When it was known that I was retiring from the *Guardian* in 1978 there were some who smiled and asked if it were possible to retire from a perpetual holiday, but others would appreciate that in many ways the life was very far from that. When people said 'Can you play golf next weekend? Can you come to dinner, can you do this or that?' more often than not, for some eight months of the year, one had to refuse because of an impending tournament. If it were in some apparently romantic place they would ask if I wanted a secretary or someone to carry the clubs. Doubtless they would have leaped at the chance once or twice but the majority, who welcome an ordered existence with their families, would soon have wearied of rarely having a free weekend, of often being at home between journeys only long enough for a 'laundry stop', as Jean used to call them.

In some respects writing about golf for a daily paper is easier but not more agreeable than it was in my early years. Facilities for the press have greatly improved, notably so at the Open championship where under George Simms and his staff they have become the best in the world. If concerned only with basic facts of the play, as some writers of necessity are, the information services are remarkably efficient. Hole by hole scores, and sometimes even the clubs used by the players, are rapidly to hand. Players with the leading scores are brought into an interview tent to give their versions of what happened. These can be informative and often entertaining but some players, even those who should know better, have lately developed the nauseating habit of omitting the definite or indefinite article when describing their rounds. Any golfer who says, for example, 'I hit three iron,' should be fined on the spot. While most golfers are reasonably honest they are human enough not to be overly self-critical. They will blame their putting when approaching was at fault because it left them far from the holes; putts missed are usually said to be longer than they were. Excuses for bad play are legion, and one soon learns to pay little attention to those who frequently use them.

However old-fashioned it might seem I have always wanted to watch the golf and grow restless if prevented from doing so. Time on the course is essential to see for oneself how it is playing, absorb the atmosphere and feel the effect of the weather, especially if it be really foul. I have always found that personal experience helps one's writing; it is difficult to feel excitement through eyes other than one's own. The golfers — and this was particularly true when information services were limited — were more likely to respond to questions if they knew you were a watcher. Generally speaking the British writers, most of whom are keen golfers, watch as much golf as their time permits.

One inescapable handicap for the writer is that he can only see a tiny fraction of a day's play. Years ago it was possible to be on the course unaware of great deeds being performed elsewhere. One might return to the press tent without having seen them but could rely on the co-operation that has always been conspicuous among the golfing press where free exchange of information is the rule. All one needs to do is call out and someone will come to the rescue. How the writer treats the facts is his own affair, but he never need be bereft of something on which to base his piece.

From the beginning I have enjoyed the friendly spirit that exists among the wide cross-section of people who have become golf writers. I have never had anything approaching a significant dispute, in spite of spending so much time with them during the season. Invariably there is an undercurrent of humour, and I have laughed more frequently with golf writers than with any other company. It used to be said that most golf reporting was done from the bar. This may have been so long ago but I soon found to my relief that it was nonsense. I can only recall one instance of a writer being so much the worse for wear that his friends used to help write his pieces. It was a sad case because he was a knowledgeable writer and a fine golfer, but his addiction finally cost him his job.

Although some may regard golf writers as parasites the work can be most demanding of energy, thought and patience, and for its frustrations and unpredictable hours. Take a matchplay event. The day rolls smoothly along, plenty to report has happened and there is time to spare. Then, suddenly, one of the leading players who seemed safely launched towards victory has to play extra holes. Mention of his fate cannot be avoided but on and on the match goes into the evening. Rarely did I watch these holes except probably in the final of a championship. One might spend an hour or more which could be more profitably spent on other work. If very late matches were of no special significance the newspaper writer could ignore them, but those reporting for the agencies, such as the Press Association and Exchange Telegraph, had to wait for the result, however late it was. These writers are the real toilers and unsung heroes of the golfing press.

Strokeplay tournaments could be equally trying. Sometimes a comparatively unknown player starting very late would lead the field on the first day of the Open. Whether one wrote at some length of his round was a matter of mood, conscience, judgement or time. If his success obviously was ephemeral a brief mention that one would look at him on the morrow might suffice, knowing that by then he would probably have vanished from the reckoning.

On the first evening of one Open I had finished a long article when a young player returned an unexpectedly fine score and was leading. Friends told me that I exploded, saying that he had ruined the symmetry of my piece (a somewhat flattering estimate), but towards the end of a long exhausting day with edition times pressing such happenings can be annoying, to say the least. Occasionally the reverse would happen and play end unexpectedly early. One year at Hoylake Sandy Lyle, who a month earlier had become the youngest player to qualify for the third round of the Open, lost the final of the Boys' championship to Toby Shannon by 10 and 9. Then all work was finished before a leisurely tea and a long homeward journey completed in time for dinner. I remember that championship for moments spent on the dunes in the breathless stillness of high summer, watching uncountable thousands of oyster-catchers swirling and wheeling over the sands of Dee with the Welsh hills making lovely patterns in the distance. Often it happened that the beauty of a setting would be an enduring memory long after the golf was forgotten.

Covering golf in America can be a mixed blessing because of the time difference. Watching in the mornings is haunted by the necessity to write and phone England about lunchtime for the first editions. Then, as the afternoon's play rises towards a climax, it has to be deserted for the foundry-like clamour of the press centre and a fresh piece written. Often play is finishing when main editions are going to press, and all one can see of the closing holes is on little television sets suspended above the writers. At one Masters I was phoning England as Gay Brewer was about to win on the last green. When I had finished I told the sub-editor that I would call again with a more detailed account of the final moments. I can still hear a flat Mancunian voice saying, 'Don't bother, Pat, we saw it on the telly.' He was over 3000 miles away; I was 300 yards from the green.

It is all very well to be out on the course when the final drama of a great occasion is unfolding but impossible to keep abreast of how all the contenders are faring. Television usually gives at least a glimpse of the significant strokes on the last few holes. Direction and camerawork are mostly of a very high order but with a few notable examples like Peter Alliss, who had the advantage of working with Henry Longhurst, the standard of commentary hardly keeps pace.

Several commentators in Britain and America still do not appreciate the dramatic effect of silence, a fundamental which Longhurst was the first to appreciate. Nothing is more irritating to the viewer than to be told what is plainly visible on the screen or to hear an excited voice saying, 'It's a great stroke, a wonderful stroke — Oh no, he has cut it into the lake!' or that a player has this putt of 55 feet for a birdie when the wretched fellow is sweating on getting down in two putts. Good television commentary is far from easy, but I do wish that some of the commentators would remember that silence is vastly preferable to statements of the obvious.

For a generation and more Longhurst, by his writing and speaking, gave greater pleasure to golfers throughout the world than anyone else of his calling. His great gifts were an acute observation of the frailties of human nature which golf can reveal so easily, the ability to describe them with an admirable economy of words, and a dry, sardonic wit. He was always quick to sense the ridiculous in a game which most people pursue in deadly earnest. When in the mood — and rarely was he not — his relating of anecdotes could be devastatingly funny, often for the manner of their telling rather than the subject, and he never needed to be coarse. Shortly after the War he was the guest speaker at Stockport, then my home club. Towards the end of his speech the captain said, rather pompously, that in his time he had known 34 mayors. A moment later Longhurst rose and said 'Mr Mayor, and' (turning to the captain) 'you, Sir, the stallion of Stockport.'

Among Longhurst's qualities was the stoic courage with which he withstood unpleasant operations in his later years. Twice in the seventies, while with him in the United States, we thought he was doomed but his resilience was remarkable, even though he would refer ironically to the close of play, coming down the 18th and so on. In the end death probably was a relief but he should have been comforted by the thought that to many people his life had been infinitely worthwhile.

The golf correspondent's life has many blessings which long ago convinced me that it was the most rewarding game for a writer. Above all it is spent in fresh, attractive, often beautiful surroundings and with congenial people. Golf is a splendid passport and through it I have made many pleasant acquaintances. Times without number when the golf was not absorbing and the rain driving or the wind bitter I have thought it was far better than being in an office and having to endure deadly rush hours. Even when unable to avoid staying in a city I would travel to the course each day in the opposite direction to the mass of traffic.

A great advantage of reporting golf is that one is not compelled to suffer tedium comparable with that which often afflicts the writer imprisoned in the confined areas where most games are played. While another writer cannot escape often hours of dreary cricket or football, in golf not everyone is floundering in mediocrity or worse. Even in dreadful weather someone will be making a brave fist of it. Sponsors might not agree but I would rather see a golfer mastering a gale with a 73 than watch a day when scores in the sixties were commonplace.

No single golfing day can be totally boring. Invariably there are a few notable strokes that can make the substance of an article, subjects to praise rather than to damn. Anyone who has suffered at golf as I have is wary of being too critical; there is no such thing as an easy four-foot putt. Golf gives abundant opportunity to digress. The most ordinary of courses with an industrial background has its measure of beauty, if only in the freshness of the grass and the presence of trees; and every course in the world is different. Often the setting has been my salvation. When not moved by the play I could fall back on describing the scenery, a single hole where a telling stroke was played, the effect of the weather on the course and so on.

It is always fascinating to observe and get to know those who reach the highest peaks in any game. Beyond a certain pitch of technical ability success in golf is a matter of the mind. Although all the most eminent players have certain basic qualities of character their personalities can vary greatly. Comparison between, say, Nicklaus and Trevino, Hogan and De Vincenzo, Player and Watson, Palmer and Littler, Thomson and Snead illustrates the point. As the years went by I came to know most of the great golfers fairly well. At times they were involved in situations that fairly wrung the emotions and this made the study of them as golfers and as people all the more interesting. As a writer I have found this the heart of the matter.

All through youth and beyond the urge to travel was strong. The planning and preparations were never a chore but, increasingly nowadays, the prospect of a journey, whatever the welcome and excellent reason for it may be, is less appealing. I do not write this from the disenchantment that can arise after having travelled a great deal but simply because the whole process is so much less comfortable. How often minorities inflict gross inconvenience on masses of people who have no responsibility at all for their problems and grievances.

My natural regret at leaving the *Guardian* after so many years was tempered by the pleasure of being at home for longer periods. I much enjoy the events I attend on behalf of *Country Life,* but they are less frequent and involve less time away.

I am thankful that my years of following golf began while there were still strong links with the generation between the two World Wars. Almost half a century ago I saw Walter Hagen play. On the eve of J. H. Taylor's 80th birthday, and again when he was 90, I made a pilgrimage to Westward Ho! to see one whose memories of an honourable lifetime stretched back deep into the nineties when he won his first championships. In 1936 I watched Henry Cotton and Gene Sarazen in an Open at Hoylake when they were at the peak of their powers. At this writing they are the senior Open champions of the United States and Britain. Sarazen's career covers sixty years and Cotton has been the most significant figure to emerge from British golf for a like period. Aside from Cotton's superb play his mind has been one of the liveliest ever devoted to the game and I have never met anyone, from the humblest to the mightiest, who was keener on golf in all its aspects. Such contacts with the past have always been precious to me in an ever-changing world.

The early years of covering the Masters were the more memorable for the friendship of Bobby Jones, and the presence of Hogan, Nelson, Sarazen, Snead, and others, all of whom excelled in the late thirties. They served to make a great pageant of the occasion when the age of Palmer, Nicklaus, Player and Casper was firmly launched. The golf of these men over many years and their strikingly different personalities were the foundation of a compelling period. I doubt that we shall see its like again.

Trevino, one of the greatest golfers the game has known and nowadays one of its few vivid personalities, remains probably the only symbol of the time when golfers achieved greatness without the start enjoyed by the younger contemporary players. Of these Watson, with his splendid technique, keen intelligence and attractive manners, personifies their finest qualities, but I fear that the age of distinctive styles and personalities is passing.

It is sad too that the age of the club professional as a craftsman, a familiar figure when I first played golf, has almost passed. Shortly before I went to live in Norfolk the late Earl of Leicester wrote to me on this subject. He had long been an ardent golfer and in 1936 was the last to join the select company of those who had assisted Joyce Wethered, as she then was, to win the Worplesdon Foursomes eight times. When I knew him his health would only allow occasional gentle golf and so he planned some holes within the park at Holkham. Many were demanding but amusing to play nonetheless.

As a member at Brancaster for many years Lord Leicester had greatly admired Tom King, the professional, and suggested that as King had recently died I write a tribute to him. King and his father had served the club since the nineties, shortly after its foundation. Unfortunately I never met him but he was one of those who regarded the profession as a vocation as well as a business.

Men like King were craftsmen, understanding the game for its intrinsic beauty and satisfaction. I doubt that he ever earned more than a modest income for Brancaster can be a lonely place many days of the year with negligible custom for a professional, but he found fulfilment there. King and the members who were his friends were to be envied. Lord Leicester said that he was the nicest person to play with, modest and self-effacing. He liked you to enjoy your game and to win if possible. Apparently he was skilled in the art of missing putts without being obvious about it so that this might happen.

There have been other instances of long reigns and direct succession in professional golf but such dynasties are passing. Young men are more ambitious and their horizons broader nowadays, and few seek the quiet country life. Ray Kimber, who succeeded King at Brancaster in 1966, is one of the exceptions. He is a countryman at heart and a devoted ornithologist. When he went to be interviewed for the job a gale was blowing and there was snow in the air. Anyone who knows the place will appreciate what a discouraging prospect it must have been for a young man with a new bride, but as they reached the club a flight of brent geese rose from the marsh and his spirits lightened. Soon after moving there Kimber saw about 40 types of birds he had not seen before. Over 200 different kinds have been sighted on the salt marsh. This was a great joy to Kimber and the club's good fortune because he remains our admirable professional.

At times the elements can be harsh at Brancaster but we who suffer the perishing winds also know days of uncommon beauty, and often when few other golfers are abroad. Then one is blessed with a feeling of solitude that I have rarely known anywhere else. Holes may have changed over the years, sometimes through the invasion of storms, but the character of the links is as intrinsically natural as it was one day when the Prince of Wales, later Edward VII, was shooting snipe there. One of his companions, Holcombe Ingleby, remarked that the land between the dunes and the marsh would make a golf course. Thus was it conceived and, because of the Prince, became a Royal Club from the outset, one of the first in England to be honoured in this way. At Easter in 1981 I had the pleasure of handing over the captaincy of HRH the Duke of Kent. He, I believe, is the first member of the Royal family to be captain of a British golf club since his father held that office for the Royal and Ancient and Royal West Norfolk in 1937.

Soon afterwards I was invited to Nicklaus's Memorial tournament on his beautiful Muirfield Village course in Ohio. Each year a great golfer from the past is honoured and I had the privilege of giving the tribute to Harry Vardon. My birthday fell during that week and Jack and Barbara ensured that I had a memorable day. It is a happy coincidence that the final recollection which time permits in this book should involve these two rare people.

Finally I am not envious of those who may be setting out for a period similar to mine as golf writers if indeed the calling, such as it may be, lasts that long. A shrinkage of newspapers, which are constantly threatened by disruptive forces, seems probable and, with the development of television and soaring costs, the need for specialist writers is likely to diminish. Neither, in the broadest sense, does the world hold promise of being as clean and as safe a place in which to live as it was before permissiveness was allowed to sow its deadly roots and crime was allowed to prosper.

The outlook may not be encouraging but at least I hope that golf will remain a joy, a challenge and an escape from the harsher realities of life as it has been for me. Fortunate are those, and they are not legion, whose occupation has enabled them to pursue their greatest interests. I am lastingly grateful to have been of their company.

INDEX